Wales: A Question for History

For Jack Alexander (b.1998)
Who Has Already Answered The Question

Wales: A Question for History

Dai Smith

seren

seren
is the book imprint of
Poetry Wales Press Ltd
Wyndham Street, Bridgend, Wales

© Dai Smith, 1999
The right of Dai Smith to be identified as the Author
of this Work has been asserted in accordance with the
Copyright, Designs and Patents Act 1988

ISBN 1-85411-125-6

A CIP record for this title is available from
the British Library

*The publisher works with the financial assistance of the
Arts Council of Wales*

Cover image: 'Painting about a landscape, sea and sky (1995)' by
Ernest Zobole

Printed in Plantin by WBC Book Manufacturers, Bridgend

Contents

Foreword

To limit a society to its systems of decision and maintenance is
in fact ridiculous [it is just] ... to propose a political and
economic order, rather than a human order ... the alternative
society that is proposed must be in wider terms if it is to gener-
ate the full energies necessary for its creation. Indeed the
political and economic changes might come, and the human
order be very little changed, unless these connections are
made.... The integration of work and life, and the inclusion of
the activities we call cultural in the ordinary social organisation,
are the basic terms of an alternative form of society.
> Raymond Williams, *The Long Revolution* (1960)

In late 1983 I completed a collection of my work which had been
loosely associated with a BBC2 television series I was then writing
and presenting. The book was published in 1984 under the same
provocative title of the programme series: *Wales! Wales?* I had
intended, on the spring tide of a then swelling Welsh historical
endeavour, to make an argument whose general terms of reference
would be securely grounded in the historian's specific practice and
findings. It was gratifying that the book received widespread critical attention and that it helped spark a debate. Since we have all
moved on, one way or the other, since then, I would hope that this
present, substantially revised and altered edition would be read,
under its new title, in conjunction with my still unreconstructed
and unrepentant volume of 1993, *Aneurin Bevan and the World of
South Wales*, which stands as its companion piece.

The chance Seren have presented to place it in print again has
led me to alter or remove a few passages written with the then
passing moment in mind, to reorganise and add to the shape of
other material, and, at either end, to provide two new chapters
'Naming Names: Beyond a Fricative History' which has a Janus
intent, and 'In Place of Wales' which seeks to tease a history-fit-
for-use out of the reverberations of the career of the genius whose
centenary we celebrated in 1997. That year was, of course,
momentous in two other respects. It may well be that it will be
seen, in retrospect, as the single most important year in the Welsh
twentieth century. Or not, since no single constitutional reform,
whether weakly conceived or strongly executed, can effect that scale
of cultural change by mere political direction or administrative
action. What the Assembly can do, if its members have the
purposeful will for it which their body's youthfulness should give

them, is create space for Welsh imagination, in all spheres of activity, to make a society, both plural and tolerant, in the distinctive style of the present day, contemporary Welsh. The new institution, if it is to succeed in this primary role, will have to remove itself from the Gatekeeper's Fear of History which so afflicts us in these last days of twentieth-century Wales. The Assembly must act as if Wales is still to be created anew and they must do so in the knowledge that no Wales is possible if what has made us, a mature and differentiated people, is denied in search of some cosmetic unity sustained by the chanted sound bites of the nursery. The continued existence of Wales *is* a question for History since the latter unfolds continuously into the future. In answering 'yes', albeit squeakily, to the Assembly proposition the citizens of Wales, and especially those who consider themselves, in both our languages, to be Welsh, have begun to answer the question in a particular way. In my view, the leadership given by the Assembly will be crucial in deciding how the question will be resolved by the Welsh. Ignorance of our modern history amongst a general populace is something we can, as a concerned society, overcome and, besides, its outcomes are there to be felt and seen in present culture; but rejection of that history, in its main thrusts and major direction, is not a tenable position. Untenable because its philosophical and political conceptualisation would, as Brecht put it in 1953, seek to dissolve the People and elect another one in its place.

The Assembly is not the last best hope of Wales since *it* can always be dissolved. The Welsh, as they now exist, are however the last best hope of the Assembly being a vital force for *they* cannot be dissolved and they alone will elect an institution which can fulfil or frustrate them. For both History will be the key factor.

Naming Names:
Beyond a Fricative History

Frication: an audible, constrained rush of air accompanying and characteristic of certain speech sounds, as fricatives.... And initial stops.

Libraries gave us Power.... Then Work came and made us free.... What price now for a shallow piece of dignity?
Manic Street Preachers, 'Design for Life'

Contemporary Wales makes a fricative sound. Caught between the consonantal imperatives of book-delivered culture and a History that has gone pear-shaped it can find no open vowelled route out of this present time, only a hiss, a rush of air, a release of wind, a sigh. As yet such songs as the Boys from Blackwood sing are the most indicative and powerful screams against the cultural vacuum we are still allowing ourselves to inhabit, in the clapped-out fag-end of industrial Wales' history; or, as *they* say, 'And we are told that this is the End'.

Almost exactly twenty years ago I sat in the audience and heard Raymond Williams deliver, in honour of another Boy from Blackwood, the inaugural Gwyn Jones Lecture at Cardiff University. The lecture series, devised by Gwyn A. Williams and myself from within the History of Wales Department at Cardiff, was deliberately intended to underline and make clear, in as high profile a sense as possible, the culture and achievements, in *all* fields of intellectual endeavour, of the Welsh people in the English language.

In that first Gwyn Jones Lecture Raymond Williams was still able to deliver a text in the context of an as yet unfolded industrial history: 1984-5 had, if you like, not yet occurred. But if the context has changed utterly the actual and the fictive histories on which he drew still cannot be so dismissed from our understanding or our imagination. The fictions that we will value, as time passes, will continue to be those which engage with the human dilemmas created by both our general and specific history. The two are inseparable. It is, I believe, what Raymond Williams meant when, toward the end of his lecture, – in which he had paid handsome, but limited, tribute to those writers who, struggling with the form and the exigencies of a mass industrial experience, had nonetheless found a means of writing 'from inside the Welsh industrial communities', and so composed a distinctive and special contribution, especially from the 1930s – he singled out a writer who, in 1978, was as vilified as he was neglected.

Gwyn Thomas was a vital signifier because he had found a form, a particular voice and mode of representation, which remained rooted within the perspective of an insider but strove to deliver up a general meaning. This surely is what happens when a novelist, at the height of his power as Thomas was in the late 1940s, makes a fiction out of history. Then, the limiting but faithful perspective of the family saga, the heartfelt but sentimental depiction of the historical romance and even the translation of individuality into the epic abstraction of political melodrama, are overtaken by a grander vision of what was, may still yet be, possible within our fiction and our history. Thomas' novel of 1949 *All Things Betray Thee*, for Williams, managed to show its 'evident historical origins' (nineteenth-century Merthyr and its crises) and yet, by distance of style and composition, it became 'a novel of voices and of a voice, and that voice is not only the history, it is the contemporary consciousness of that history'.

In 1978 Raymond Williams thought that 'in a new kind of crisis' the reach beyond 'the industrial experience alone' required 'a reaching for new perspectives and new forms' in 'the accents of a fidelity at once visionary and historical'. Twenty years. And in that time, as the material foundations which elicited such remarkable creative achievements were hacked at from without and withered away from within, we have largely exchanged literary fantasy for fictional vision and myths for history. In the corrupt miasma that has settled over the Welsh mind like swamp gas, Wales itself has become A Question for History: one which, if not answered, will take us, drugged and oblivious, into the next millennium. The questions have been posed before. It takes courage to answer them to their face, not knowing if there is any consolation beyond the ability to reply.

That is what happened to both Welsh intellectuals and to the wider Welsh people in the interwar years: economically crushed, socially deprived, politically battered, they were, as Gwyn Thomas, in particular, saw and testified, also liberated. Liberated, that is, to adjust 'the key of the scream we utter' for there was nothing romanticised, or fantasised, about the several species of hell and human misery which Thomas' characters were privileged to be liberated to consider and to articulate. Gwyn Thomas' truth was the truth of a librettist in need of a chorus or of a sculptor faced with a block of marble. But what he worked on for public view he also stressed in private, and particularly at the end of the 1945 Labour Government's dalliance with a politics beyond mere administration, a democracy fit for the governed not merely for governance. His American admirer, the poet Norman Rosten, wrote him a number of fan letters at this time, a time when the poet was also a mentor to a younger American novelist who had shared a writer's work apartment with him in Brooklyn, the soaring Norman Mailer. Thomas, thanking Rosten for a gift of his latest verse, replied on 12 December 1950:

> Anyway, on Tuesday night – I was due to lecture to the British Poetry Society at Cardiff. I had not given a subject. The title space had been left blank, a privilege afforded to the more garrulous swamis in this belt. The arrival of your volumes transformed me into an evangel, sent me to the meeting with a sense of mission. I would announce and illustrate the work of a poet whose strength of voice, depth of pity, proclamation of a healed and united mankind would shake them out of their seats. It did. Most of the audience were miners down from the valleys of Rhondda, Garw and Aberdare, men whose essence could have gone to dyeing your verse the brilliant colour it is. Every wind of a torment from hell and British Toryism had moulded the shape of their faces and hearts. Your words moved into them like food or love, with passion, without a moment's doubt or pause. You might have been born for the sake of speaking to just that group at just that moment. I confined my readings to *The Fourth Decade* and this letter would be far too long if I gave you the list of the verses which they wished me to read again or to read over themselves, alone and at their own tempo when the meeting was done. There is a lyrical quality in the longings and angers of these men that made them, with a perfect appositeness, your audience. As one of them said to me after: 'Great, great, to have sung out in one fine note the song that is pressed out of us bastards in tiny groans.'

There is that fricative sound again, the groan of what he told Rosten was a 'brave, lyrical and sardonic people' whose 'spirit' he wished 'to express'. The astonishment, indeed puzzlement, which his plural narrators – his 'Willie, Ben, Walter, Arthur and me' as multiple persona – evoked was compounded by a prose at once demonic and demented: that cross between James Cagney and Savonarola which had no obvious British equivalent. It was touchingly recognisable and maddeningly distant, almost an echo of a reality. It is the same haunting loss of that knowledge, and of its potential, – thrown away, hidden, available – which runs tantalisingly through the first and early novels of industrial South Wales' last great 'insider' practitioner, and which, like a late bursting out of flame in a dying fire, marked out his two late masterworks.

Ron Berry, who was born in the Rhondda in 1920, seven years after Gwyn Thomas, and died there in 1997, is a writer whose time for fame will come. He lived long enough to know he had a steady core of support and a growing band of admirers, despite all kinds of commercial and official neglect. The close critical attention which one such late champion, John Pikoulis, effectively performed for his last work, *This Bygone*, in 1996 (in *New Welsh Review*) will need to be done now for the five novels Berry published between 1960 and 1970. This will surely trace how a 'brave people' had learned to survive by becoming increasingly more sardonic than lyrical. The move from savage indignation to a wearier cynicism, one that can be detected in the shift from Thomas to Berry, is there to be seen in the language itself or rather in the mouths which now speak the heightened language of consciousness. For if Gwyn Thomas' characters all sound alike, and like him, for 'no language was too good for my people', or for their aspirational dreams, then, for Ron Berry, the bitten-off, truncated and authentic dialogue of his characters, young colliers in particular, is positively monochrome compared to the rich, adjective-laden prose riff which he narrates, wilfully and unapologetically from book to book – the amniotic ocean of human tide flow in which his real time world aimlessly floats.

His early novels attacked the flaccid juxtaposition of a declining industrial society (the 1950s and 1960s) and the conveniently forgotten or displaced world whose features are still there despite appearances of change. In *This Bygone*, though, we are taken straight back to 1937 and down to the beginning of the Depression's end in the first years of the Second World War. It is that rare thing, a novel completely about a time past which has not a whiff of historicising fiction about it. It relies on its historical distance not for perspective but for compassion for all the things that are to come, and which inflect the lives and actions of his protagonists, and so are felt and yet not known. It is the story of the youthful collier, Dewi Joshua, the life he learns from work underground and the life his two loves will shape above it. The novel is, amongst other things, the most authentic account of work at the coalface ever written by anyone anywhere.

Ron wrote the following to me just after the book was printed and whilst BBC Wales was engaged in making a film about his life and work:

Gomer [the publisher] sent an early copy of *This Bygone* a week ago. Parcel post delivered my batch yesterday, and here's yours, near enough my swansong too, I think, barring a sort of corpus transfer, and despite recurring discontent.

Can't imagine the final product of my TV 'life' although Wynford [the director] says I shall be able to see it quite soon. They foraged like escapee mink, without the hereinafter of being alien and hunted. Never realised there were disciples either. Mine are past tense, gnarled, friendly as grass. Most in Treorchy cemetery. In a roundabout way it's why I made *This Bygone*. Yesterday lives. As if yesterday. Just gone. Almost.

This least sentimental of all Welsh writers had not one iota of nostalgia in him for the past as past. He detested anyone who wished to make any kind of cultural capital out of it. And he was sure, because of his own knowledge, that professional historians would inevitably homogenise it even if the best of them refused to pasteurise it. Nonetheless, the past as our only guide to a future that was not directionless absorbed him and its loss was such an implicit betrayal that it quickened him with anger. In his last works he wanted to name names, not in order to give spurious voice to the voiceless but to establish beyond the doubt of any form of fictive representation that, as the title of his posthumously published autobiography has it – *History Is What You Live*.

That, too, is a wondrous, captivating piece of writing – and of course, from his pen, an artifice. It sits and lives, however, within another tradition – the honour we do to ourselves by naming names, or rather, in any society which aspires to create 'a human order' by refusing to succumb to the varnish of the present, by naming the names of lives which are otherwise lost on the wind, whistling between the stolid consonants of mere existence.

It is a kind of history, whether as fiction or not, which we must now begin to write to allow those *without* a close knowledge a connection that can make them see and feel their roots without recourse to being re-potted in their own country. It is, in the end, the most profound human impulse, one without which there is only a fatal lack of self-worth. Wherever there is a social fever, a crisis of war or conflict or revolutionary change the impulse to record like this is rightly irresistible. It is a reaching out past autobiography to a biographical impulse which connects. The significant memory is always of others.

Edwin Greening was born in 1911 in Aberaman, near Aberdare; he would later fight in the Spanish Civil War. His late memoir of the 1926 General Strike and Lockout, through the eyes of the fifteen-year-old collier boy he then was, studs its impressionistic tale with the nailed-down detail only real names, insistently recalled, can effect.

Soon we were at the bottom of Blaengwawr pit with its vast bricked arches. We pushed the three big planked doors and walked past the silent stables. The horses were now pastured on the Aberaman Offices fields. We walked along the timbered gallery that wound its way towards Tonllwyd and Cwmaman which ended in the big marshalling yard for the trams which were sent on to Aberaman colliery proper. We crossed this double parting and made our way to the coal face of the 7 feet seam of the 'Dug-Out' district of Aberaman colliery. From this point the galleries showed signs of nearly three weeks stoppage of work with bent and broken timbers, fallen rocks from roof and side and the ever present throat-drying lung-destroying stone dust.

Everywhere the utter silence, not a scurry of a rat nor the buzz of that subterranean cockroach known as a Shoni-Dau-Gorn. Only the swinging lamps and the tread of the men and boys who constituted the labour force of the Dug-Out district of the Aberaman colliery in May 1926. Most of them are dead now but they were Will Greening, Edwin Jenkins, Martin White, Jack Pritchard, Reg Frame, John Finn, Charlie Finn, Will Finn, John Lewis, Gwyn Lewis, Myrddin Lewis, Tommy Ray, Charlie Lewis, Will Lewis, Bob Edevane, Eithon Richards, Norman Richards, Dick Lewis, Emlyn Lewis, Tommy Jenkins, Jessie Sollis, Jack Payne, Tom Davies, Fred French, Ted Price, William Jones, Wilfred Jones, Will Robinson, Windsor Robinson, Davy Lewis, Rhys Lewis, Will Lewis Britz, Patsy Crowley, Cyril Jordan, John James, Arthur James, Evan Smith, Stuart Smith, Ike David, Ben David, Will David, Will Cornelius Williams, Evan Williams, Will Williams, Walter Filer, Len Robinson, Bert Gill and many others.

The Dug-Out district of the 7 feet seam of Blaengwawr-Aberaman colliery in May 1926 was a dirty, ugly, dangerous place as dangerous and ugly as a Dug-Out on the Western Front in the Great War of 1914-18. My father and I collected the hatchet, shovels, sledge-hammer, wedges, timber forks, mandrils and curling boxes and tied some of them together and labelled them. After a last inspection of the coal face we struggled out of the pit with our load and put them down in the cellar.

That evening, Will Vaughan, Alf Webber and I were bird nesting by Ynyscynon pit where now runs the Canal road, Cwmbach and as we pottered around the reeds of the old canal we heard the throb of drums and the sound of gazooka music. We ran back to the small bridge at Well Place and saw coming down the now crowded street a curious band of many-coloured marchers led by a drum major. The band came down Well Place and wheeled round with drums throbbing and gazookas in full blast. It was the Cwmbach Marcaroni Jazz Band on parade and our first sight of a jazz band. It was the first sight or sign of what was to be in the Aberdare Valley and the coalfields of a vast out-pouring of popular music and display, but in mid-May 1926 when the coal lock-out was in its first days it was impossible to perceive the events that would catch the imagination of the ordinary people....

Early on Monday 2nd August 1926 I went to Will Vaughan's home and from there we went to the Blaengwawr Inn. It was about 7.30am of a beautiful day. There the Club Street Mexican Band assembled. The 40 Mexicans were dressed in cotton black and white trousers, bespangled waistcoats, red sashes and tall straw sombreros made from fish frails or plaited straw baskets given by Jack Francis, Richie Hurt and Rose Burge. With kettle drums and bass drum we made our way in small groups to Aberaman brickworks and climbed Mynydd Coed Cae Aberaman to the grove of Scots pines which still stands on the summit. Will Vaughan and I with Jack Evans, Aneurin Jenkins and Trevor Snow went right up to the top but the older men lagged behind and were hidden in the morning mist. When the main body emerged from the mist the scene looked like an incident from the Mexican revolution of 1912, but instead of being led by Pancho Villa our Mexicans were led by Charlie Smith of Club Street, Aberaman, a Powell Duffryn labourer and ex-regular soldier. We rested at Llanwonno Church and came down into the Little Rhondda at Ynyshir. The Wattstown football ground was a mass of bands. An official told me that 114 bands were competing that day. I calculate that there must have been 6,000 bandsmen and followers alone.

The bands paraded around Ynyshir and Porth. At about 6.30pm the Mexicans put on their usual magnificent display but they did not get a prize.

Then about 7.30pm they all retreated to the Station Hotel, Ynyshir. Will Vaughan and I with my uncle Arthur Jenkins, his son Aneurin and cousin Jack Evans, both Mexicans, went to Standard View Street nearby, the home of my late uncle Gomer's family. There we had a great welcome of fish and chips, bread and marge and tea with condensed milk.

At 8.30pm the Mexicans formed up in the main road of Ynyshir with lots of bands from Pontygwaith, Stanleytown, Llwynypia, Ferndale and Maerdy and with kettle drums rattling and the bass drums booming we set off 30 yards apart. The great parade of the Rhondda, Aberdare and Mountain Ash bands began to a great clapping, shouting and the barking of dogs. We marched through the dusk of a beautiful evening through the shabby, narrow half cobbled streets of the Rhondda Fach. Crowds lined the streets and the trams came to a stop.

Immediately in front of us was the Harem of the Sheik of Maerdy with their quaint eastern music of ocarinas, and eunuchs, slaves and turbanned Sheik. Behind us were the Napiers Black Watch. Heartened by the excitement of the crowds the Mexicans went through their full repertoire of marches – 'Down in the Sand Hills of New Mexico', 'Marching Through Georgia', 'King Cotton', 'Colonel Bogey', and 'Moonlight and Roses'.

We passed through crowded Ferndale, the Harem went onto Maerdy, the Mountain Ash bands turned left and we right at Blaenllechau and soon left the excited villagers behind us as we climbed the rough mountain track of the Ffaldau. As we left the Rhondda I turned to look at the yellow street lamps of the Rhondda Fach, and did not realise it then that the Rhonddas, those two great coal mining valleys had reached the watershed of their economic development. Their stupendous growth since 1809 which led to their having 166,000 people in 1921 was over. Now hidden from us all on that summer night in 1926 was an equally stupendous decline soon to come in the 1930s.

Led by my uncle Joe Evans (Llew Dar) we crossed the moonlit Mynydd Craig y Bedlwyn. The Phillipses of Bedlwyn Farm must have been amazed to see the sudden appearance of a band of Mexicans ambling past in the moonlight. We skirted the dangerous Bedlwyn quarry and came carefully down the old Cwmaman colliery incline and marched home through the streets of Cwmaman and Godreaman to the home base of the Blaengwawr Inn. Bronzed, hungry, tired but happy I reached home, supper and bed. That day the 2nd August 1926 was my 16th birthday. We had marched and sang 30 miles that hard but happy day. And the Lock-Out had started its 13th week and 4th month.

And it is what Ron Berry, of course with the more intense dramatic effect of a major artist, insists that we hear and see again as he varies the pace and thickness of his brushstrokes to re-present the shapes, relationship and ends of the industrial world he was born to remember for us.

From Cefn Nant y Gwair you can see a mile of railway track curving down to Blaenrhondda station. Robins, hedge sparrows, blackbirds, song thrushes, chaffinches, yellow hammers and wrens nest in the deep cutting leading up to the tunnel, where Granny Berry's first husband was killed in 1887. Violets bloom early in damp sheltered spots along the cutting. Earliest catkins, too. Farther down the track, minnows spawned in a small stream which runs into Selsig. Set apart from the village, Glenrhondda Institute looked elegant. Concerts and dances upstairs. Two billiard tables and a snooker table, Reading Room and a

Committee Room downstairs. The caretaker was Ned Bowen, formerly the village crier. Ned hobbled on club feet. St John's Ambulance classes every winter in the Institute. Among a 1,000 books in the Reading Room, *Leaves of Grass* on the same shelf as Edgar Wallace. A blend of two brooks, Nant yr Ychain and Nant Berw Wion, flows past the Institute, entering a stone arched culvert to join Selsig over the far side of Blaenycwm Road. It's a caveman's treat, crouching through the culvert with a box of matches. The hollow oak this side of the culvert, that's where a brown-haired girl allowed six boys to try her in turn, in 1932.

In 1984 the deserted Institute was vandalised and burnt to the ground.

Across the brook and the lane from the cashier's bungalow, a favourite twin-trunked sycamore. Climb the trunks cat-burglar style. Way up in the green welter, you're invisible. After dragging at a cigarette, Johnny Murphy came down through the branches. He kayoed himself. Mrs Cashier bathed his head. Glorious in full foliage, that sycamore. Soft bark, easy for carving names, arrows, hearts. In autumn thousands of propellers spin down into the brook.

Willow twigs from inside the railway fence made the best whistles. Plenty of spit and patience, tap tap with the old man's cobbler's knife, suck and gently screw, slip off the bark, a craft of ordinary jungle boys. Jack Miller had a silver birch catapult stick, square elastic at 1/2d a foot from Sam Wiltshire's shop in Pentre, and a soft leather pouch cut from the tongue of a boot. Years later, Jack kept terriers and lurchers. We drowned a geriatric greyhound, faithful deed stemming from the horizon vision of Bedouin Taffs....

However, now we're up here on Cefn Nant y Gwair. Robens and Beeching are elsewhere, honing themselves for hatchetwork. The pits are producing coal and its steam engines blowing up-valley, through the tunnel to Swansea. Blaenycwm football field hasn't yet been levelled at the base of Pen Pych mountain. Gorllwyn tip behind Hendrewen Road is black. About 70 years will moss, lichen and grass it green. Over on the left, across the ravine, another slag tip pours from the mouth of Graig level. This tip had grown since 1859. Graig incline swoops down to the screen, where Blaenycwm's only artist, J.T.G. Chunks Lewis, began earning his keep. Oilboy Chunks with his bucket and brass pump, caked grease shining from his ankles to his lapels, the one-eyed water colourist oiling tramwheels ten years before the pits were nationalised.

Graig level killed a few men, besides silicotics, arthritics, ripped flesh, smashed bones and damaged souls. Also one suicide. Percy Prior walked off a footbridge. The coal train from Fernhill dealt what he wanted. Percy had 100 per cent dust. I worked with Percy the slasher, his willing collier-boy on the shovel. He wore a spiked candle-holder in a brimless bowler hat, wax dripping over this thick eyebrows when he lay outstretched on his side, holing under and over the stank. Grubtimes, 11 to 11.20am, Percy eating bread, cheese and raw onions with cold tea. In reflective mood while picking congealed wax from his eyebrows, he planned coal-getting. Percy trumped (bribed) the hauliers for extra trams. We filled six or seven trams a week more than any other pair in the Graig. Legitimate bribery as practised throughout the Welsh coalfield, part of our socio-economic fabric. Huge, gaunt Percy from Somerset, whose widow married their lodger, Jackson Hope, another powerful man sent to his coffin by pneumoconiosis.

Black historied all right, the old Graig level, where we slaved in dust and water, where I worked with or in the same headings as Sid Hullen (dust, dead), Jimmy Shanklyn (rheumatic fever, dead), Frank Carpenter (wry-necked and droop-shouldered from injuries, dead), Walt James (dust, dead), Cliff Williams (TB, dead) Glyn Richards (ex POW of the Japs, ailing ever since, dead), Jackie Griff (dust, dead), Percy Prior (dust, suicide), Eddie Jones coch (dust, dead), Will Weekly (Compo, injured spine, dead), George Thomas (dead), Goronwy Evans (dead), my father (dust, arthritis, dead), Tommy Lewis (dead), Tommy Brunker (dust, dead), Harry Thomas (one kidney, dead), Arfon Thomas (compo, dead), Sioni Parry (dead), Dai Jones Widow (dead), Harold Evans (dead), Jesse Parsons and Lee Parsons (dead), Eddie Jones Widow (dead), Shink from Trealaw (dead), George Paisley (dead), Will Martin (dead), Frank Paisley, powerhouse collier (dust, dead), Jack Lewis (dead), Jack Smith (health ruined by his late twenties, dead), Will Harry Lisle (dead), Glyn Evans Bach (compo, dead), Jack and George Galloway (dead), Danny Griffiths (dead), Morgan Jones (dead), Albert Benning (compo, dead), Willie Thomas (dead), Bert Thomas (health ruined, dead), Doug Davies (compo), George Pickens (dead), Ianto Griffiths (dead), Ron Deane (compo, dead), Bert Page (dead), Owen Jones (dead), Glan Jones (health ruined, dead), George Cox (compo, dead), Charlie Deane (dead), Iago Pickens (dead), Phil Pickens (dead), Twm Davies Clip (dead), John Rossiter (health ruined, dead), Griff Dyer (dead), Fred Evans Chick (dead), Ernie Maggs (dead), Tom Thomas Ty Glas (dead) Lew Hopkins (health ruined), Max Lisle (TB), Will Butch (compo, dead), Ernie Petrie (ex POW of the Japs), Trev Williams Little Horse (dead), Ned Thomas (injured spine, dead), Felix Carpenter (dead), Levi Beynon (compo, dead), Winston Richards (dead), Long Bryn Lisle (compo, dead), Ossie Harry (dead), Willie Harry (dead), Phillie Swift (TB, dead), Tom Parry (dead), Arthur Williams (dead), Cyril Nash (compo) ... fragment round-up from four years in the Graig level. Release came via Hitler in

1940. Just a small level, the Graig, where lads were punished by
grinding toil, and before that weakened by the diet of beggars.
These men are unsung in any chronicle of existence.

In 1978, right at the very end of that first Gwyn Jones Lecture,
'The Welsh Industrial Novel', and long before a formidable body
of academic criticism on industrial fiction had begun to form,
Raymond Williams reminded his listeners how, for the imaginative
writers involved, there had been such 'difficulties' of form and
subject matter – difficulties, he added, that we know 'too well,
having also closely inherited them'. And so closely, still I would
say, that the difficulties, and the opportunities remain with us. It
took, perhaps, fifty years or more for a literature about the post-
Civil War Southern states to emerge that could overcome those
intractable difficulties of form and content so as to allow us to see
that history, not 'as it may be studied' but how 'it was experienced'
into the present, and, if we date the close of the industrial dynamic
of Welsh society from, say, the 1960s it may take another decade
or so before distance allows *that* charged history to speak to us,
close again, in fiction. And maybe, too, this time it will come as
music or drama or, more likely yet, as painting and film or in a
plural not singular manner of artistic presentation. In whichever
way it comes we must, somehow, find a way of telling and show-
ing and honouring what we have been, and may be yet again.

'We state the facts' said Jameson. 'We state them now softly,
now loudly. The next time it will be softly for our best voices
will have ceased to speak. The silence and the softness will ripen.
The lost blood will be made again. The chorus will shuffle out
of its filthy aching corners and return. The world is full of
voices, harpist, practising for the great anthem but hardly ever
heard. We've been privileged. We've had our ears full of the
singing. Silence will never be absolute for us again.'
Gwyn Thomas, *All Things Betray Thee*

★   ★   ★

... History is the raw material for nationalist or ethnic or fundamentalist ideologies, as poppies are the raw material for heroin
addiction. The past is an essential element, perhaps *the* essential
element in these ideologies. If there is no suitable past, it can
always be invented. Indeed, in the nature of things there is
usually no entirely suitable past, because the phenomenon these
ideologies claim to justify is not ancient or eternal but historically novel.

... The state of affairs affects [historians] in two ways. We
have a responsibility to historical facts in general and for criti-
cising the politico-ideological abuse of history in particular.

I need say little about the first of these responsibilities. I
would not have to say anything, but for two developments. One
is the current fashion for novelists to base their plots on recorded
reality rather than inventing them, thus fudging the border
between historical fact and fiction. The other is the rise of 'post-
modernist' intellectual fashions in Western universities,
particularly in departments of literature and anthropology, which
imply that all 'facts' claiming objective existence are simply
intellectual constructions. In short, that there is no clear difference between fact and fiction. But there is, and for historians ...
the ability to distinguish between the two is absolutely funda-
mental.

Eric Hobsbawm in a lecture at the Central European
University in Budapest, 1993

There are any number of reasons to be optimistic in Wales as this
century closes. At first sight not many of them are closely
connected to any historical or traditional definition of Welshness:
though it must be said, yet again, that much of that is an 'invented
tradition' of relatively recent times. And where it is not – the
language question, cultural modes, the very landscape we live in –
there is no rock that does not crumble as we shrink away from the
hard places which increasingly encroach on all our Welsh spaces.
At the end of the millennium traditionalists, of any sort, who yearn
to make a new Wales in the image of an idealised Wales, with characteristics derived from a continuum, have, at best, to compromise
heavily on the ideal. If radicalism has defined politics in Wales this
century there is little to suggest it will root easily in the opening
years of the next. If particular occupations, essentially dominated
by males, infused their work-derived ethic through whole communities, there is no sign that the emerging workforce will be anywhere near as distinctive or as homogeneous. If forms of popular
culture, notably collective and amateur from music to sports, once
translated local pride from street to stage then the emphasis on a
private quality of appreciation and professional demonstration of
skill has given us a global Esperanto of telecommunicated endeavour which dwarfs our former public intercommunication. If the
Welsh language itself survives or even flourishes it will largely be
because learners have embraced it as native speakers diminish and
linguistic bastions shudder. If religious faith widens or deepens,
even in our secular society, in imitation of its spread elsewhere,

then it will not be under the banner of a nonconformist religion that once marked out Wales as sharply as Roman Catholicism did Ireland.

New energies will not necessarily revitalise older givens of Welshness. Wales in the late 1890s shared experiences that were shot through with a commonality of religion, language, work and sense of place. Wales in the late 1990s is busying itself with plans for city-regions, Euro-Capitals, formal bilingualism and inward investment of foreign capital to tide over a low-skilled workforce until all the factors gel. It is not, in most ways, an unattractive vision but it begs the question – 'Who then will the Welsh be?' – it dares not ask. For over a decade the question which *was* posed so firmly and so often in the 1970s and early 1980s has been replaced by the soft affirmations of national identity which are second nature to the unelected and the unrepresentative. So, plenty of images of Wales and affirmations of Welsh identity have been showered upon us even as the nature of the country as experienced and expressed by the bulk of its inhabitants through four or five generations has been irredeemably changed. Even more to the point, the capability of Welsh people to influence such change or to respond meaningfully to it has been heavily restricted by the loss or destruction of the key institutions which they once forged to allow a democratic voice to be heard, yet these material changes are what will, eventually, create the new circumstances for the culture which will come to re-define the Welsh. Meanwhile those who have been the principal beneficiaries of economic and social banditry since the mid-1980s are now caught in a dilemma that only has one outcome: they must seek to maintain a cultural stasis that acts to legitimate their present power by presenting *all* other socio-cultural change (as articulated by others) as a threat to the very existence of the nation (as articulated by themselves): but they can only stand still by inventing a future dedicated to a mythical past. The alternative culture, that is already shaping, is an uncertain one because it has lost its material purchase on the present. It, too, must look to the past to find the motivation to drive it on. The difference is that its past lies within the borders of history not myth. What that history really was will inevitably decide who the Welsh will really be and so it is to the cultural debate of the last two decades that we need to turn to comprehend the ferocity of the intellectual conflict and, maybe, glimpse the future that the deniers of our actual history also fear and hate.

Paradoxically, by the end of the 1980s it seemed as if the debate was all over. The study and practice of history was more widely disseminated in Wales than ever before. The production of first-rate historical work was proceeding apace. The popularisation of historical explanation had had clear social impact. For the first time, the volume of work allowed us to talk of a 'Welsh historiography' and, hence, discuss not only the uncovering of material but also the rivalry of interpretation. In addition to the multi-volumed Oxford and Longman series, still on-going, and the one-off subject-specific monographs and the single volume, all-encompassing Histories of Wales, and the textual study series from the Open University, and the volumes of collected essays, in Welsh and English, from various publishers, and the vital academic journals which had quite revolutionised the subject – notably the *Welsh History Review* and *Llafur*, from 1960 and 1972 respectively – there came a welter of learned surveys of all this writing which, heavily footnoted and referenced as if in proof of their very contention, established the intellectual hegemony of the Welsh historical profession. The weight of this assertion can be traced, too, in the ways in which other forms of writing – from travelogues and journalism to fiction and poetry and criticism – were temporarily transfixed. Nor, for a while yet, did anyone challenge the two central assertions that had been made, and detailed, about the history of modern Wales – that the industrialisation and urbanisation of the country had transformed the whole way of life in Wales and that, this century, its principal means of expressing, articulating and dramatising its new self was in the English language.

This is what Gwyn A. Williams, in his volume of 'fractures', *When Was Wales?* wrote in 1985:

> Into that industrial Wales poured anything from two thirds to three quarters of the actually existing Welsh population. They shifted massively into the Southeast.... These people were drawn into a society which was repeatedly modernising and revolutionising itself, planting communities and uprooting them, building itself into an export metropolis of a world economy and merging inexorably into the overarching culture of the world language of English. This threatened to create two, and more, 'nations' out of a Welsh people.

And John Davies, in 1990 in his *A History of Wales* used his chapter titles to suggest geographical Trinities whose mystical unison might yet allow the centre to hold but, scrupulously, let his main text speak for itself:

In 1851, Wales had 1,163,139 inhabitants; it had 2,523,500 in 1914, an increase of 117 percent in sixty-three years ... in 1850, two out of three of the inhabitants of Wales spoke Welsh – a total of about 750,000 people – and most of them had no knowledge of any other language. By 1914, there were almost a million Welsh speakers; yet they represented only two fifths of the population, and four out of five of them had some command of English.....

To the vast majority in 1850, the world was full of omens and enchantment and of the supernatural acts of God and the devil, and many magical rites had functional significance. By 1914, the agents of modernity – education, mobility, machines, policemen, science – were rapidly leading to the 'disenchantment of the world' as mysticism yielded to rationalism.

Industrialisation and urbanisation and the new mentality which developed in their wake, were the root causes of this transformation.

However, though historians themselves accepted the force of evidence, even if they weighed it up in different ways, two extraneous factors prevented knowledge of that history becoming part of civic transformation.

The first was that the society which had been created by such history was itself passing out of history and, secondly, that if it lacked contemporary force then, perhaps, its historical pre-eminence could also be downgraded. After all, this was the only way in which a Wales conjured up by ideology could conceivably come into being. By the 1990s, if myth remained the ideologues' counterfeit coin, essentialism had become the plastic currency in which they now dealt.

★　★　★

These habits seem to be guided by a powerful if imprecise notion that works of literature are autonomous [but] ... literature [cannot] be chopped off from history and society. The supposed autonomy of works of art enjoins a kind of separation which, I think, imposes an uninteresting limitation that the works themselves resolutely will not make.... Neither culture nor imperialism is inert, and so the connections between them as historical experiences are dynamic and complex. My principal aim is not to separate but to connect, and I am interested in this for the main philosophical and methodological reason that cultural forms are hybrid, mixed, impure and the time has come in cultural analysis to reconnect their analysis with their actuality.

Edward Said, *Culture and Imperialism* (1993)

'Essentialism', as principally defined by Edward Said, is a mode of representing actuality, principally through texts, as if they could float free of social and historical moorings to become eternal and timeless in their meaning. Instead of this holistic creation he called for 'a profoundly secular perspective ... beholden neither to notions about historical destiny and the essentialism that destiny always seem to entail, nor to historical indifference and resignation'. This is a plea for the human right to choose difference allied to a belief in human agency, both held together by the human process which is history. It is precisely what Gwyn A. Williams, utterly committed to the historian's craft and the significance of that craft for society, meant when he talked of 'the Welsh ... making and re-making themselves in generation after generation ... usually within a British context. Wales is an artefact which the Welsh produce. If they want to.'

In the way of these things, in a Wales some of the Welsh want irrespective of our history, his remarks have been used as if *only* the agency mattered, and to hell with the context. The great historian would never have been so naive as to believe, with those who took his complexities and turned them into slogans, that you could 'invent Wales', any old Wales it seems, whenever and wherever you wished. Febrile plays and films from the end of the 1980s and into the present decade fantasise about a here-and-now Wales in order to evoke a future untrammelled by the confining jumble of a burdensome past. That future, however, is not convincingly available. Writers have spun fantasises because their work has lacked precise connections into, knowledge of, a completed, an achieved history. Fantasy has been a substitute for a past they have not imagined and a future they cannot, therefore, conceive. We have had a decade and more in which fictive characters have fed on their own dreams not ours, and so illuminated only the backdrop of the writer's mind.

Literary criticism over these years has also struggled to come to terms with the connections between literature and society. Separate accounts of Welsh language and English-language writing only seemed to confirm the other divides in Welsh life which the industrial transformation of Wales had brought in its wake. The bilious rage this aroused in some sections of the Welsh intelligentsia enlivened but scarcely illuminated the debate. The desire for simplistic outcomes, fair shares for all and equal dues, just flew in the face of all the available evidence and, when it was conceded, as it must needs be, that Welsh-language writing had not grappled with the overwhelming experience of the twentieth-century Welsh in the way that had happened in English-language writing: why, then the debate changed to argue for the significance of influences and interrelationships across languages so that the unfortunate, regrettable, but, yes, undeniable 'internal difference' could be lessened. My point here is not to argue against some salient points made and certainly not, ever, to suggest that the Welsh language, in many manifestations, did not permeate the historical experience of modern Wales. It is rather to repeat that it was, nonetheless, in English that the characteristic literature, politics and social intercourse of that forming society was conducted. Of course there were significant exceptions – though generally marginalised by origins, location or political creeds – but the literary divergence is, historically, a clear-cut one. To seek a different way of being and writing in the future is the right of anyone in Wales disgruntled by our present confusion. It is, though, no one's right to alter a past reality. That actually is sacred for when, and if, all the primary and secondary and even tertiary hallmarks of Welshness vanish from any contemporary society the one sure thing that will remain to be possessed is the history we share and dispute.

One of the areas of dispute in recent years has been over the question of whether 'Wales' must imply a species of unity or, if not, whether those who choose to be Welsh can be diverse without being divisive, mature without being triumphalist, minoritarian without being overbearing. I believe the history of Wales will prevent the emergence of a wish-fulfilled Wales but I also believe that if the Welsh know their own history they will not concede that their country requires or needs totalising definitions of an essentialist kind. If the sightless mask of essentialism in Wales was literary criticism then its white stick was a form of social anthropology. The empirical basis of the latter was information gathering through social survey statistics and field interviews. Its relationship to the weaker tenets of journalism was uncanny. Newspaper leaders periodically hailed its findings because they, too, inhabited a Wales in which turning over a long-discredited cliché somehow passed for truth-telling. Years after the staple joke and common lore of industrial South Wales had been about men and women crossing and cris-crossing over from valley to valley on Friday nights to enjoy new-found freedoms, and decades after the phenomenon of working women had altered home-life and conceptions of 'Mam', intrepid investigators and faithful reporters laboured to tell us how very, very much the Valleys differed from their outdated image. What was missing was any sense of the relationships between people, across generations and gender, between a landscape and a life, a past and a present. No feel for this meant no grasp of why Tower should emerge as the first workers' co-operative pit and the last deep-mine left in Wales. To think that was a mere matter of economics was not to think at all, as that splendidly named Welshman, Tyrone O'Sullivan, could have informed them. Only to be informed would have been to acknowledge the past that did make the Tower story a successful one and, once again, whatever the empiricism, the cultural imperialism at work was out to substitute a theory of disempowerment – that Labour and Union industrial leadership had misled their followers – for the reality experienced by the disempowered: that a loss of self-built institutions compounded the powerlessness attendant on economic decline. If they read history they would see how the 1920s had underlined this and the 1930s reversed it. Conditions changed but human agency remained, and required more than 'committees of notables' to allow its purpose to be felt.

★   ★   ★

About half a century after most of Ireland won its independence, Irish historians no longer wrote the history of their island in terms of the mythology of the national liberation movement. Irish history, both in the Republic and in the North, is producing brilliant work because it has succeeded in so liberating itself. This is still a matter that has political implications and risks [but] the fact that a new generation has grown up which can stand back from the passions of the great traumatic and formative moments of their countries' history is a sign of hope for historians.

However, we cannot wait for the generations to pass. We must resist the *formation* of national, ethnic, and other myths, as they are being formed. It will not make us popular ... [but] ... it has to be done.

Eric Hobsbawm, 1993

There are any number of reasons to be pessimistic in Wales as this century closes. The debate we have held amongst ourselves grew shriller and more personalised as the ideals of the 1970s shrivelled – the miners' strikes and victories of 1972 and 1974 were only harbingers of the heart-rending community struggle and defeat that was the 1984-5 strike; the devolution swell of the late 1970s foundered as surely in Gwynedd as it did in Gwent, and was more supported in West and Mid Glamorgan than in either Welsh extremity. The *ad hoc* bodies that formed and re-formed during the fall-out of the miners' year-long fight vainly grasped at the straws which appeared to be bringing their respective, 'historic' Waleses together. Yet the very coupling of the Communist Party in Wales with the National Left groupings of Plaid Cymru was nothing if not emblematic of the way in which such tendencies, once fringe but very much attached to a Welsh polity, were themselves in free-fall. The mainstream structures of democratic Welsh politics would now be systematically dismantled or, at best, reduced in power and intent. Confusion was worse compounded as Welsh public life turned into a novelist's nightmare – material and characters so steeped in self-aggrandisement and so capable of double-talk in pursuit of power and wealth that neither magic realism nor post-modernism could hope to capture the ineffable spectacle of a nation led by scoundrels in the name of patriotism.

As the new philistinism spread through Welsh society the most penetrating question the managers of the Brave New Wales could think to pose was the one they found most appropriate in the weights and measures departments of life – 'How will I know when you have succeeded?' To which the only real answers were – 'When you know what it is we should be trying to do; when you know what can be measured and what cannot, by its nature, be weighed; when you understand that a society is not an empty shelf that can be stocked or re-stocked or just discarded; when you realise that if you only ask one kind of question you will have only one kind of answer.'

So we measured and tabulated and exchanged statistics as if they were insults or plaudits and built Heritage theme-parks at a rate of over five hundred in a decade. Somehow the great debate passed over the head of people who continued to just live through some of the most momentous shifts in Welsh life in the last one hundred years. Newspaper leaders regularly highlighted the advances made by the various Welsh language movements (for they were never single in purpose or style) in the public perception, and just as routinely invented layers of hostility that had not, and largely do not, exist. Yet as the linguistic signage (an unlovely 1980s term, as redolent of its time as any) proliferated on the streets, a whole culture, in both languages but mostly in English, was put to the sword economically, despised socially and ignored for its palpable achievements. Oddly then, the much-patronised heritage industry, albeit patchily, offered this beleaguered, but still majoritarian, Welsh people a glimpse of hope. Not the rather forlorn and exaggerated hope of tourist dollars and wide-eyed visitors but the deeper, rooted and localised sensibility that who they were and where they came from had a value that was immeasurable. After all, they had little else but their own history to take forward. The question posed by that history for Wales as a whole was how it could be connected to the new political economy of Wales – connected or disdained and discarded. There were enough self-interested and self-appointed in Wales to opt for the latter and, for a time, they may appear to win. The victory would be a Pyrrhic one for their own materialism is itself built on cultural foundations, on the propagation of Wales plc, and, without the full and open recognition of that once industrial and urban, working-class world which, more than any other, shaped the modern Welsh, it would be built on sand. Then some society will live here, and even thrive, but, except in the memory, it will not be a Welsh one.

The real task is to turn the sentimental possibilities inherent in Heritage into the civic gains available from acknowledged History. Some of that can be accomplished by educational means, and especially within the framework of life-long learning; and, of course, the support for the teaching, study and research of the history of Wales needs to be restored to the levels attained in the 1960s and 1970s so that new generations can have a chance to produce work similar in impact to that proclaimed during the so-called 'Renaissance' in Welsh historical writing, underway from the early 1960s. That conveyor belt is now shuddering as the supply of practitioners dries up. It is my contention that that historical conveyor belt is the most secure life-line to a Welsh historical future – and that that phrase is not a contradiction in terms. The history can only be conveyed if we make and sustain a culture in which we allow history to liberate us from an eternal present.

Pessimism does not necessarily entail despair. One of the most salient facets of the first half of this century is that when it was over the Welsh did not appear to require the kind of intellectual purgative that revisionist history in Ireland would have to supply for our near neighbour. The reason was a simple one. History itself had made the Welsh a secular, rational and de-mystified people. Historiography was only lacking in the positive sense of telling that story and it soon began to do so. Historical process had cleared away the other lumber. When the political and social desires attendant on that particular experience floundered from the 1970s those who had always detested the 'distortion' it had produced in Wales moved to propagate an alternative world, one that had been made marginal but could now compete for the spoils. History was quickly identified as the story which needed the new spin. In 1989 *Sbec*, then S4C's free TV Guide, published a 'ten-part pull-out supplement building up to a 160 page guide to Welsh history'. It was bilingual. And it had, in Wales' two languages, an alternative timescale in which two 'Wales', of equal validity, just occasionally collided:

OL-NODYN

DYDDIADAU PWYSIG YN HANES CYMRU

1929 – Ethol y wraig gyntaf yn Aelod Seneddol yng Nghymru – Megan Lloyd George yn Sir Fôn.

1931 – Dim ond 37.2% o boblogaeth Cymru a fedrai'r Gymraeg yn ôl y cyfrifiad.

1933 – Sefydlu'r Bwrdd Marchnata Llaeth yn cymell ffermwyr Cymru i gynhyrchu llaeth.

1934 – 265 yn cael eu lladd ym Mhwll Glo Gresford, ger Wrecsam.

1935 – y BBC yn cynhyrchu o Fangor.

1936 – Rhyfel Cartref Sbaen yn dechrau – o'r 174 o wirfoddolwyr o Gymru, bu farw 33. Carcharu Saunders Lewis, Lewis Valentine a D.J. Williams am eu rhan yn yr ymosodiad ar yr Ysgol Fomio ym Mhenyberth, Pen Llyn.

1937 – Mudo o Dde Cymru yn cyrraedd ei frig. Rhwng 1921 a 1940, gadawodd 430,000 o bobl Cymru, y golled fwyaf mewn poblogaeth drwy Ewrop gyfan.

1939 – Agor yr ysgol gynradd Gymraeg gyntaf yn Aberystwyth.

1941 – Bomiau'r Almaenwyr yn lladd 387 yn Abertawe a 165 yng Nghaerdydd.

1945 – Bu farw David Lloyd George yn Llanystymdwy.

1947 – Eisteddfod Ryngwladol Llangollen yn cael ei sefydlu.

BACKDATE

KEY DATES IN WELSH HISTORY

1929 – In the General Election, the Labour Party wins 25 out of the 36 seats in Wales.

1931 – Death of Welsh miners' leader A.J. Cook.

1934 – Male unemployment in Rhondda 60%, in Merthyr Tydfil 69% in Dowlais 73%

1936 – Start of the Spanish Civil War in which 174 volunteers from Wales fight, and 33 of these die. Saunders Lewis, Lewis Valentine and D.J. Williams of Plaid Cymru imprisoned for their part in the attack on the R.A.F. Bombing Station on the Lleyn Peninsula.

1937 – Mass emigration from South Wales at its height (between 1921 and 1940, 430,000 people leave Wales, the highest population loss in Europe).

1939– An economic report suggests that Merthyr Tydfil be abandoned as a town and its population transferred.

1944 – First 'Welsh Day' debate in the House of Commons devoted to Welsh affairs

1945 – Welsh Labour MPs prominent in the first majority Labour Government (Aneurin Bevan as Minister of Health and James Griffiths as Minister of National Insurance). David Lloyd George dies at Llanystumdwy.

1947 – Coal industry nationalised and celebrations held throughout South and North Wales coalfields.

Equal validity, yes. Equal impact, no, for as Bevan once insisted 'There is no democracy of facts'. Democrats and citizens cannot allow history to be derailed by patriots. Communication of the whole of our history and our culture, in its actual and palpable form, is now of the essence if the institutions we will inhabit are to serve the Welsh and not the idea of Wales.

★   ★   ★

I grew up [in Chicago in the 1950s and 60s] on the WFMT voice. It was [a radio station] ... full of calm, reason and – most important I think – self-esteem. The voice seemed to say: 'This is the way we do things here. The music we play, the shows we air – we are proud of them. They reflect our vision of the world....

The idea in the air was that culture was what we, the people, did. The idea was – and is – that we were *surrounded* by culture. It was not alien to us. It was what the people did and thought and sang and wrote about. The idea was [an admixture] of the populist and the intellectual. The model ... was an autodidact: a man or a woman who so loved the world around him or her that he or she was moved to investigate it further – either by creating works of art or by appreciating those works.

Our heroes, to we who grew up listening ... were those with vast talent and audacity, and no respect.

[Especially] ... WFMT meant listening to Studs Terkel and his humanism and enthusiasm and, finally, delighted wonder at the whole damn thing.

David Mamet, *The Cabin*, 1991

When I was a boy, and steam trains still ran, there were no open or connecting carriages. You entered your particular carriage and sat on one of the moquette rows, four passengers to a row, which faced each other. To all intents and purpose you were locked in until the train shuddered to a stop at the next station. Except for one thing, one fascinating, tempting thing – above the carriage door in a hyphenated space just big enough for a hand was a taut chain. And on the wooden panel painted in red were the words:

Do not pull the Communication Cord
Except in case of Emergency

This was the cord which connected the isolated passenger to the driver. The only means of communication. To misuse the means was to be fined beyond the pocket of any boy, and most families.

In a sense we are all now in those isolated carriages staring at the taut communication chain. We live increasingly separate lives. We are an endlessly mobile people. Whizzing about in our sealed, private spaces to our sealed, private homes. Think of how little we use our public spaces, how emptied of residents our city centres are, and of how full on Saturday nights, outside night clubs, pubs, cinemas, they are, of colliding, distinct atoms, of you, of us, hurrying past to go home to sit in front of a private screen.

And even if I exaggerate just slightly it still underlines how vital it is that we make some connection between our social being and our individual lives. The act and the art of communicator is as crucial to a society's well being as the science or technological advance of communications.

In his book *Keywords* (1976) Raymond Williams pointed out that the general meaning of 'communications' – to make common something or other to many – came to mean, as the industrialisation and urbanisation of Britain proceeded, something more akin to 'lines of communication' or 'means of communication' – in other words, roads, canals, railways – transport. Now, at one level this was the key component in transforming our societies, because it did force the atoms together, and made us 'in common'. Think of how a map of Victorian Wales would, within, a generation, from 1850 to 1880, have changed from a virtual blank, so far as a cross-hatching of railway lines is concerned, to a series of lines drawn so closely together they almost merge into a dark mass. And down and across those lines of communication flowed people, from all over the world, to live in the new townships and bigger cities of the coalfield and the coast. This brought together people who did not know each other, did not share generations of family or village memories, did not, in the street, recognise each other and did not possess the forms of *retreat* into a sealed off, privatised world of domesticity and of entertainment that we do. There was the book, the printed word of course, but mostly that would be found, and often read, in libraries. Private possession and reading of books was largely, and until the appearance of paperbacks, the mark of a professional or middle-class existence. So the new world of South Wales, if it was to develop as a community and not just exist as an aggregation of people, if it was to find a way for people to live together as citizens and not just as workers, had also to communicate in a different way.

This experience was one undergone by other immigrant societies the world over. It happened in Chicago – and Cardiff in 1905 was called by a French observer 'ce petit Chicago' – as it happened on the lower East Side of Manhattan, in New York City, where successive waves of Germans, Italians, Jews, Poles and Russians congregated in the decades before the First World War. No coincidence that out of *that* environment, out of *that* babel, came some of the greatest communicators the world has seen this century – out of a world of street politics, of theatre and vaudeville and over-crowded tenement buildings came Tin Pan Alley, and the world of streetmusic publishing, and later records – a universal language to cut across the mutual incomprehensibility imposed by language. From those unpromising beginnings came James Cagney, born in 1899, the Irish-American punk who in movies was instantly recognisable as any kid on any corner in any miserable city in the world. Cagney, like Chaplin, did not need words to communicate his broke but gutsy personality – he stuck out his pigeon chest, and, backside almost horizontal with his head, *strutted.* Across the world, and especially in South Wales, that struck chords as resonant as George Gershwin's haunting hymn to urban life, *Rhapsody in Blue*; it was, beyond and including Cagney, a tap dance that had tap roots into the new peoples' lives.

Out of this need there came a shift in the meaning of 'communications' – a peculiarly twentieth-century shift – one that saw us all understand it as the 'communications industry', print and film and broadcasting, 'the media', and now videos, the information superhighway, the internet, the digital revolution that will, give an unprecedented range of radio and television channels. What this means is that the careful doling out of the air waves and transmission channels across the limited spectrum that the old technology imposed is at an end. The broadcasters are positioning themselves like camels with shrivelled humps to get their share of the 'spectrum glut'. And we, at home, confronted by a myriad of choices will have to decide whether this is real freedom, real communication or another way of dividing us. Does the receiver have to be passive, a consumer in a cocoon? Should the transmitter be the *broadcaster,* not the narrowcaster, intent on helping along the process of sharing that we label 'community' and to which end the act and art of the 'communicator' becomes increasingly central? Content was once as crucial as form and the wonder of the 'whole damn thing' was once conveyed, was once communicated, was once made common and shared because otherwise it could not be a socially coherent force. Just over a century ago we would have been born into a world, here in Wales, where no-one had ever seen an international rugby match in Wales since the Welsh Rugby Union and all the trails of glory it would later signify, did not exist; the valleys, though already heavily populated in places like Merthyr and Aberdare, had not been filled up with the terraces that, within two generations, would come to stand for 'what this place looks like'; the pithead gear was not yet towering, latticed and iron; and the population was not yet, as soon it would be, the fastest growing in the British Isles. There were no music halls, variety theatres or cinemas, no panoramic photography of the streets or hymn-singing football crowds. In short the images of Wales, soon clichés and communicated to the world, were just not there yet to be disseminated. By the time we arrive at 1995 and the National Lottery it was second nature to a communications body like the BBC (London branch I hasten to add) to decide, when promoting the venture live from Wales, to wheel on male voice choirs, ex-miners with their lamps and the pit head gear of your neighbourhood Heritage Park.

All of which is to say that the past reality has indeed disappeared but that the perception of it down those historic lines of communication remains more potent than the present reality. We might call this a failure in communication. The sense we have of ourselves in Wales is so confused that we scramble our signals to the outside world. Partly this is because we have, in this latest phase of our social and cultural modernity, yet to reconcile the non-stop roller-coaster of wonder that was South Wales down to the 1920s with the subsequent long-fall into economic disaster and then national subsidy that has been our lot for most of this century. Take a trip down the M4 between Swansea and Cardiff: at one point you'll pass three clustered signs, in English and Welsh, directing you to the Museum of Welsh Life, Barry Island and Cardiff/Wales Airport. A perfect trinity to sum up our past and our uncertain present. A folkloric past in aspic; a pleasure dome originally built as a 1920s Workers' Playground; and a ticket out of the place. We'll need to choose how to reconcile that trinity.

In innumerable ways, and in ways most historians have not yet begun to trace, communication, imparting and sharing in common, has been layered through recent Welsh history. Quite simply people needed to make sense of their lives together in bad times and good – not all could find individual escape routes, and social coherence could only be found through a common purpose. Image-makers in film, theatre, on television, with paints and prose and poetry, through photography and by sound of all kinds, are not in the business of just reflecting our existing reality. They are, if the communication with us is intense enough, shaping the way we have been and will be. There is no longer, if there ever was, something that just existed, that was there to be communicated, and then understood. The communicator is at the epicentre of our culture. The cultural communicator – in song, in dress, in advertising, in video, in magazines – is a manipulator of future behaviour. You might call this by another word, lamely applied now only to politics, propaganda. And if propaganda, seeping into a social and cultural context is still, publicly anyway, anathema in any civilised, plural society, then public service broadcasting in a communications-dominated world really does find itself at the heart of the matter of late twentieth-century Britain and Wales.

The Italian, Marconi, sent the first successful wireless signal between the South Wales mainland and Flatholm in the Bristol

Channel in 1897 and shortly involved the greatest Welsh communicator of the pre-wireless age in financial scandal. By the 1920s when David Lloyd George had fallen from power forever, the technological revolution in communication which radio represented had hit Wales no less than other parts of the British Isles. Initially sets were expensive and make-do ones were cobbled together, but the demand did not cease. On the new 3-valve radio sets in the 1930s you could hear news, comedy, drama, variety theatre, sport and royal pronouncements. It was an incredible means of uniting people of different outlook and location but, more importantly, and however pompous the early BBC may have sounded, it offered social and cultural opportunities for people literally deprived, by income or geography, of live theatre, opera and the great sporting events. In the summer of 1930 as economic crisis and social despair deepened in South Wales the Carnegie Trust, a philanthropic body that had placed books in the Miners' Institutes across the coalfield, turned their attention to the new-fangled radio. They established fourteen centres, from Aberaman to Kenfig Hill, where people could gather, together, to listen. Their report said:

> The wireless set has brought much pleasure and variety into the lives of many people who, before it came, had little to talk about except the perennial subject of how to make ends meet. As one man remarked, the wireless had brought 'happiness' into the place. [The sets are] ... intended to be used for amusement and recreation as well as for instruction. It would be entirely wrong for anyone to suppose that the wireless set was to be looked upon as a kind of schoolmaster. Such an attitude would show a complete misapprehension of the whole business. The thing which wireless can do is to bring into every Institute the living voice of some of the best speakers of the day, discussing all kinds of subjects, subjects which have a broad human value and are not confined to any one view of life or any one attitude towards it.

Over sixty years later I think we can take that as a definition of broadcasting purpose that still stands. Of course television continued the domestication of our cultural habits – with curtains drawn and visitors forbidden to knock in the very early days – and the enormous spread of possibilities will undoubtedly continue to make private, or family, watching, the norm despite the renaissance of cinema and the rise of an interactive technology. But how we use that technology will prove to be a function of our role as citizens *or* as playthings. We will need to decide whether great sporting events, themselves the product of late Victorian popular culture and not the slick invention of some PR expert, are an integral part of our national identity, something we have created to share, or another consumer goodie on which, if we have the means, we can gorge our more limited selves. But will those kinds of occasion be worth having if we do not sense that we share them in common because they have communicated their worth to all of us?

Broadcasting in Wales will increasingly need to stress the achievements and tradition of the majority experience in twentieth-century Wales in the language of that majority, the English tongue that has become our principal Welsh means of communication. Only a clear minded and full-hearted understanding and acceptance of our modern, complex history will be sufficient if we are to move forward. A nation without the public memory that history is can have no more sense of its identity than an amnesiac patient has of a former, forming life. There *are* those who would wish the historical slate wiped clean; it can't be done, and they will end up communicating only amongst themselves since communication is a two way process in which ears are as vital as mouths. And eyes, of course.

Such communication, particularly broadcasting, will need to be continuously vital in our culture in Wales in the way a Chicagoan radio station was in the life and mind of *its* listeners; and in the consciousness of one of them, David Mamet:

> WFMT has lived long and has served and continues to serve the community in an essential way. It has persisted and grown. The station sounds to me today much as it did when I was a kid: a voice saying 'Culture' is just that which we do. 'Here are some things in our heritage which we enjoy, and we think you will enjoy them, too.' It was and is a beautiful voice, a self-respecting voice, and the voice of home.

Changing Wales

Her intuition had divined a condition of life that existed irrespective of countries and national boundaries.
Alun Richards, 'The Former Miss Merthyr Tydfil'

Wales is a singular noun but a plural experience. The Welsh are different from each other because of their history. The paradox they face is that they look to that history for traditions, the continuity and the assurance that a society uncertain of itself requires. There has long been a quest for unity where little exists, past or present, and a shunning of the diversity that is the true mark, in every sense, of this nation's maturity. Rival monologues of the past are substituted for historical dialogue. Myths, nostalgia, kitsch and celebration are bottled for consumption by adults who publicly consent to designate their own groups and sub-groups as the essential part of the whole they can, by their very nature, never effect. Until there is a full understanding of the hold-all terms 'Wales' and 'the Welsh' as historically and socially constructed matters which have, in turn, interacted with and acted upon whatever material reality has been in Wales we will continue to live in shadows of our own making.

The problem of Wales is not the Welsh but the problematic of 'Welshness'. Perhaps it is the size of Wales that drives so many of the Welsh to look for a holistic society, a totally defensible bastion against the world, like Masada, where a bond can never be dissolved, only transmuted by suicide. Some of the Welsh now feel this way about their allegiance to a linguistic definition of Wales. But if the adherents to language are the most exclusively 'native' of the Welsh, their mirror image is often to be found in those who settle in Wales, usually in the exceptionally pretty parts; for them allegiance is more to a land of beauty which still possesses – as we are told in exquisite prose and verse whose fragmentation bears witness to inner pain – a spirituality, a lambent mythology of the past revealed in the present, holding the outside world at bay. Wales rings with the self-righteousness of those who make claims for it according to the image of the country necessary for them.

There was a time when the politics and culture of Wales were vitally exciting precisely because those who espoused the country's cause – say the pre-1914 socialists who challenged the public sway of Liberal rule and nonconformist pretension – wedded their arguments to a complex reality. Wales was not then 'a problem'. It was seen within a wide framework of religion, politics, the state, cities, industry, education, unions; the problems facing the people who lived in Wales were confronted on a broad scale. This species of nationality has, since the 1920s, been deemed inadequate. It is certainly messy. It is not easy to answer the question – 'Who are the Welsh?' – unless their identity is made very rigid (language, birth, residence) or very elastic (anyone who chooses to consider themselves part of the nation).

But what is a nation? To that question, too, the Welsh have given many answers, and if ideas of an unbroken historical tradition or a poetic genius can scarcely withstand the probe of logic or scholarship, it does not seem to affect one whit their continuing manufacture. The nation is, as Benedict Anderson has coined it, an 'imagined community'. However, people do not all necessarily 'imagine' the same community. 'Public' definitions may collide with 'private' realities in America or even England without serious questioning of national identity, but the 'imagined community' applied to Ireland or, in muted fashion, to Wales can become a monolith imposed on or offered to the subjected or blind people. Monoliths are easier for outsiders to recognise, and there is a patronising kind of sympathy to which small countries like Wales are prey which prefers to accept such an easy answer than hear a babel of voices.

Also, the manner in which Wales developed from the late eighteenth century meant that in politics, economics and culture the country was knitted closer and closer into a 'British' fabric of government and society. The very success of that tale prevents any quick disentanglement of the threads of 'Welshness' and 'Britishness', no matter how ardently some of the Welsh may desire this. The mainstream experience of the 'modern inhabitants of Wales' – has been about multi-faceted tension and not its dissolution. Maybe the latter will be our next stage. If so, it will surely not come by whistling against the winds of our actual past.

That sense of potential is, for me, the best welcome Wales can provide. It is an exciting place in which to live, to analyse, to share. I do not see Wales as a talisman or as a tradition or even as an alternative – utopian, ecological, linguistic, picturesque – to what exists already, here and elsewhere. It is an actual territory, forged by a complex historical process that is not yet worked out. Its experiences are clearly not separate from other experiences in and beyond the British Isles, but it has experienced such common, human history in ways – linguistic, cultural and social – that make it the Welsh experience.

There have been tragedies within this country – none greater than the fate which overtook the Welsh language from the late nineteenth century, none more doleful that the economic depression of the inter-war years – which perhaps only farce can convey. In the hands of a Welsh Borges or a Cymric Rushdie our experiences might be transmuted into the gold of mythopoeic history. Enlightenment might follow. Instead we seem to have been content to parade half-truths in an historical mythology of obscurantist illogicality. There is, of course, plain history, but the historian, too, deals in fiction, even if, like the private eye he resembles, he can only coin his wisecracks within the legal tender of a framework of rules. In this look at the way Wales has been, or perceived to have been in the last bewildering century I occasionally bend the rules because, to quote the nineteenth-century American novelist William Dean Howells, 'A man is not born in his native country for nothing. I wish I might persuade you'. Such persuasion needs to be specific and personal, for authenticity requires the induced sincerity of the one-eyed observer.

Any definition of Welsh experience, native or otherwise, is inseparable from a sense of place. Perhaps this is why so much topographical lyricism is sung over the beauties of the Welsh countryside. Confronted with the startling rock-strewn vistas of North Wales mountains or the enticing sweep of Cardigan Bay you can see the point. It is undeniably and essentially Wales, but it is not the Wales that sings to me. Empathy with the sea, lakes, mountains and rock strata may serve one kind of purpose but scarcely scratch the surface of a lived, human history.

I could define 'my' Wales in terms of pit-head winding gear, domino rows of terraced houses falling down hills that pass for mountains, and the thin defiance of a brass band on the march. The clichés are too close to the truth for most of us to avoid them. The disappearance since my youth of most of these 'primary' sociological characteristics may finally purge us of our clichés with their preservative gel of nostalgia. Our definitions will become sharper, but their primary node will remain urban.

The greater part of the landmass of Wales lies north of Merthyr Tydfil and west of Llanelli. It shrugs off the leaden-footed South and embraces only a very select urban progeny: spas, market towns and seaside resorts, enlivened by academic terms and summer tourists but, mostly, as private as the solitary walks for which they seem designed. North-East Wales, in location and in accent, teeters on the edge of the Merseyside conurbation, all red-brick, flat land, sluggish canals and low hedgerows. Wrexham is the biggest Welsh town outside the South, framed between hills to its west and the umbilical motorway, permanently external, to the parental east. Local patriots cling to it as tenaciously as those who love unlovely Newport or crow over feisty Llanelli. But this is all small-town stuff and there is good reason to argue that until now Wales has never possessed an urban heart.

True, Swansea between the wars was able to foster artistic talent. It had developed a style as a town which hugged together a Welsh ruralism and a Welsh provincialism in two tongues. Its smugness was rescued by its jaunty style. The devastating bombing raids of World War Two smashed its higgledy-piggledy nature and it continued to ruin its chance of any urbanity with almost every new building that has gone up, or not, since. The insufferable superiority of interwar Cardiff, established on no more elegant a source than the detritus of Docks money, decades after that supply had dried up, was compounded of suburban swank and an ineradicable accent which cut into aural sensibilities like wire through cheese.

Yet Cardiff now has the feel of the capital city it has been in name since 1955. It now has a decidedly all-Wales focus, underlined further by the Assembly. It has long left behind its merely commercial image. Cardiff is now a real possibility as the accepted Capital of Wales. It is more 'Welsh' in outlook today thanks to the spread of bureaucracy and the communications industry than it has ever been. It lives both to its own rhythms and within the expectation of those who use it as the Capital of Wales. Its metropolitan artificiality, so recently created, is perfect as a setting for the Wales in flux that will be our condition to the end of this century. Or, to adopt the lines of the Cardiff poet, Dannie Abse, it will serve, for our future, as a place 'where the boy I was not and the man I am not met, hesitated, left double footsteps, then walked on.'

The past, too, can sidestep us. The sense of our past should not be just a matter of complacency or pride, it should be one of burning recognition. What moulded the Wales in which we live now is often half-forgotten but never completely so, because everything that Wales now is can never be separated from the experience of the part of it called, in a still-dismissive generalisation, the Valleys. That experience – of industrial growth and population explosion – altered the essence of Wales by its material irruption. Easily the highest percentage of native born Welsh people live here (well over 90 per cent of the population compared to figures of only 60 per cent plus in North-West Wales and less than that in the North-East Border counties) and, despite an aging demographic profile, their work seepage, rather than removal, across the only motorway that penetrates Wales will ensure their full integration into the technologically-driven economy of the next century.

The Valleys are not malleable. They still stand out in accusation of the past like a painful backbone that refuses to be slid quietly via the analgesic of nostalgia, into a diminished future. This is not a question of mere economics or even survival. The Valleys are needed to take forward a culture. There is nothing in this culture which denies change. There is everything in it which refuses the dehumanising of people in the name of any abstraction or their reduction in the name of a respectful celebration of a 'heroic' past.

The Valleys – the industrial, working-class history of the majority of the Welsh – have not marked their inhabitants alone. They have endlessly fascinated and frightened others by their successive levels of deprivation and their self-induced visions of human possibility. For a long time now, they have been observed without having been seen, comprehended without being understood.

Their history and their myths must be joined together until a third element appears – and that is the relationship of 'Wales' to Wales. Historical paraphrase has been less adept than poems or paintings or music in bringing off the conjuring trick. Perhaps it can only be 'experienced' before it can be 'informing'. Even then a tangled skein of personality, nationality and intellectuality will not allow, I suspect, an illuminating identikit for the Welsh to be handed out in our schools. Besides, formal education does not invariably illuminate. It depends on what and by whom you are taught. Blinkers have often been regulation wear in Welsh classrooms and it has been customary for Welsh writers to lament (along with the Scots and the Irish) the lack of teaching and learning about their native country in their schools, colleges and universities.

In one sense, though, this did not apply so far as I and many others were concerned. There was, in our education, a form of Welsh history and Welsh grammar and Welsh geography and Welsh literature. Some of it even spilled into the twentieth century to demonstrate 'relevance'. Mainly, however, it was a knee-jerk response to the accident of national locality. None of it seemed to confront the implicit sense of a Welsh experience all around me, in my family and in the places I lived. When that was made 'accessible' it came across as a kind of comic grotesquerie or as an inane celebration of virtues (in song, in sport, in what were variously labelled national characteristics and pastimes). What interested me and those I lived amongst were, contrariwise, all the elements of a popular culture which was, and still is, quickly denigrated as Anglo-American commercialism; later came the flood of general ideas and literature which swamps adolescence.

But I never doubted my Welshness in, or outside, Wales. Equally it never occurred to me that I would ever choose to spend any time working on the history of Wales, let alone come to study and write and broadcast about it professionally. For one thing I took it, and myself, for granted. For another what was exciting intellectually seemed to be about other places – and for me particularly the history of England, France and America. Only slowly did it occur that the techniques being used elsewhere to explore social and cultural history were not dependent purely on having available sources and a backlog of secondary literature. The lack of both of these was, I would discover later, a serious handicap in Wales, but it was a by-product of larger neglect rather than an inherent deficiency. Either way it seemed more useful to continue to widen intellectual horizons than to stay safe within the one I 'knew'. However, what began to nag at me in alien Oxford and in much less alien New York was the feeling that I was, though irredeemably rooted in Wales, intellectually ignorant of the recent history that had shaped my Wales. As I mooched in the library stacks and catalogues of Columbia University, I realised how patchy was the written history of nineteenth- and twentieth-century Wales.

In retrospect it is obvious that a revolution in Welsh historiography was already underway. I felt the first blast when I opened a copy of *Merthyr Politics: The Making of a Working Class Tradition*, edited by Glanmor Williams, sent to me in New York on its publication in 1966. Here were essays which spoke directly of industrial South Wales in a sophisticated historical manner. Glanmor Williams, in his introduction, noted how unbalanced was the amount of historical writing on rural Wales when the actual weight of history had shifted to industrial Wales. As I read that, even the winds that howled in across a wintry Atlantic sounded welcoming. No one today would be unable to read up the history of modern Wales, in survey or learned monograph or academic journal. The teaching of twentieth-century Welsh history is commonplace now in the schools and colleges of Wales as it was not, at any sustained level, thirty years ago. However, what is still not to be gainsaid is the comparative lack of impact of this reworked history on the general intellectual and cultural climate of Wales in the 1990s. The implications of the written history, in books and journals, has not filtered through to challenge contemporary assumptions about the origins of present attitudes and policies in Wales.

This is, in part, because more direct solutions had been discovered. Welsh life in the 1960s and 1970s was declared irredeemably fractured without the healing power of the Welsh language and the institutions that could succour it. The simplicity of this message, allied to an insistence that 'Wales' had been exploited as a colony of imperial 'England' and given a false 'British' consciousness, was its strength. Its weakness was the fact that it was largely a historical fantasy blended with a socio-cultural myth. Its attached politics, therefore, could not emerge fully even if South Wales was called a 'disappearing culture'. 'Cultures' do not disappear; they are acted upon by, and react against, the process of social formation from which they can never float free. The future of the politics of language in Wales proved less 'the revolutionary socialist analysis' of the 1960s and 1970s as the comfortable 'repressive toleration' of the years which followed.

The obvious alternative for those concerned to emphasise the unwritten history of the twentieth-century Welsh was to engage in a counter-blast of celebration. There was, after all, a wealth of material with which to refute the denigrators of Wales' majority culture. The sheer courage and humanity of those communities had been matched by an amazing capacity for playfulness and emotional release. Were brass bands and educational classes, autodidacts and platform eloquence, political magic and pigeon-fancying, male-voice choirs and rugby teams and voracious reading *not* 'culture'? Above all else the institution which had given cohesion to a community was absent: the South Wales Miners' Federation ('The Fed') was, in its heyday, the single most vital element in twentieth-century Wales but, in its relative decline, it had been ignored. The danger with this counter-approach, pursued energetically by some historians in the 1970s, was that explication and presentation occasionally outweighed critique and analysis. It provided a mirror image of Welsh-speaking Wales which has, through crisis and shrinkage, been self-absorbed and fiercely bonded when threatened.

In 1983 the distinguished Welsh novelist Emyr Humphreys published an impressionistic but learned survey of Welsh history. *The Taliesin Tradition* took as its theme the survival of a continuous Welsh tradition in the face of all contrary odds. He ascribed this to a 'poetic tradition' which had invested the native language with the power and authority to sustain 'national being'. For Emyr Humphreys this was the essential aspect of Welsh history. In order to explain its unfolding, however, he had to welcome the blurring of history and myth. 'The manufacture and proliferation of myth must always be a major creative activity among a people with unnaturally high expectations reduced by historic necessity.... In Wales history and myth have always mingled and both have been of equal importance in the struggle for survival.'

This confines the functional role of myths – whether it be Owain Glyndŵr's 'nationalism' or the 'legend' of Tonypandy, or Prince Madoc's 'discovery' of America in the twelfth century – within an unfolding history, and is the deliberate mythologizing of 'dedicated minorities prepared to bend their entire life energies towards the salvation of the whole nation' (Emyr Humphreys). Naturally, in the crucible of myth, the nation blends together. History is rather less receptive to alchemy. For the organic nationalist spirit, history must not only 'mingle' with myth but, if need be, must have its reality subordinated to the historical requirements of the nation. This is, perhaps, acceptable politics for some. It is not good history. The details buckle and bend into unaccustomed shapes to accommodate the burden of longing. In this view the reality of Welsh life cannot be allowed to obscure the meaning of Wales. And the meaning of Wales is 'a cherished myth' since only that can support the fantasy of historical integrity. This verbal dexterity is concerned with obscuring the perpetual divisiveness in Welsh history by emphasising only recent fractures – the 'murder' of the Welsh language, the embrace of 'affluence', the kowtowing to 'Britishness' at the expense of 'Welshness'.

A lexical sophistication about hold-all terms such as 'the general public' or 'the middle class' or 'public opinion' or 'the English national character' or, indeed, 'France', is not hard to discover. The size and vigour of France, as of America, and, once upon a time, of England, allows the diversity of individual or social exis-tence and of national definitions. The latter can serve both ends of the political spectrum, though more usually the Right. The term 'British' has often been so used, usually by the English when they wish to give a political or a military thrust to their social and civil overlordship. Or at least that is what Irish nationalists, Welsh patriots and American sociologists think. The thought is broadly correct, so far as it goes. Only it ignores the multifarious, actual interrelationship of peoples also held by the word 'British'; it rules out the historical experience of unity found in the description of themselves as 'British' by working people in strikes, unions, depression and war; and it blurs the complex question 'Who are the English?' Clearly, they are a people who, in the last two decades have taken the sneering appellation 'Brits' and blithely applied it to themselves without a hint of self-awareness or irony. It is a prime recent example of the Anglo-Saxon capacity to deflate verbal enmity through absorption: neither admitting knowledge of meaning nor seeking anything more than a sense of inclusion for others which the others absolutely do not wish to share – for even the Welsh and the Scottish who claim to be British will not sport the vulgar tag, 'Brits'. But as always, sophistication goes out of the window when nationality knocks on the door. Those who think themselves to be other than what they are supposed to be are assumed to be the victims of a history and of a conditioning in which they have had no say. The tangled skein of social history is thus reduced to a dreadful accident or a cunning conspiracy. Either way it must be conjured out of existence by myth. Unravelling is harder. And all the more necessary for that.

Without a doubt the 'professional' Welsh, blinded by their own desires, misread Wales very badly in the 1970s. The reasons are as much sociological as ideological. The decline of the coalfield entailed a withering of major political and cultural energies. Politics was replaced by politicking. Imagination atrophied. History was now wilfully redefined so that it stood only as a commentary on what should have been. And that was, in the 1960s and 1970s, a resurgent Welsh-language world in which not only official status should be granted (as it largely was) but where 'lost' worlds had to be regained. Despite a pragmatic, economistic nationalism on offer from Plaid Cymru, the broad understanding behind the resurgence of political, cultural and linguistic nationalism remained the same, implicitly, as it had been, explicitly, in the 1920s and 1930s: the Anglicisation of Wales was an avoidable disaster, the industrialisation of Wales had deracinated the native Welsh, mixed them into an anonymous conglomerate of 'half-people' and effectively de-humanised them. They, and Wales, could only be saved by the restoration of 'Welsh' values through the vehicle of the language. South Wales had once linked its material being to its sense of itself as a potential power for change (as with comparable English and Scottish areas). Now, in reduced circumstances, the indictment and the appeal were often strong, especially amongst the young.

The 'little red book' of a generation in Wales was Ned Thomas'

The Welsh Extremist (1972), which argued a sensitive and impassioned case for the worth of a Welsh-language world as a focus for humanity and civilisation in the twentieth century. He had, of course, to address the unpalatable fact that this did not, then, include most of the Welsh. In fact this did not matter too much since the book, though in English, was not addressed to them but rather over their heads to the Englishman, 'who is concerned not with power and size but with quality of life.... He should be in no doubt that his own equivalent in the Welsh-speaking community is ... held down.' Welsh-speaking Wales was, then, 'a pole of humanity', and, though later in the 1970s Ned Thomas insisted that his remarks did not apply to 'individuals whose language is ... an accident', he repeated that 'as the description of a social process' his words on South Wales stood. They were:

> As the educated Welsh-speaker looks at the new affluent working-class of South Wales he is bound to see people who have lost a culture and gained only a higher standard of living, people made particularly vulnerable to commercially-fostered pseudo-values by their own rootlessness, people who have lost the dignity of a language and acquired a despised and comic dialect of English.

The arguments in *The Welsh Extremist* were not particularly novel despite the cloak of the epithet and the irony of the noun (i.e. a *Welsh* extremist would be considered reasonable if he were not 'Welsh' but 'English'). Its sentiments could be repeated by catechism from that canon of English tradition which had looked, in various ways for a century or more, to defend an organic, natural English civilisation against the destructive tendencies of 'mechanical, mass life' or 'industrial civilisation'. In the 1930s the critic F.R. Leavis and those associated with his literary magazine *Scrutiny* had seen 'English literature' (or a selective version of it) as a holy writ which could save 'English' civilisation from all the commercial, predatory values besetting their society. The working class, the constant object of their fear and pity, could not be saved from itself by the false gods of Marxism, which, they argued, was only a mirror for the ills besetting the unhealthy culture of the day. The 'fugitive' group of right-wing agrarian ideologues in the Southern states of the USA reached similar conclusions about their vanished world. And in Wales Saunders Lewis, poet, critic and President of Plaid Cymru, took comfort from European authoritarianism in his advocacy of cultural elitism and social hierarchy.

Of course, by the 1970s Plaid Cymru was no longer advocating, with the cold logic of Lewis, the 'deindustrialisation of Wales' (Mrs Thatcher would accomplish this, for different purposes, after 1979 and make a mockery of the notion of a 'new affluent working class') and, indeed, it had become a reformist party with its feet set firmly on the shifting ground. The industrial South was designated a key area in future political advance. That region's own *Welsh* existence was no longer denied outright or admitted only in association with the traces of an older Welsh-speaking culture still detected in it. In the next (1977) edition of *The Welsh Extremist* Ned Thomas could add: 'There is incontrovertibly now a distinct English-speaking culture that is Welsh in the South Wales valleys, but it has shown little sign of dynamism except in connection with a political nationalism which is attached to the notion of a resurgent Welsh language.'

The historical skewing of this view was not as important as the linked insistence on a culture-based politics which saw language not merely as a mode of communication but as the essential underpinning of a social order. The language is then freighted with 'the quality of life' which will, somehow, replace the 'size and power' that the political and class struggle of South Wales' history has, it would seem from total omission of the facts, never confronted or controlled. This is a middle-class Welsh Nirvana which, essentially without threat to 'size and power', is exactly the Wales its 'England' (another unreal confection) wants. There is a character in Welsh-language lore known as Dic Sion Dafydd: a man who betrays his origins and his language by aping his English 'betters'. He is, in turn, despised by those from whom he came and those who he would be. The savagest irony to be visited on 'the educated Welsh-speakers', as a type, was their failure to see that it was with the eyes and the mouth of Dic Sion Dafydd that they saw and spoke of English-speaking working-class Wales.

Such a response took on more importance because the ground had, indeed, shifted. Industrial working-class Wales was, as its socio-economic base shrank, less articulate in its politics and culture. The meaning of history was being reassessed in order to accommodate it to the ideological myth by which 'Wales' could not emerge until history itself was infiltrated. The majority of Welsh people were being given a story about themselves which either trivialised the defences of communal and familial solidarity that they had erected against the ill-will of power or which denied them the memory of the real control they had occasionally wielded together through common struggle. Politics was not always the mere administration, often corrupt and time-serving, it sometimes became. 'What I can't get anybody to understand,' complained a character in Alun Richards' 1960s play *The Big Breaker*, 'is that better men walked these streets. There were chartists shot dead where we stand now, *chartists*! Men of purpose and design, and later, others. Ablett, Cook ... What men! What purpose! *To change the nature of society* ... Ah, and they broke themselves in the attempt, broke themselves, the real ones. And what comes to the top of the pile now....'

Class institutions – unions, independent education, active local politics, and even a communalising street life – had shrivelled. The institutions that had generally ignored this life in its heyday expanded and, in self-fulfilling relationship, stood increasingly unchallenged as the guardians of culture in Wales. The subsidised paraphernalia of a minority language with majoritarian pretensions declared its Wales to the world. The Welsh middle class, as opposed to a working class it despised or patronised, needed to tend its qualifying epithet since 'Welsh' was, in its case, exactly descriptive of its cultural formation and social function.

Where English-speaking Wales could articulate itself it was reluctantly acknowledged. Mostly, though, it was not an important fact (except when, devastatingly, it came to vote and upset, temporarily, the designers) because it no longer inspired fear and had no purchase on the cultural artefact Wales had become. The production of Wales that was proceeding apace in the Cymricising suburbs of Cardiff, in academic and journalistic circles, on the subsidised pages of a Welsh-language press and on the air waves, had no real need to take account of those who did not fit into the picture. In a sense, they could be deemed to have lost the right to choose the rules of the game precisely because of what they chose to be. What *real* compulsions were affecting them was hardly considered.

Paradoxically the very indifference and self-confidence of these people were, as far as this redefinition of Wales was concerned, now set to work against them. During the 1960s and 1970s urban and industrial Wales unashamedly lapped up the possibilities of material consumption. The relatively small scale of the gains should not obscure their importance: they were not petty when put into the context of the lives of a generation of men and women who had suffered, as children and adults, economic devastation, world war and austerity. Besides, the idea that the traditions they and their forbears had helped nurture and support were becoming hollow did not occur as a crisis. The miners' strikes of 1969 and 1972 were fuelled, in South Wales as elsewhere, by anger at the undercutting of relative prosperity and by constant reference to the orally transmitted experience of fathers and grandfathers. ('They won't do it to us'; 'This is revenge for 1926'.) The media could appreciate this *after* it happened. Others could interpret it as the awakening of a sleeping giant. In fact the moment was both historically regressive – based narrowly on the miners, on their historical development and on the restructuring of wage agreements in the 1960s – and entirely explicable in terms of the communities that, mostly, now commuted to the valley mouths, sought white-collar jobs and shared in common British/Welsh preoccupations. The 'revolt' of the early 1970s was a moment not a process. The crisis that would in the 1980s affect the vast majority of Welsh people was an economic, social and political crisis. That remains an enormous dilemma. The 'Condition of Wales Question' was not for most of the Welsh about Welshness at all, it was about unemployment and jobs, about bad architecture, about bureaucracy and political participation, about dead-ends and opportunities. But in the 1990s nothing in Wales was subsidised more than 'culture' for toothless dogs can bark at will.

This question of culture in Wales today is still inextricably caught up with the arguments over language. The latter becomes a badge, possession of which, especially by learners, is a sign of good faith. One such learner fulminated at the 1983 National Eisteddfod that the Welshman/woman who did not try to speak Welsh was, in terms of 'Wales', an un-person. The opinion was voiced by R.S. Thomas, poet, nationalist and, in this as in other matters, a fundamentalist. Fundamentalism demands that reality, the chaos of uncertainty, be fenced in. R.S. Thomas has turned 'Wales' into what Jonathan Raban calls 'an analogy for most people's experience of living in the twentieth century ... a special, spare grammar and vocabulary in which certain statements can be made as in no other language'.

R.S. Thomas doubtless agreed with Saunders Lewis in 1962 when the latter broke his silence by delivering his famous radio broadcast that spoke of the fate of the language as being of overriding importance. Mere politics was a secondary consideration even for nationalism. This also legitimised a concentration on single-issue and lobbying, demonstrating politics that gave the Welsh language an official boost. Government commissions conceded the strong arguments for positive discrimination that the new language society – Cymdeithas Yr Iaith Gymraeg – urged in word and deed. Few now argue against the necessary life-support machine needed by Welsh if it is to survive, let along grow in numbers, into the next century. There *is* a present for the Welsh language, and a future.

Nonetheless, over this most delicate of issues, assumptions about the past often cloak more interesting, perhaps more helpful truths. The first linguistic census for Wales was that of 1891. It showed that only 54.4 per cent of the people living in Wales spoke Welsh. The figure can almost certainly be revised slightly upwards, but the inescapable fact is that the Welsh-speaking people of Wales were not in an overwhelming majority in their own country in the first decade of this century and, more important, that the number of monoglot Welsh was dropping like a stone. The converse of this was the rising number of both monoglot English and of bilingual speakers. In other words English was a language spoken and understood by 84 per cent of the population of Wales by 1901, although it is the following decade which sees far and away the largest flood of non-Welsh immigrants into the coal mining valleys. Unarguably the English language did not have to struggle to penetrate into Wales.

This remains for some of the Welsh an unpalatable fact. They point to the use of that board hung around the necks of school children for daring to speak their native tongue in school – 'the Welsh Not' – and to the teaching of English in general. However, the evidence we have for the 'Welsh Not' (as with its equivalent in Ireland and the Highlands of Scotland) is oral, impressionistic and, crucially, almost entirely confined to voluntary schools where it was operated by parental desire. The device, generally, was no board but a small piece of wood held in the hand as visitors to the Museum of Welsh Life at St Fagan's can verify. The State Education that was legislated for in 1870 became compulsory in 1880 and was widespread by the 1890s. Where the 'Welsh Not' *was* employed in these 'British' schools it was also stamped on by higher authorities immediately. The agitation for the teaching of Welsh in the schools of Wales was underway before the 1890s and enjoyed considerable official backing from that day to this. Besides, the adult population of Wales who knew English in 1901 would have been largely unaffected by any educational policy, pro or con. To put it bluntly, Welsh *may* take a new lease of life from Welsh schools nowadays, but it was not mortally wounded because of schools in the past.

What happened was that English became, at a crucial time and in certain areas, not only the preferred language of civil life – entertainment, social discourse, magazines and popular newspapers – but also the vehicle for a more democratic culture. Industrialisation had allowed the Welsh, in Brinley Thomas' famous diagnosis, to 'colonise their own country'. As the population of Ireland was halved between 1841 and 1911 so the population of Wales doubled. Welsh language culture thereby flourished. However, its integrated association with nonconformity in religion and Liberalism in politics tied it to a distinct sense of what a Welsh community should be. That sense was increasingly challenged by impersonal, material forces which threw up a proletariat, made it of mixed origins, saw that it was secularised, frequently 'uncontrollable' and discovered its socialism not in Welsh – which stayed a sickly plant until after World War Two – but in English. The pamphlets of the Kerr Publishing House of Chicago brought Marx to Wales: 'As I was reaching adolescence,' wrote Aneurin Bevan, 'towards the end of the First World War, I became acquainted with the works of Eugene V. Debs and Daniel de Leon of the United States.... I was reading everything I could lay my hands on. Tredegar Workmens' Library was unusually well stocked with books of all kinds. When I found that the political polemics of de Leon and Debs were shared by so loved an author as Jack London, the effect on my mind was profound.' Nobody translated *The Miners' Next Step* into Welsh.

The decline of the Welsh language is not made less so by pretending that the factors involved were avoidable. Neither enlightened administration, patriotic fervour nor compulsory Cymricisation could have altered the clash between cultures (not nations) that the process of linguistic change represented in Wales. Welsh, despite the presence of identical abstract factors, from schools to 'inferiority complexes', did not succumb in the North and West to the English tide. Radnorshire, Montgomeryshire and South Pembrokeshire were largely without Welsh before the twentieth century. Glamorgan contained as many Welsh speakers as the rest of Wales put together as late as 1951. Nowhere more than in the discussion of language and its usage in Wales, past, present and future, do the Welsh need more understanding, more toleration and more humility the one to the other. If bilingualism, except formalistically, is likely to remain an impossible dream, dual lingualism, or the truly bilingual and the monoglot together, offers distinct and sensible hope for a modern civic society. Others thought, and think, differently.

The great linguistic shift that occurred in Wales was a trauma, but all was not lost, for Welsh-speaking Wales tended a memory and a hope. In part, perhaps, it had to define itself against the Welsh who so readily became English-speakers. They too, have a past to cherish if then they are to have any relationship, other than a ruptured one, to their future. Ned Thomas was right, though maybe for reasons foreseen differently in 1972, in his insistence in *The Welsh Extremist* that any future Wales and the Welsh language may have 'must depend very largely on the English-speakers in Wales'. Their culture, then, requires a firm analysis in its own right for English-speaking Wales has long had its own life in its own terms. It is not a half-baked, imported substitute and its own history is not best served by dwelling on the contemporary fixation over languages. The divide that took place in Wales was not merely linguistic. It was also a fracture in the economy and society which led to a difference in collective psychology. There is plenty of evidence from Welsh language sources in the nineteenth century (and up to the 1960s perhaps) to suggest a widespread feeling of 'inferiority' (though this reversed from the 1890s) but the concept does not apply at all to the industrial, predominantly working-class world, emerging full-blown in the South in the last quarter of the nineteenth century. This difference is what Wyn Griffith recognised in his study of 1950, *The Welsh*, and what he, and so many others, have mooned over:

> The mining valleys of the South are full of life, eager, vivid, mercurial and yet determined, a life somehow Latin in quickness. The North is quieter, slower in pulse, less accustomed to living in large aggregations, less penetrated by different nationalities. In between North and South there lies a thinly populated agricultural area which diminishes the contact between them and acts as a stable centre, a mean between the two extremes. Is there a common factor, something which can be recognised in isolation, in all this variety?

The split was such that comparative study of the two Welsh cultures by translating literally from one language to the other as if to move from Welsh to English, in a reality beyond the text, was to look through a glass door rather than into a mirror, is an unconvincing exercise if its purpose is to seek to unify rather than to explain. Instead analogy is required between similar cultural experiences. The 'problem' of South Wales in its relationship to Wales is not unique. Leslie Fiedler in his study of modern American literature, *Waiting for the End* (1964), crystallised the universality of the issue. Fiedler was considering the pain recent Jewish-American writers

had caused, and suffered, as they set about transforming the 'literature of ... reassurance, intended to be consumed by an in-group
which knows it is abused'. The transformation would mean, after
1914, 'pledging allegiance to social or cultural ideals larger than
their Jewishness, whether Bohemianism or socialism or humanism
in its broadest sense'. This is precisely what happened to the industrial Welsh who also became, through a blazing social drama, 'representative (in all their particularity) ... of ... all mankind'. Some of
their post-1930s 'regional writing' then ceased to be 'sub-literary'.

> But this only begins to happen when regional writers stop being
> apologists and become critics, abandon falsification and senti-
> mentality in favour of treating not the special virtues of the
> group from which they came, whether those virtues be real or
> fancied, but the weakness it shares with all men. Such writers
> seem often to their followers, their very friends and parents,
> traitors – not only for the harsh things which they are led to say
> about those fellows, friends and parents in the pursuit of truth,
> but also because their desire for universality of theme and appeal
> leads them to begin tearing down from within the walls of a
> cultural ghetto, which, it turns out, has meant security as well as
> exclusion to the community that nurtured them.

This process runs counter to the predominant 'praise-tradition' of
Welsh literature (in both tongues). Leslie Fiedler's words provide
the best gloss on the kind of writing South Wales, in its forming
heyday, required if it was to show its mature capabilities. Certainly
no mere plodding history or fleeting lyric can manage to express
the Faulknerian story of industrial Wales. But it is not the language
which is at fault but an unsubstantial vision of form. It may be that
even now we are too near to the shape of all that historical experience to be able to re-present its full meaning in imaginative fiction.
We handle more readily the bastardised forms of historical romance
which are given a licence to mythologise at will in selective areas.
Mannered prose filled the margins of books of colour photographs
which even managed to prettify the industrial valleys – not a coalface in sight. Or any other face come to that. The Welsh on the
ground have often been given short shrift as their 'Wales' is transformed, agonised over and consumed.

Nobody has made better use of this dying fall than the writer
Alun Richards (b.1929). His finely crafted novels and short-stories
have pulled aside the curtain to expose vanity and illusion in equal
measure. Against this, he highlighted the continuing capacity of
people to rescue the humanity of their lives through all the small

moments and trivial structures that provide an opportunity for grace. In his books the Second World War's impact on 'Welsh' society is not put to one side as if it were only a passing cloud of fire, and the popular culture of spectator sport, raw and vital, elegant and heart-stopping, is seen, in the only way possible, from the inside. The closely observed detail of his fiction works like a yeast to produce a literature able to hold a people's changing experience in its parables of form and style. They are clearing away the lumber that prevents any proper making of art. His work is our best warning yet against the carnivorous faking of a cultural cannibalism that consumes real experience and digests it into pap.

Alun Richards, in his biting short story 'The Former Miss Merthyr Tydfil', spotlighted the lame transition from history to artefact in the artistic career of his bourgeois shape-shifter:

> They normally spent Christmas in Wales, sharing themselves out between her mother and his people but this year her mother had expressed a wish to come to London and Melville wanted to use all his spare time for painting. The irony was that he'd completely changed his style since his exhibition. Now he painted Welsh industrial scenes exclusively and his little canvases were all expressions of some aspect of valley life. Pit wheels, ravaged coal tips, cameos of gaunt chapels and back-to-back homes now made neat little patterns whose colours somehow formed an idealised picture of a way of life that was gone. There was something immensely nostalgic about his work, however. It had a prettiness and charm and clearly evoked memories in which people still delighted. It was as if part of experience had been reduced and falsely crystallised into manageable proportions, and although she could not quite express it, Ivy was aware of a parallel with those glass baubles she'd seen as a child. When you shook them, they produced artificial snowstorms, snowflakes swirling down upon some miniature log-cabin and showing a little world enclosed with all the properties of a cosy dream....
>
> ... There was not a terrace or a pit shaft that escaped him now, it seemed, and his best known study, a group of lads playing dickstones outside a blacksmith's shop with a haulier and blackened colliers in attendance, had been bought by a famous London Welshman who'd described it as 'indicative of the true spirit of our people'. She'd been there when he said it, as had Melville's mother, but what relation it had to anything Melville had ever known about, Ivy could not imagine. If his mother had seen Melville talking to a collier in the old days she'd have phoned the police! But there it was, these memories which were now paying off a treat. Everybody was very complimentary,

including his mother, whose attitude towards Ivy had softened over the years. Now she spoke of Ivy as one who'd overcome tremendous odds. You'd think she was from Biafra, not Ruby Street, but there, they were all alike in their incapacity to see things as they were.

The recent history of most of the Welsh people is still being allowed to drift with them into a lobotomised anonymity. Not in the name of Wales or the Welsh or any other spurious hold-all concept but for the sake of their humanity, in honour of their obscure existence and of, to quote Gwyn Thomas, their once 'refulgent dreams', it is necessary to assert the validity, and, in the flare of history not the fog of myth, the importance for our history of the Wales that became English-speaking.

The passage of time which encompassed such a change was not all one of loss. The riches it brought should not be spurned. Speaking of a different people who came at exactly the same time in history to live in the shadow of that architectonic icon of leaping change, Brooklyn Bridge, Irving Howe, one of their sons, wrote:

> Much of the East Side [of New York] is beyond recall, and must remain so. There is nothing glamorous about poverty, nothing admirable about deprivation, nothing enviable about suffering. Whole areas of human possibility and pleasure were blocked off by the immigrant milieu, in part because it needed the repressions of discipline, in part because it had to cope with material want. And the toll in self-denial was often very high. Human beings should not have to live with the enforced austerities that many Jewish immigrants accepted as their lot.
>
> Yet even while registering these impressions, one suspects they do not get to the heart of the matter. There were strengths, great strengths ... a rich and complicated ethic ... a readiness to live for ideals beyond the clamour of self, a sense of plebeian fraternity, an ability to forge a community of moral order even while remaining subject to a society of social disorder, and a persuasion that human existence is a deeply serious matter for which all of us are finally accountable. Not that these strengths were unique to the immigrant Jews or that there is any reason to suppose they might not survive the immigrant milieu; but for many children and grandchildren of the East Side, it was through this world that one first came to glimpse a life worthy of the idea of man.

★   ★   ★

It is not so easy today to see what made the industrial South so

attractive to generations of men and women. Present contemplation of the Valleys is inseparable from the melancholy sense of lost
chances. Orange-bricked tower blocks muscle their pointless bulk
into the sky above empty moorland. On the plateaux between
Valleys housing estates that must have resembled Italian hillside
settlements in the architect's model turn dirt-grey in the rain and
wind that blows through their vandalised precincts. The residents
note the irony and rechristen their reservations – High Chapparall,
Ponderosa, the Lost City. In the towns spawned by the wealth of
the valley bottoms, buildings reflecting the confidence and purpose
of the past are allowed, for the profit of redevelopment, to crumble
into terminal decay, to be replaced by an architecture of mindless
imitation, dressed up with mottled tiles and tinted glass.

A flood of tat and pap has rushed in. Cellophane and car parks
distance the poverty and decline. Speculators in property now line
valley streets. Antique dealers, whose converted junk shops are the
first step to a trans-Atlantic container, wait as innocent and as
voracious as vultures. Stripped pine-dressers and tiled wash stands
queue up to leave. The nostrils of passers-by tingle from the smart
of caustic soda. Latticed winding-gear represents the picturesque.
Gutted chapels shelter petrol pumps or craft centres or DIY stores.
It is hard to feel empathy with this mixture of public anonymity
and commercialised vulgarity. And yet places that now appear
trapped by the lack of any style were once avenues of human
release precisely because of what their chaotic physical aspect had
once represented.

'I was fascinated by that light in the sky', wrote B.L. Coombes
as the first words of his autobiography of 1939, *These Poor Hands*.
Bert Coombes, a Herefordshire farm-boy who went to work in the
coal mines of South Wales just before the First World War, had
been looking at the distant glare of the Dowlais blast furnaces
above Merthyr long before he made his trek from countryside to
industry: '... in the cold and wetness of the winter evenings, when
we had finished feeding the animals and had cut enough chaff for
the next day, we crowded near the fire of damp logs that Mother
was coaxing into flame with the bellows. I would look at our feeble
fire and think, with longing, of the heat and brightness that must
be about those distant flames.'

Bert Coombes left the miseries of agricultural work as soon as
he was old enough to do so. His quest for 'good clothes, money to
spend ... fresh places and faces, and – well, many things' was one
he shared with hundreds of thousands of his generation. Coombes'

family rented a smallholding and so were immeasurably better off than the farm labourers who 'had no right to call a word their own'. Even so, he hurried to the place where, an older friend told him, 'a young feller ... ain't got to call no manner of man sir up there – no, yuh ain't ... an' yuh could see to read in the streets ... so yuh could.' The relative freedom of a democratic culture was something Coombes learnt to cherish beyond all else in the three decades that took him from the onset of one world war to another. It was a freedom stitched into the material of industrial life. At first, though, it was through his physical senses that he experienced the new world as he arrived, in the rain, at his lodgings in a mining village:

> A lot of elbow-grease must have been used to cause the polish on that door. Despite the rain which was falling, the brass rod at the bottom shone and the step was milk-white....
>
> I was taken inside ... and helped to deposit [my] battered box near the bottom of the stairs, where it contrasted with the shining passage, the bright stair-carpet, and the brass-rod on each step. The kitchen was a'dazzle with brass. There was a row of brass candlesticks on the mantel and a strip of brass along the edge, as well as a thick brass rod beneath and another wide strip covering the upper part of the chimney opening. That fire did not peep from under the second bar, it filled the grate as high as was safe, and its white heat showed in the reflections on the fender.
>
> The warmth and comfort were something to which I had not been used.

This wide-eyed wonder never quite left those for whom industrial and urban communities were a novelty. At the turn of this century the communities themselves were in-the-making and the novelty was one of both people and environment. So far as working people were concerned convenience and consumption quickly outweighed any nostalgia for a rural life. A Cardiganshire woman, on a brief visit home from the Rhondda around the turn of the century, was recalled, in words that Bert Coombes echoed, as saying:

> We're fools to stay in a place like this. In Treorchy there's electric light. Just put your finger on the switch and the place lights up.... Turn on the tap in the scullery and there's plenty of water.... There are pavements to walk on.... The street lamps are on all night. There are plenty of picture-houses for somebody to have some fun. If you haven't any dinner ready you just send the children round to the Bracchi [Italian] shop for fish and chips. On Saturday there are cheap trips to Cardiff. O yes, we're mugs to hang around here.

And they did not. Cardiganshire's population declined from 73,000 in 1871 to 59,000 by 1911. In the early 1890s Cardiganshire-born people in Glamorgan numbered over 14,000, a quarter of the population of their native county. When the twentieth century began there were almost 16,000 'Cardis' in Glamorgan and more than a third of those were in the Rhondda.

What happened in Wales during the last century is easy to describe statistically. A small population of about half a million in 1800, over eighty per cent of whom lived on the land, had become, by 1914, a people over five times that number, eighty per cent of whom lived in towns and cities. Large areas of Wales were still untouched by industrialisation, and urbanisation was both spotty and restricted. Nonetheless, the bulk of both the Welsh and the immigrants who arrived from about the 1860s were affected by industrialisation, and this was especially true of South Wales. The balance between an industrial and an agricultural workforce had already tipped in favour of the former by the middle of the century, but in the sixty years after this 388,000 people left the Welsh countryside – most of them for the coalfields of the South. What this process of social and economic change did to Wales, to the idea of Wales, to the Welsh and to those who became Welsh is still at the heart of our contradictions and our potential.

Between the 1750s and 1850s the Welsh economy came to resemble a patchwork quilt of tradition and modernity. Some of the squares were hand-stitched whilst the newer, brighter colours were machine-made. The Welsh countryside had long been a mixture of arable and pastoral farming. The lowland areas concentrated on the limited production of barley and oats as staple crops. On the greater expanse of upland areas animals grazed: the Welsh cattle-drovers had a long tradition by the early nineteenth century. Isolated sheep farms were dotted all over Wales. In large areas of the country this remained the situation as the century progressed. Great estates and great houses dominated the economy and politics of Wales and, indeed, the lives of their hard-pressed tenant farmers whose own farm servants, often relatives, 'lived in'. An underclass of farm labourers eked out a bare subsistence. From the 1870s Welsh agriculture became increasingly pastoral – livestock was kept to be slaughtered for use, to produce eggs, cheese and butter for sale and, in short, to supply the wants of the developing urban centres. By the 1890s it was no longer the main support of human life in Wales and the substitution of banks and mortgages for landowning landlords, small farms for landed estates, and machinery for labourers was well under way.

Industry – in the shape of coal outcropping, iron ore mining, fulling mills and a network of domestic labour in the woollen trades – had penetrated the basic economy by the end of the eighteenth century without imbalancing it. Nor was it clear that the eventual imbalance would occur in the South. For a time it seemed as if North Wales would prove the forerunner. Its mountainous, seemingly remote nature belied its accessibility in the early days of British industrial growth. It was, in fact, adjacent to the fount of British industrial formation and capital investment – Lancashire, in particular Manchester and the port of Liverpool, and iron-working Shropshire. The early ingredients required for quick-raising industrial dough were all present in the region – water power, minerals, a labour force, and good harbours that were, quite soon, connected by road and rail to the hinterland.

The region's output was basically for export, although there was some local trade in the smelting of metal and the splitting and dressing of quarried slate. Copper was mined at the Parys Mountain and Mona mines in Anglesey where, in the 1790s, it reached an early peak. Barges took smelted copper and brass away, much of it to supply the ships that plied the trade in slaves and sugar in the eighteenth century and which were sheathed in copper. Flourishing trade and colonial wars helped the copper industry along. And in North-East Wales the Midlands ironmasters pioneered works at Brymbo and at Bersham that founded an iron making tradition which lingered on, as at Shotton, into the late twentieth century. This, in turn, stimulated the mining of coal in the area for the local iron-works' needs: in Denbigh and Flint, there were 14,000 miners employed by 1914.

However, it was the slate mines and quarries of North-West Wales that above all threatened a decisive shift from a rural to an industrial culture. Slate was a monopoly trade in British terms. It produced a rash of slate ports and slate railways, by which the slate was carted to ships stacked to the gunnels for transportation. Welsh slate covered the spreading roofs of the proliferating work-towns of the nineteenth-century world. Liverpool merchants, English slave-owners and Welsh lawyers grew rich, powerful and titled on the proceeds. Towns like Blaenau Ffestiniog and Bethesda spread in heaped-up terraces around their quarries and housed a distinctive, Welsh, quarryman's culture that was half-artisan, half-proletarian and wholly its own.

The production of slate reached its height by the 1870s and the quarrying work-force, widely dispersed throughout Gwynedd, never exceeded 16,000 in number. They remained a self-contained industrial enclave, scarcely disturbed by immigration or mechanisation, until the break-up of both industry and workforce in the wake of the three-year lock-out at the Penrhyn quarry (the largest in the world, with 2,500 men employed) at the very beginning of the twentieth century. Their heroic struggle to control the nature of their own work and to organise themselves for that purpose in a reconstructed union has been justly celebrated in poetry, fiction and history. Nonetheless, if they had continued to live and work within a viable slate industry they – like the factory woollen workers of the Welsh border country who had also been towed along by a great sea-change until the 1870s – would have constituted no more than a minority Welsh experience. They did not threaten the self-defining Welsh world of the nineteenth century either by size or by nature.

North Wales, which had seemed to be an integrated industrial area of great potential, never managed to move beyond the stage of disparate industries. In common with other European regions it had a number of natural advantages but in North Wales they did not quite gel together. The crucial agent which enabled 'take-off' elsewhere was lacking.

Nowhere in Europe did *national* industrialisation or economic growth occur, whether naturally or by state direction; instead there was an explosion into industrial pre-eminence of regions *as* regions. The agent might be wool or cotton or linen or, say, pig iron. From the middle of the eighteenth century increasing demand for iron led to the exploitation of timber for charcoal to melt the ore. Water was required to power the machinery. Eventually coal would perform the functions of both timber and water, and, from the middle of the nineteenth century, be required for its own, steam-raising, properties throughout the industrial world. In regions with these natural advantages a skein of financial and technological expertise was unwound to create a network of roads, canals, railways and harbours. Such regions became, for a while, self-sufficient. As long as their expansive, industry-generating phase continued, new discoveries could be absorbed and fresh requirements met *in situ*. Their power and influence spread outwards in concentric circles all over Western Europe.

These industrial regions and sub-regions of Europe were out of step with the nations in which they were situated. From the Ruhr to Lancashire, from Northern France to North-East England, from the Sambre-Meuse basin to South Wales, they had more in common with each other than they did with their 'nations', established or emerging. They were already the future. South Wales, slowly at first and then with increasing momentum, was such a European region in the way North Wales – deficient in coal, too dependent on the earlier industrial developments of North-West England, and not well situated for altering patterns of trade – was not.

This was not obvious at first. Indeed, if there was an economic dynamo attached to South Wales at all in the first half of the eighteenth century, it was across the channel in Bristol. This city was still called 'the Welsh metropolis' in 1818, and every Wednesday, at the Welsh Market House, as well as at the annual September Fair, the produce of the South-Wales vales and uplands sought an urban outlet there. The money required to finance the capital outlay of heavy industry in South Wales came largely from Bristol merchants and investors. Their cash helped overcome the inadequate roads, rough terrain and overall backwardness of the area. Their motives were conditioned by what they saw happening at Merthyr in North-East Glamorgan where, by 1800, a town of over 7,000 people had grown up in less than forty years. It was the largest urban concentration in Wales, and remained so until the 1880s.

The great iron-works in its encircling districts – Cyfarthfa, Dowlais, Penydarren and Plymouth – rapidly made Merthyr the Iron Capital of the world. Entrepreneurs, compounded of genius and ruthlessness, founded dynasties based on technical skill and exploited labour. New techniques for refining ore into bar iron were utilised in works that took advantage of the economies their huge size gave them to capture expanding markets. Above all else, prosperity was founded in continuous war – by the Seven Years War against the French from 1757-1763, by the wars to stop American independent government from 1776-1783, and then through the wars against revolutionary and Napoleonic France from the 1790s to 1815. By the time the wars ended there were eight giant iron-works in an eleven-mile radius from Hirwaun to Blaenavon, and smaller works had sprung up all around them. These were the suppliers of munitions. They cast guns and shot. They filled their bulging order books with the demands of the navy. Profits made in spices, slaves and plantations were recycled to make more. The iron industry of South Wales was the love child of war and empire.

The new century's lust for metal was insatiable. In the lower Swansea Valley, on the banks of the Tawe, copper ore was shipped in and smelted. Water, limestone, timber and coal were abundant. Before 1850 there were eleven works belching noxious white smoke within a three-mile radius of the town soon nicknamed 'Copperopolis' for its metal exchange and near-monopoly of world trade. Just to the west a British monopoly trade in tinplate was developing around Llanelli and its neighbours, which produced half a million tons by 1891. From the 1790s canals had sliced through the hills to the north in order to supplement the tramroads' carrying capacities. Before mid-century the Taff Vale railway ran from Merthyr to Cardiff and a third of the total British exports in pig iron went out from a South Wales that produced forty per cent of Britain's pig iron. Iron from Merthyr carried railway trains in St Petersburg and paid for substantial shares in American railway stock. Iron opened up coal drifts, financed castellated Gothic mansions and sucked in workers for its spreading requirements.

Nonetheless, despite the concentrated fury of the iron industry and its brazen siblings, the Welsh population by the 1850s was still spread thinly and relatively evenly. Its increase in size from the eighteenth century was a common European phenomenon and, as elsewhere, continued to put pressure on the land as a prime sustainer of the growing population.

Throughout the nineteenth century the Land Question dominated Welsh politics. The economic grievances of Welsh-speaking, non-conformist tenant farmers were dovetailed into a wider sense of political and religious exclusion. The subsistence crises of the early nineteenth century resulted in popular disturbances, none more disturbing than the so-called 'Rebecca Riots' of the 1840s led by farmers in West Wales, during which toll gates were attacked. By the end of the century a political 'take over' had been almost completed in the Welsh countryside and the Liberal Party could justly think of itself as *the* party for Wales. It was, however, the complaints of farmers rather than of the agricultural labourers which had been espoused by governments, as the 1896 Royal Commission on Land makes clear. The Commissioners, over a three-year period, had held 1,086 interviews all over Wales, only 21 of which were with agricultural labourers, although this under-class on the land comprised, of course, the majority of agricultural workers. Their numbers fell from 73,300 to 44,900 in the forty years from the middle of the century but the conditions of those who remained – their squalid housing, lack of schooling, relative illiteracy and exploited social deference – disturbed even those for whom the image of Wales by the 1890s was one of green, rural harmony disturbed only by industrial growth.

The enemy of the farm labourers, and especially of their periodic attempts to form unions, was their fellow-countrymen in the farm-owning class. The labourers only 'enjoyed' a collective presence, a sense of community, at particular times in the year – the fairs of May and November when men and women hired themselves out in the streets of the market towns where the farmers congregated. A Welsh sea-captain remembered how 'it was a disgrace to a Christian country to see a parcel of men and women in a row on each side of the road and farmers surveying and engaging them as he would buy cattle'. The railways that tied the land together and brought the markets of the urban areas into the reach of the farmers also provided avenues of escape from this degradation. Within half a century over 50,000 labourers made use of those iron rails to move out of their condition of dependence. Iron was as much of a social lubricant in the countryside as in the towns of nineteenth-century Wales.

Iron remained a major manufacturing presence in Wales down to 1914, but, as with the smaller copper trade, ores were by then being shipped inland to replace the local ores which were being worked out and did not, anyway, suit the processes of steel-making. The early advantages had gone and iron works, increasingly moved to the coast, were in as parlous a state as the slate industry, which had also irredeemably marked an area and formed a culture within a limited circumference. The major difference for South Wales lay in the fortuitous existence of some of the richest and most varied coal seams in the world. This fossil fuel would, from the 1840s, seem an endless source of provision for the basic steam power required by all industries well into the twentieth century.

The Customs Officer of the tiny hamlet and river inlet known as Cardiff gravely recorded in 1782: 'No coal is exported from this port nor ever will be because of the expense of bringing it down from the interior part of the country.' No customs officer's written words were to be so ignored by immediate posterity until Herman Melville took his melancholy office in New York in the 1860s. Coal would be pursued as relentlessly in nineteenth-century Wales as *Moby Dick* would be neglected in nineteenth-century USA. There were over 500 coal mines being operated in South Wales by the first decade of the twentieth century. Cardiff was for two decades the greatest coal-exporting port in the world and, by the 1880s, finally and lastingly outstripped Merthyr as the biggest Welsh town. Coal was now the favoured handmaiden of capitalism in Wales. The possibility from the 1850s of undertaking deep mining opened up the steep-sided, geologically faulted central valleys of the coalfield. Bonanza times transformed a rural hinterland into one, vast industrial landscape. This was an industrial explosion that blasted Wales out of the continuum of its history.

The slack left by the decline in the iron industry was taken up by coal. The falling away of demand for Welsh slate and the laying off of quarrymen was counteracted by coal. The woollen industry of West Wales – factory-based in industrial villages in the heart of the Welsh countryside – was, in its manufacture of flannel shirts and drawers, dependent on the coalfield population for demand. The siphoning off of waged, adult labour on the land was effected by coal. The growth of agriculture as a marketing industry was impossible without the voracious needs of people whose prosperity lay in coal. The railways, the docks, the ships and all their workers, the banks, the schools, the shops and the buildings – and all who came to construct and staff them – were the creatures of coal. The first great pulse of the full process of industrialisation was felt by the middle of the nineteenth century; the sonorous diapason of iron and coal began to entice generation after generation with its seductive promise. The ratio of population in Glamorgan and Monmouthshire to all other Welsh counties changed between 1801 and 1911 from one to four to three to one.

Where did the work-force come from? There were Irish in Merthyr and Tredegar in some numbers by mid-century but the bulk of the immigrants were, until the end of the nineteenth century, Welsh by origin. As the coalfield imploded, men followed the coal, bringing with them their skills learned in iron-ore mining, slate-quarrying or working the coal for smelt. The demand for labour soon pulled in anyone strong enough to stand the work. The collier, like the quarryman, prided himself on the tempered skills of the craftsman but, though mechanised mining was yet to come, his industry was more straightforwardly extractive and so, in effect, open to anyone. Wales became an importer of labour to speed her export of material wealth. Men came from further and further afield – from counties adjacent to the coalfield, then from the English border country and the Midlands, from Cornwall and Devon and Somerset and wherever the call of high wages and excitement stirred the imagination.

By 1861 there were 18,000 Irish living in South Wales. Glamorgan's population was 66 per cent native to that country, 11 per cent from other parts of Wales, and 23 per cent non-Welsh over half of whom were from Somerset and Gloucester. Decade by decade the population swelled at an unprecedented rate and the number of non-Welsh migrants to the coalfield grew in proportion to native Welsh until the latter were outstripped in the last great decade of absorption (1901-11). During those ten years the population of Glamorgan alone rose to over one million, of whom one third were born outside the country. Over half of the men employed in South Wales were engaged in the coal industry.

The percentage increase in the population of Glamorgan in the half century since 1861 was the same as that of England and Wales over the century itself. No wonder that the 'coal-owners' paper', *The Western Mail* of Cardiff, could editorialise on 1 January 1901:

> Every period and age dwindles into insignificance when compared with the nineteenth (when) Wales at a bound emerged from the obscurity in which it lay in 1800.... With the development of the coal and iron trade began a gradual exodus from rural districts until the latter have been depopulated and Glamorgan, Monmouthshire and East Carmarthenshire gorged with toilers and moilers as thick as bees in a hive....

Arguably, as we now survey the results of this capitalistic hubris, Wales was never properly industrialised. It was not merely that it was a regional phenomenon but also that wherever it occurred in Wales it was a primary matter. There was no secondary or spin-off industry to complement the production and export of low-cost, bulky material. Certainly the manner of industrialisation within Wales was, in national terms, utterly uneven. It was a lopsided Wales that swaggered into the twentieth century. Unarguably, it was Wales that felt and looked different.

But within a generation all the indices of growth were reversed. The slump of the inter-war years so altered the shape of employment and mobility – the work-force halved and almost half a million people were blown out of Wales by endemic unemployment – that the image created then, imprinted by the grainy documents of print and film, blotted out in the public memory the febrile confidence of the Wales which preceded it. The innocently posed and panoramic street scenes of Edwardian Wales fail to match the authenticity created by the more sophisticated photography of the thirties.

Wales at the turn of this century is immortalised in the sepia tints of a thousand postcards slipped into cellophane envelopes and stacked for sale in the shoe-boxes of antique dealers. What we see is, invariably, a world bulging with tabernacles, bursting with smoke, chimneys, coal trucks and, well, Bert Coombes' expressively vague 'many things'. Edwardian Wales photographed itself as it wished to be seen – progressive, lively and arrayed in a merited glory. Rarely do we note individual faces or people who take much more than a walk-on part. How different from the 1930s where every scene is ordered to tease a response, from a drawn visage to a kitchen's disorder in which the grime seems ready to come off if you scrape your fingernail across the print. The documentary representation of inter-war Wales, as with the Depression stills of Roosevelt's America, is designed to authenticate experience and, thereby, to *involve* the spectator. It sets out to elicit emotion not, like a family snap, to invoke self-admiration.

The result has been that the quintessential Welsh experience of industrialisation has been lost in the welter of angry sentiment which the pictorial cliché was designed to provoke. Since the 1930s, too, documentary reportage, statistical surveys and academic theses have shared the small change of explanatory cliché. The blunt, seemingly out-of-proportion complaints and opposition emanating from the Valleys were, thus, the effect of a 'tight-knit' society. Intransigence was a product of geographical 'isolation' or of 'occupations' that 'conditioned' social and political responses through 'work culture'. Dejection and passivity were connected to the 'immobility' of those not 'motivated' enough to leave. The Valleys of the inter-war years were, and are, summed up in their 'new' impoverishment: the images are fixed in our heads – valiant, foolish, even prehistoric in their removal from present concerns. But those images are, in actuality, only just removed historically from the frontiers of all the forces that made Wales a modern world. The process had taken the Valleys over the border first. The central act of the drama that ensued happened in the Valleys.

This should be the crucial memory rather than the spiralling economic fall. For a very long time South Wales had been a nineteenth-century pressure house in iron and coal, the very bones and marrow of industrialisation. The overwhelming, detailed materiality of quickening life was based on that industry. This was like no place the people who flocked in had ever seen before. Merthyr Tydfil, by the 1830s, was foretelling in its own mess of cottages, inns, chapels, brothels, sewers, schools and works that the

Welsh were to be an industrial people. In cameo, here, and with an abiding resonance in Welsh literature and history, people were jostled through decades of economic and ecological crises. The riots and strikes and raging politics which sporadically interrupted the capitalist purpose of this world were a rehearsal of what many more were to discover for themselves. When the Welsh working class is conjoined to Merthyr the noun is 'birth' and the adjective 'first'. What occurred in Merthyr even before the 1840s can only really be comprehended through such metaphor.

However grim and brutalising South Wales remained well into the twentieth century, some of the people who had been through the early years of towns like Merthyr looked back, from the 1890s, and congratulated themselves on the improvements in health, in municipal services and the repression of crime. Fruits of good fortune – the profits of commerce – withered so rapidly after the First World War that the middle classes' role in setting a public tone, in shaping a community of shared interests and social grada- tions, has been almost forgotten. Perhaps this was because the middle classes of the Valleys themselves managed to ignore the towering statistics of infant mortality, deaths in childbirth and the mutilation and destruction suffered in the pits. Ironmasters and coal-owners mostly scurried away to sylvan retreats, their capa- cious residences shrouded from the industrial chaos by screens of birchwood and monkey-puzzle trees. The slightly lesser (but very aspiring) breeds built their gabled and baywindowed villas in just sufficient number to mark their territory off from the encroaching dwellings of the workers.

There was, then, a small, yet significant, commercial and profes- sional segment who set out to develop a framework of social reference for their sprawling townships. They often succeeded. The original truck shop of the company towns gave way, as the nineteenth century went on, to high streets of emporia able to supply more than basic needs. The shopkeepers were a clan apart. They stand, slightly stooped from so much attention to the customer and the ledger, in photographs memorialising their indi- vidual establishments. Girl assistants and grocers' boys flank these white-aproned, moustachioed merchants. Behind them, in the cavernous gloom of their shops, an ordered cornucopia of goods is spilled in display – racks of cane brushes hanging down past rows of tin buckets; hooks twisted into flitches of bacon or the vermilion and white undersides of carcasses; windows piled high with biscuit tins, packets of tea and rice; aisles crowded with dusty sacks and hooped barrels of earthy potatoes or sifted sugar and powdery white flour; pine shelves stacked with scrubbable coconut-matting; yellow-waxy counters embedded with brass rulers to measure out dress material, floral curtains, lace cloths; cupboards of hats and collars and the soft, creamy fringed mufflers that brought a touch of ease to a collier's neck and titillated his susceptible vanity.

Here, then, was a burgeoning population, crushed and concentrated into limited space where the immediate, physical miseries of working-class life were acute, and frequently insupportable, but also, even in the mean streets themselves, put into direct contact with the tawdry, glamorous, available paraphernalia of a mass, urban life whose vistas bedazzled as surely as the blinking scenes of a diorama. This visual and tactile magic gripped more tightly than anything left behind in the country. It was, for the eye, an illusion which could even transform the strings of terraced housing, basically drab and utilitarian, into a bewitching perspective in which they moved, like humped-up Chinese dragons, across the irregular mountain sides whose quirks and faults caused streets to rise steeply at right angles to each other or plummet down the hillside with each house like a brick in a tower that is forever falling. This was not regimentation, but configuration of dwellings and landscape. The streets undulate in speckled bands of red and grey or sit up, broken-backed, in a juddering line of march. Around the corner, from a high mountain ridge of contemplation, looking up from the river, the spectator would see a tumble-down, overhanging spate of purple-black slate roofs, slotted one on the other until they all seemed joined.

Minds grew fat in this forcing house. They fed on the over-arching promise of the power and mobility of railway viaducts. People listened through day and night to the clangour of wheel on rail. Underground, the days flickered in the dark for an army of colliers. Above ground, nights went soft with the yellow fuzz of iron-stalked gas lamps. Pit-head wheels rapped out a spinning message of work and wages. Daily the pit hooter beckoned with its steamy rasp. The movement was constant, frenetic, cyclical, ambivalent. Human meaning was buried in a puzzle of relationships. People were defined by the public, tangible world that was ceaselessly growing with them. The visual mood was surreal.

Fantasy nudged you on almost every corner. Play-castles with Provencal turrets peeped through the foliage on to an industrial Disneyland whose separate 'worlds' all collided. Self-confidence and amazement would, in time, be replaced by doubt and familiarity but a generation or more of that fluid population which streamed into South Wales remade their identity and discovered an appropriate style after the initial, neighbourly shelter of fellow migrants, established faiths and old acquaintances.

This new world needed to be named before it could be known, and cheek by jowl with ancient place-names now unrecognisable from their rural origins, South Wales received a novel, non-Welsh nomenclature to match its brand new existence. Before Edwardsville or Merthyr Vale there was nothing. Like Pottsville and Carbondale in Pennsylvania, they came straight from the godhead of industry. These villages, segments in reality of a gigantic Welshburg, were soon the only known reality for most of the Welsh and for the immigrants to Wales: Treharris and Hopkinstown, Williamstown and Tylorstown, Wattstown, Edmundstown, and Cynonville, and the hopefully named Mountain Ash and Ferndale – trailing a transposed rurality with them into a jumble of alleyways, red and yellow brick, and switchback street roads where people found a common identity to take back to the family hearth. There were soon generation gaps through which the middle-aged snarled in discontent at youthful rowdiness, now paraded continually and not only at allotted fair times or harvest gatherings. People explored the possibilities for enjoyment of an urban space that was both crowded with life and, it seemed, without horizons of limitation.

Cardiff, the city on the coast into which the valleys poured their coal, had already by the end of the last century become irritatingly non-dependent on traditional Welsh life. It was, too, unmistakably the node around which the Welsh future would be based. Exhortations to remember the rock from which it was hewn came regularly from visiting politicos and dignitaries. The city, with its fun-palace battlements and glittering arcades, was on an ego trip whose heights were induced by the assured notion that here, too, was a marvel of the world to place alongside those 'freaks' who, as the tallest, strongest, shortest, fattest, filled the theatres with sleights of hand or feats of strength which broke the bounds of normal expectation with every new, possible impossibility. To the city of sights and giants and available consumption came the spectators who, thereafter, had another measuring stick.

At the Cardiff Exhibition of 1896 in the pavilions that housed models, ceramics, engineering exhibits and a 'working coal mine' alongside an oriental bazaar, the organisers dutifully placed another intriguingly different item – a display of 'Old Cardiff'. The effects of the new city (less than 1,800 people in 1800, more than 180,000 in 1914) upon an equally new populace, there and in its pullulating hinterland, caused great anxiety for some in Wales. At the blessing of the Assizes in the spring of 1909 the chaplain to the High Sheriff of Glamorgan took as his text 'Thou leadest me besides the still waters' in order to illustrate the need for wise guidance, since 'the rapidity of growth' and the strains of 'modern life' had led Wales to 'her own peculiar difficulties' as 'the simple life had been renounced':

> How had the Welshman stood the strain? The poet had become the man of action and force. He had great abilities, and today he had great ambitions, and he had shown himself able to deal with great affairs. He had developed the need for 'higher education'. However, people snatched from rural areas were overwhelmed by the new life when taken away from 'the waters of quiet' and needed time for self-examination and prayer, for Wales was at the present time at a crisis in its history ... typified by the city of Cardiff which had risen like a miracle almost in recent years with magnificent buildings of which Welshmen should be proud. ... Wales [must] beware lest she put her trust too much in such material wealth.... The public men of Wales had a great task to perform.

Wales had spawned a generation of such public men by 1909. They stressed the qualities needed to maintain a community cohesion. It was to be held by the anchor of past values bred in the Welsh countryside. The scale of things defeated them. Their idea of culture was challenged by the popular, living culture of people increasingly removed from their former ties of custom, tradition, religion, language and social deference.

Producing Wales

> Wherever we look at medieval Wales it seems to dissolve into plurality; its history appears to be no more than the sum of its individual parts ... [but].... [a] sense of continuity through time from the original and true proprietors of Britain contributed powerfully to the self-identification of the Welsh. It was reinforced by the belief that all Welshmen of noble stock shared common blood and thereby common status. In a society dominated by the terminology and concepts of lineage and status, it was in terms of community of blood and descent that a sense of common identity could be most readily expressed ... [to which] ... was added another potent ingredient in the making of national identity, that of a common mythology, a sense of shared traditions, myths and sagas. It was a mythology which was jealously cultivated by a professional order of bards and remembrancers.... As with all such mythologies, its aim was to provide an interpretation of the past which was compelling for the present and prophetic for the future.
>
> R.R. Davies, Wales 1063-1415 (1987)

On 23 January 1906 Dave Gallaher and the New Zealand rugby team he captained were about to board the liner *New York* at Southampton Docks on the first leg of their journey home. They had played thirty-two games throughout the British Isles since their arrival in September 1905. Now, as the All Blacks climbed the gangway, they were assailed by a boisterous rendition of 'Hen Wlad Fy Nhadau', the Welsh national anthem, and a choral question-and-response that involved Gallaher and the Welsh leek to the latter's benefit. The choristers, decked out in the red of Wales, were thirty rugby-mad Welshmen studying in Southampton.

Neither their sporting passion nor their colours and favours would have seemed representative of Welshness to their grandparents. The song they sang was, as an anthem, even younger. Their marks of Welshness, apparently so venerable, were almost as young as they were themselves.

If Gallaher and his companions had travelled inland from New York City when they arrived in the USA, they would have discovered a thriving Welsh-American community whose own sense of Wales did not accommodate rugby football. On the contrary, when in 1893 Wales had defeated the three other home countries for the first time, *The Cambrian*, a leading Welsh-American newspaper, declared that the only advantage derived from rugby was Welsh success since, in all other respects, 'there are tendencies observable in its popularity which point to national danger'. In due course the former would eclipse the latter but, in 1896, after his nationalist policies were rebuffed politically in the South of Wales, the 'northyn', David Lloyd George, would bemoan that region's 'morbid footballism'. In late nineteenth-century Wales, rugby was more than a game, it was an incubus. *Y Faner*, a Welsh-language newspaper in Wales, commented in 1885:

> The hankering for kicking 'the black ball' has fallen like a plague on the boys of the South. Day and night, for the poor and the wealthy, the religious and the irreligious, football is the talking point.... And several of the daily and weekly newspapers employ correspondents to cover it, and set aside long columns for the purpose of giving detailed reports of such bestial sports. Aren't things like this indisputable proof that this 'Age of Light' is returning to the 'Land of Darkness'?

Twenty years before this, 165 Welsh people had sailed to found a colony in Patagonia at the nether end of the Southern American continent. In part, they were impelled by a conviction of impending doom for the survival of Welshness in Wales. During the last century almost 100,000 Welsh people crossed the Atlantic and settled in the USA. However, it was not doom and gloom which drove *them* away but a hope for more immediate economic betterment. Most of the Welsh who became Americans migrated after the Civil War ended in 1865. They took with them an idea of Wales that was already formed, and their culture was strong enough to take root for a generation or more. Of course Welsh-Americans lived in a time-warp, whereby what they conceived as Wales was being bypassed in Wales even as it was to be, inevitably, swamped within America. Like rugby, the Welsh national traits succoured in America were invented in the nineteenth century to suit the requirements of an emerging sense of Welsh nationhood.

It was of course the official or public side of Welshness which was embraced, those traits that leading members of the community, in America as in Wales, considered acceptable and, therefore, by the logic of national protection, 'natural'. The Welshness they promoted was a judicious mixture of national antiquity and conventional morality. Thereby the Welsh emigrants to America would become worthy citizens of the New World by virtue of their inherited characteristics, and the Welsh in Wales, who were the template for this Cambro-American pattern, remained Welsh insofar as they upheld these expectations. Both communities shared the dismissal of other features of contemporary Welsh life as intrinsically un-Welsh or potentially anti-national. To be Welsh and a British imperialist or an American citizen was no problem; to be Welsh and a Catholic or a Socialist was. The original show in Wales would run longer and play to bigger audiences as it reworked some of its lines to accommodate latecomers, but the production of 'Wales' that was staged in America was done with imported props, favourable reviews and an audience that was defined by exclusion.

Our picture of Welsh-American communities is mostly derived from the essays, speeches, sermons and newspaper editorials of those who set the norms for Welsh-American life. The Welsh language, Welsh character and all of Welsh culture were invested with the traits of sobriety, respectability, utility, musicality and rationality that nineteenth-century Wales saw when it looked in the mirror. Welsh-Americans imitated the Wales-at-home in the frenzy of their chapel-building; in the propagation of literature and literacy through Welsh (and English) newspapers; in their celebration of communal Welshness at singing festivals and eisteddfodau; in their success in industry, both as entrepreneurial owners and as a craftsmanlike work-force; and in their virulent anti-Catholicism – the anti-Irish riots in Pennsylvania in the 1870s were echoed in Wales in the 1870s and 1880s. They were as profoundly promonarchical – they applauded both Victoria's Jubilee and the Prince of Wales' Investiture in 1911 – as they were eager to become US citizens: an estimated seventy-five per cent queued up for naturalisation. This characteristic paradox was shared by their native Welsh kindred, who were equally happy with British Imperial sentiment and Welsh national fervour.

This flaunting of Welshness was widely believed in and supported. Nowhere more so than in the epicentre of Welsh-America – the city of Scranton in North-East Pennsylvania. Yankee ingenuity having failed in the mid-1840s to found a thriving iron industry on local ore and Pennsylvanian anthracite, the Scranton brothers imported Welsh skill from nearby Danville in the shape of Tredegar-born John Davies. First in iron, then in coal. Scranton soaked up for decades Welsh industrial skills perfected in Wales. The Welsh, along with other British migrants, arrived to teach Americans how to fire a furnace, puddle iron, split slate, cut coal and roll tinplate. The Welsh who had come in the seventeenth century to Pennsylvania as Quakers, and in the early nineteenth century to New York State as farmers, now colonised the Wyoming and Lackawanna Valleys of Pennsylvania as iron-makers and, above all, as anthracite miners. By the 1890s Scranton had moved from being a tiny hamlet to become the thirty-ninth largest settlement in the USA. Clapboard houses and telegraph poles littered the clumpy hills on either side of the river. And below the hills the coal breakers signalled, in a ring, the presence of the mines in which the Welsh and their children worked.

Scranton had the largest concentration of Welsh in America – 7,500 people who had at least one parent born in Wales, making up ten per cent of the town's inhabitants. The Hyde Park district housed the Welsh and there were two whole blocks stuffed with Welsh-run stores, banks, businesses, professional men and churches. There were lively newspapers, in Welsh and in English, and Welsh societies and eisteddfod occasions, large and small, abounded. Scranton's Welsh community saw itself as the prime upholder of Welsh nationality in America. Leading members took politics, in the Republican cause, very seriously, for the Welsh leaned heavily on the successive waves of migrants – Irish, Poles, Lithuanians, Ukranians, Slavs, Italians – and their social and occupational positions began to be threatened as skills became shared or, through mechanisation, were at less of a premium. The Welsh were not averse to utilising their advantaged positions and sense of social superiority to immigrants who could not assimilate as easily the Protestant Anglo-Saxon norms of America. Most of the Welsh could speak English, and many of the new Welsh immigrants were anyway predominantly English-speaking, so upward social mobility into white-collar occupations was no problem for the American-born generation. Less amenable jobs were filled by the new migrants but, as a visitor to a Scranton mine, first worked by the Welsh in 1868, noted in 1910, its work-force had become: 'managers and superintendents, Welsh; foremen and bosses, Irish; contract miners, Poles and Lithuanians; outside labourers, Slovaks, Ruthenians, and Italians'.

Other, perhaps less palatable, things were happening to the community: a rapid Americanisation, in culture and in language; a decline in religious attendance and in the literary as opposed to the musical, side of the eisteddfodau; and a level of roughness and lawlessness that led, in the 1860s and 1870s, to literally murderous forays against the Irish. The Welsh fought each other, too, before and after drink. There were Welsh saloons as well as Welsh chapels and, it was alleged, a brothel in Scranton which specialised in catering for the Welsh (quite how is probably a matter for sexual linguists). There is nothing surprising in any of this, but it was incisively removed from the written history of Welsh-America in favour of anodyne lists of hierarchical achievement until historical analysis in the 1980s replaced ancestor worship.

The most telling connection between Wales and America is the similarity in the daily lives of the bulk of the Welsh industrial migrants. They were largely untouched by the concerns of the minority whose higher contemporary profile ensured their unrepresentative presence in written history. The majority, whether they were becoming 'Welsh' in Wales or 'American' in America, led lives whose structure was more dictated by work patterns than by Welshness. They succumbed to the dubious pleasures of popular song, of baseball or rugby, enjoyed the trinkets of a consumer society and the early flourish of a leisure industry. This was the case on both sides of the Atlantic.

Many deplored it. Many more just carried on with living in one place as they had in another. In the 1890s a Pennsylvanian Welshman bewailed those of his community who 'had learned in Aberdare, Merthyr and Rhymney to drink beer like water and to get as drunk as tinkers'. No one knew that better than the minister of the Congregational Church in neighbouring Edwardsville. He was the Reverend T.C. Edwards, whose church was the biggest Welsh church in America. He was a native of the Cynon Valley, had been a minister in Cardiff and was a noted figure in the Eisteddfod. He took the bardic name of 'Cynonfardd' and, in cultural terms, was probably the single most important Welsh-American of his time. The Reverend Edwards was also a notable campaigner against the liquor trade. He had to be: many of his congregation were notable non-abstainers. In 1905, as the Religious Revival swept Wales, Cynonfardd was busy filing legal orders to close saloons whose licences were up for renewal. The saloon keepers resented the Welsh busybody. One of them paid a Pole, anglicised as Edward Savage, to reply. He did so by dynamiting the church.

Welsh-America survived as 'Welsh' by ignoring such intrusive reality or by compartmentalising the occasions of their lives. Edwardsville Church was rebuilt. An eisteddfod is still held in honour of Reverend Edwards, though no one speaks Welsh. Roots are uncovered in newspapers, societies and guided tours of Wales. It is a selective Wales that they wish to know. In 1913 the Archdruid of the Welsh National Eisteddfod went to the American Eisteddfod at Pittsburgh where he invested Cynonfardd as America's first Arch-Druid. The mock-heroic moment was more expressive of trumpeted Welsh confidence than any real heroics in far-distant Patagonia and, in its concentration on the lineaments of national culture deemed essential for 'Welshness', supports the conviction of the South Walian who visited his American cousins in 1912 and decided they were 'ten times more Welsh than they were at home. They are Welsh to the core'.

This conceptual elasticity had, before 1914, achieved an even greater triumph at home in Wales where, notwithstanding its alien origins and strictly regional boundaries, rugby had been welcomed into the Welsh national fold. The Welshness that lived so brightly yet so briefly in America could not regenerate itself by incorporating a new item of national identity, but in Wales there was, before 1914, every chance to do so. Moreover, there were compelling reasons to see national traits in the *valued* developments of modern Wales so that a middle class could root its social being in a national identity.

Rugby football was an almost unique purveyor of these possibilities in late nineteenth-century Wales. It was quintessentially a middle-class game and, with very few exceptions, remained so until the late twentieth century in the other home countries. Further, it was, in origins and early personnel, not associated with anything Welsh at all. Even within Wales many of its early players and administrators, at club and international level, were neither Welsh by birth nor by language. Many were 'Welsh' only through the aspiration to play for Wales.

Scarcely a Welsh XV from 1880 to the turn of the century had less than three or four players who were born to non-Welsh parents outside Wales. First generation Welsh international players were legion. The sons of Somerset, Devon and Gloucestershire provided wit, initiative and innovation. Frank Hancock, scion of a brewing family and born in Wiveliscombe, Somerset, in 1861, migrated to bustling Cardiff where he 'invented' the four three- quarter system of play whose startling success led to his own captaincy of Wales in 1886. If he had played against England that year he would have been on the opposite side to his brother, P.T. Hancock. His arch-rival as Welsh centre was the incomparable A.J. Gould of Newport, the most-capped and indisputably supreme player of his generation; his father Joseph, who bred a family of rugby-playing athletes, had moved from Oxford to Newport to do business in that dynamic town. Dick Hellings who, despite a broken arm, scored a try for Wales against England at Gloucester in 1900 was a Rhondda collier – born in Tiverton, Devon, a county which gave Harry Packer to Welsh rugby as player and selector. The Welsh packs of the 1890s boasted the speedy Wallace Watts, born and bred in Chipping Norton, the versatile Arthur Boucher, another Somerset man and the 'brains' of Welsh forward play, Tom Graham of Tyneside. No wonder the Welsh Rugby Union wished the national qualification for the Welsh XV to be merely a playing career within Welsh club rugby. For such men, with *bona fide* working-class players only emerging after the foundations were laid, rugby and Wales were ways of moulding society into the form of a 'club'.

These men were the doctors, lawyers and businessmen who found homes and a living in Wales in its boom years after the 1860s. In common with Welshmen who had absorbed the current interest in team games through public school or university or simply residence in England, the early players were young men entering on a professional life who enjoyed the social bonding provided by athletic pursuits. Their desire for male sociability was shared by contemporaries in societies as geographically removed as Ireland and America, as connected in their joint divergence from a traditional past as South Wales and the South-West of France. In the two latter instances it was rugby which became the passion rather than any other sport. The reasons are, partly, accidental: soccer was established too far away (in working-class Lancashire and, later, in northern France) to be a direct competitor; it was rugby which, through a middle class in the coastal towns, whether in Bordeaux or Newport, was established before a working-class interest, as players or spectators, was aroused.

A sport that was proletarianised through overt professionalism could prove vital and attractive to a working-class audience, both spectators and players, but would never serve as a social cement in a society such as South Wales where the commitment of public men, politicians and business people, churchmen and patriots, was to the *idea* of a community of interest. Rugby football had to be, and remain, amateur if its function as the sport of first a community and then, by extension, the nation was to he upheld. The role the game was able to play, by manufacturing a sporting fraternity that cut across class divisions, gave it such an initial boost. The craving for physical leisure and dramatic excitement on the part of the thousands rushing to work in the coal mining valleys did the rest.

Villages and townships established their own communities through rivalry and much of the mayhem associated with the game in the 1880s and 1890s did not please the middle-class patrons who controlled the rules and customs of the sport. Rugby's popularity was such that their strictures were never entirely effective but the game's penetration of popular culture anyway ensured that so long as they were not rebuffed, working men would accept the self-imposed disciplines of a mass, spectator sport. To this end the covert professionalism of heavy 'expenses' for star players was quietly taken on board; a split between amateur and professional, such as occurred in England through rugby league in the 1890s, would have ended the special need of the sporting middle-class in Wales – an opportunity to play an amateur game with their English/Scottish/Irish peers without losing a socially *inclusive* game. This was well understood by 1914, when the first edition of *The Welsh Outlook*, a new social and cultural journal, appeared in Wales. Faced with the growing interest in professional soccer in Wales since the early 1900s, it opined:

> Rugby is ... the game of the Welshman. The international records of the past twenty years show that the Principality can hold an equal if not superior hand in the game.... The Association code in Wales is new and alien and comes in on the back of its popularity elsewhere: it is the game of the alien of the valleys whose immigration and de-nationalising tendency is one of the major problems of our country [and] the social context of the game [is] cosmopolitan....
>
> Wales possesses in Rugby football ... a game democratic and amateur – a unique thing to be cherished and ... the concern of thinking men who value the complex influences making for higher levels of citizenship.

Rugby had become 'Welsh' not because a Welsh Rugby Union was founded in 1881 to select national sides to meet the other Unions of Britain but because, within twenty years, the social function had merged with sporting success to become a focus for nationality. Already, by the early 1890s, club sides had sprung up in almost every nook and corner of the expanding coalfield. Soon they challenged, and often beat, the (slightly) older clubs of the larger towns. These in turn had begun to welcome working men into their ranks and to agitate for their inclusion in Welsh XVs. Creative play had brought Wales her first, elusive, Triple Crown in 1893. The heavier forwards and bruising play of the other nations contin-ued, nonetheless, to trample on the 'pretty' play of the Welsh until the 'Rhondda Forwards' – a readily employed euphemism for any collier, tinplateman, steelworker or docker – were fully united with 'clever' – generally middle-class – backs. In the three seasons after their Triple Crown success under A.J. Gould's captaincy, Wales won only one game a year but in January 1896 just after Wales beat Scotland in the mud, a blackened Gould told a throng of his admirers, 'Why *I'm* like a collier, look at me!' The following year he led a similarly chosen Wales to only her third ever victory against the might of England, and there were four forwards in the pack who were, literally, from the Rhondda. On this basis victories began to flow and a second Triple Crown in 1899-1900 was followed by five more before 1911.

The more Wales won the more the other countries accused Welsh rugby of covert professionalism and, worse, of 'cheating' by employing the stamina of the working-class to ensure victories. Resentment was often deep. But in Wales the taste of victory was the rubber-stamp required for the national verification of rugby football. This was also proving the case for that radically different nation – New Zealand – whose 1905 All Blacks conquered all that the mother country had to offer. When they came to play Wales on 16 December 1905 it was more than a world championship that was at stake, or even national pride. The issue was national defin-ition in the 'modern' world through sport.

This is why the victory against New Zealand in 1905 was presented to the world as a sign of Welshness itself, irrespective of the recent origins of the game or the actual origins of its partici-pants. Indeed, the fact that the Welsh fullback on that December afternoon in 1905 was from Nottingham, the pack leader from Lincolnshire and the captain born in Westbury-on-Severn, Gloucestershire, was supremely irrelevant to the team's entry, as rugby players, into the Pantheon of Welsh national mythology, an entry which had been prepared for them in the myth-making course of the nineteenth century.

Two days after the Welsh XV's 'historic' triumph the leading Welsh newspaper of the day devoted an editorial to the feat:

> When you consider for a moment what Wales had to do, and when you think of how she did it, there arises in every man the feeling of highest admiration for qualities that find the most popular expression. The men – these heroes of many victories – that represented Wales embodied the best manhood of the race. And here we are met with some of the greatest problems in the development of distinct nationalities. We all know the racial qualities that made Wales supreme on Saturday: but how have they been obtained?... The great quality of defence and attack in the Welsh race is to be traced to the training of the early period when powerful enemies drove them to their mountain fortresses. There we developed, then, those traits of character that find

fruition today. 'Gallant Little Wales' has produced sons of strong determination, invincible stamina, resolute, mentally keen, physically sound. It needs no imaginative power to perceive that the qualities that conquered on Saturday have found another expression in the history of Welsh education: that long struggle against odds that has given the Principality her great schools and her progressive colleges. The national traits are equally apparent in both contexts.

By 1905 these 'national traits', for which no imagination was necessary, were enmeshed in a web of national piety spun from over a century's imagining.

The first great burst of Welsh national trappings had come towards the end of the eighteenth century. They were the product of the intellectual 'awakening' of the eighteenth century, translated to Wales, and a severe crisis of the agrarian economy which had been additionally shaken by the major impact of still patchy industrialisation. Scholars, bibliophiles, antiquarians, lexicographers, poets, patriots, crowd on to the canvas. In London, societies of the Welsh, learned and convivial, began to flourish. Welsh intellectual life quickened. The renaissance of interest in things Welsh after the 1770s is indeed remarkable. In part it owes something to the Romantic interest in the remoteness of Wales: both geography and history obliged with a mix of wild beauty and mysterious antiquity. Welsh historians have pointed to the lack of institutions – educational, political, metropolitan, bureaucratic – to preserve a Welsh folk-culture felt to be disappearing, and how this need was met by groups and individuals on a passionate and uncoordinated basis. There was, undoubtedly, an attempt within Wales to unite a sense of nationality with a fervent political radicalism (Jacobinism) at a time, the 1790s to 1830s, of irrepressible, if sporadic, conflict and riots in the countryside and in the towns.

There was a great deal of genuine scholarship and discovery. Some that was not as well-founded owed more to the lack of a tradition of critical scholarship in philology, the provenance of Welsh texts and the state of historiography than to any slapdash or ill-conceived approach. However, in the use made by others of this 'rediscovery' of Wales, we move into murkier waters. If the Welsh nation was 'required' to possess certain traditions or aspects that were dependent on a history that could not be fully ascertained, then myth, invention and even deliberate forgery would fill the gap.

The Welsh rediscovered the legends and lore of their history in the eighteenth century. Descent from Brutus and the Trojans and

the Arthurian saga, commonplaces of the Middle Ages but dis-
credited in the sixteenth century, were again waved airily around.
More important was a better-founded emphasis on the real thread
back to the sixth century – the language, and, too, a resurrection
of the Welsh Bards as a direct line of descent from the Ancient
Druids. In the fertile brain of a Glamorgan stonemason, Edward
Williams (1747-1826), who took the bardic name Iolo Morganwg,
the tradition took on a contemporary resonance. He cashed in on
the eighteenth-century's Druidic obsession by declaring himself
and a friend as the two last Welsh bards. The Gorsedd, or 'throne',
of the Bards of the Isle of Britain was then literally invented by him
and equipped with a ceremonial order. It was first tried out in 1792
in London and then spread, in small groups, through Wales until
in 1819 it was grafted on to the National Eisteddfod. The latter, a
meet for competition in music and poetry, had had a sporadic, and
genuine, existence in Wales since at least the twelfth century. In the
eighteenth century a revival of bardic versifying had taken place
and had been boosted gradually by societies set up to propagate all
matters Welsh. By the 1820s the eisteddfodau were the principal
vehicles for presenting the accumulated Druidic backlog to Wales
as its own true image.

Everything then came fast and furious. After the 1858
Eisteddfod at Llangollen – the first really major occasion – the
National Eisteddfod was established. Railways saw to it that its
proceedings – in Welsh and English until 1953 when the all-Welsh
rule was introduced after almost twenty years of agitation –
attracted large and appreciative audiences. But what they saw and
what they sang, though suffused in national and heroic imagery, was
the nineteenth-century's version of the Welsh past.

The Red Dragon banner of Cadwaladr, used by the Tudors to
claim overlordship of Britain? This was competing, unsuccess-
fully until the twentieth century, with the three feathers of the
Prince of Wales as a national symbol and flag. The leek *was* an
ancient symbol of the Welsh princes, but the daffodil? This
appeared in 1907 through an error, and was incorporated in the
1911 Investiture by Lloyd George. Druidic insignia and regalia?
Designed by Iolo and incorporated into the ornate costumes of the
late Victorian era by Sir Hubert von Herkomer and Sir Goscombe
John. Welsh costume itself? The tall black hats and blue or red
tweed cloaks worn by Welsh women in the 1790s in remote mountainous areas were left-over English fashion of the 1690s. They
were turned into a Welsh national dress of red cloak, petticoat,

bedgown and tall black beaver hat, for use on 'national' days, by the philanthropic patriot, Augusta Waddington, Lady Llanover. Little girls wear it every St David's Day (1 March) and in the last century Dame Wales became the Welsh equivalent of John Bull in cartoons, adverts, dolls and post-cards. Wales as the Land of song and harpists? The immensely popular triple harp, symbol of nineteenth-century Wales, was an Italian baroque instrument introduced in the early eighteenth century, and it was that century which produced, too, what became known as traditional Welsh music and songs. The great choral societies were the products of industrial Wales, and *penillion* singing (accompanying the harp in a descant) only emerged in the nineteenth century.

The one clear note of Welsh unity today is heard when rugby international crowds open their throats to bellow 'Gwlad! Gwlad!' half-way through the undisputed Welsh national anthem 'Hen Wlad Fy Nhadau' – 'The Land of My Fathers'. The song has everything the emergent Welsh nation required – bards, freemen, patriotism, singers and an exhortation that the 'old language' should live forever. Sir John Lloyd, doyen of Welsh historians in the early twentieth century, closed his 1931 *A History of Wales* with the words of the anthem

> *Gwlad, gwlad, pleidiol wyf i'm gwlad!*
> *Tra mor yn fur i'r bur hoff bau*
> *O bydded i'r hen iaith barhau!*

and commented: 'North, south, east, and west, Welshmen will be found singing at patriotic gatherings ... the strain of "Hen Wlad Fy Nhadau", of which the broad and simple melody was composed by Evan James of Pontypridd, and the words written by his son James.'

If Sir John had written his book in 1890 he would not have been able to conclude it on such a note for, as he himself wrote, it had only 'become the Welsh national anthem within the last forty years.' Its own history encapsulates the shift from mythical fantasy to practical use. As late as 1898 a leading Welsh journalist was lamenting the lack of an anthem for Wales (the 'British' one appeared in 1740 and was the earliest). The Jameses had submitted their song, composed in 1856, at the 1858 Eisteddfod. It was listed under a selection of Welsh airs and though quickly popular it was by no means an automatic choice as a national song until the last decade of the nineteenth century, by which time the trappings of an invented history were themselves disseminated and used. The Jameses and their song were taken to the bosom of triumphant, respectable, nonconformist and patriotic Wales – a society whose leaders had successfully won the first piece of legislation to apply specifically to Wales in 1881 when public houses were closed on a Sunday. The composers of the anthem, however, had kept beer shops, pubs and inns all over South Wales and James James died in the arms of his son in the Swan Hotel, Aberaman, in 1902. The facts were less important than the sentiments inspired.

The *actual* history of the Welsh up to the early nineteenth century, by which time they numbered about half a million, cannot be adequately summarised in a couple of paragraphs. What can be said, however, is that whoever the Welsh were at any particular time, they did not share more recent conceptions about Welsh history or nationality. Initially, they did not even consider themselves 'Welsh' (the term used of the 'Cymry' by Saxons) but British. Before the Roman settlements, and afterwards, there were tribal divisions and loyalties. When the Roman Empire's authority, delegated and otherwise, began in the sixth century to dribble away in the face of the breakdown of the Empire's central authority and the increasingly concerted attacks of the 'Barbarians', there were communities of the Cymry all over Britain. Those in Scotland, over a period of time, were cut off from fellow Welsh-speakers in the western part of Britain which, gradually, became Cymru or Wales as its territorial limits were made synonymous with the area within which the Welsh were confined by military contingencies. Out of the chaos of continental invasions, alliances and counter-attacks the identity of the Welsh in Wales was established. By the ninth century tribal rulers, chieftains and princelings were marking out their more localised tracts in disputatious rivalry. Attempts to unite all those in Wales under one rule or one body of law fell apart in these quarrelsome hands. The scale was small but the pattern was not unusual in the Europe of that period.

The distinctive marks of the Welsh were an early embrace of Christianity before the Anglo-Saxon invasions had shut off Rome and a language that was, by the sixth century when our earliest surviving poetry is dated, already producing skilled and subtle literature. In the early Middle Ages, the bards would act as propagandists and interpreters of Wales for their patrons, princes and lords. By then the 'fall' of the Welsh from their earlier 'British' glory was a constant refrain. Codified laws were presented as a handed-down tradition of distinctive Welsh law-giving. The geographical areas of Wales, nonetheless, remained distinct, under local, princely rule. After the Norman invasion, the Welsh/English border country and the lowlands of South Wales were parcelled out by those owing allegiance to the Norman dynasty in England.

In the twelfth and thirteenth centuries a succession of resolute Princes of Gwynedd, in that stony North of Wales where the marcher lords of the Anglo-Norman kingdom had failed to penetrate, strove to bring all Wales under their banner. They could only do this if the messy localism of separate Welsh communities was sorted out by instilling in their rulers and sub-rulers the order of hierarchical allegiance demanded by the Anglo-Norman kings of the Welsh princes. That kind of fealty the Gwynedd dynasty was prepared to pay. Within Wales they sought to exert the same gradation of rule by referring to themselves as Princes of Wales. Through diplomacy and war they came close to bringing off the trick, though not without upsetting other Welsh rulers and causing internecine, familial and civil strife. Wales might have emerged as a mini-feudal kingdom in a feudal Europe but for two things – the first was the growing unease of an 'English' kingdom undergoing the same process at the ambitions of their Gwynedd subject-princes; and the second was the deep mistrust felt by other Welsh princes and lords for the 'modernising' tendencies emanating from Gwynedd's thrusting dynasty. When Llywelyn the Last was killed in 1282 at Cilmeri, near Builth Wells and far from his northern base, political initiatives designed to unify Wales disappeared for centuries.

Add to this the 'failure' of Owain Glyndŵr in the fifteenth century and the 'absorption' of Wales into England in the sixteenth century by Henry VIII's Acts of Union, and the history of Wales itself, in the eyes of many subsequent patriots, also disappeared or, like Arthur in his cave, went underground until a better day. From this perspective a sober argument about the necessarily limited nature of Owain Glyndŵr's revolt in the troubled fifteenth century or an examination of the 1536 Act of Union in terms of an administrative strategy widely desired by the Welsh gentry, falls on deaf ears. Never mind that a Bible in Welsh – and by extension the provision of a literary basis for modern Welsh prose – appeared in 1588 as a result of the Protestant Reformation signalled by the 1536 Act, or that the words in Welsh for 'nationalism', 'national' and 'nationality' appear, for the first time, in the late eighteenth century and, in regular usage, from the 1850s. If people wish to believe that for centuries a sense of Welsh nationhood has persisted, as a natural outcrop of the Welsh people, then that faith will not be shaken by careful contextualisation of evidence which traces the material production of a culture of nationality.

Nonetheless, it is worth repeating that you cannot be or become something you cannot imagine or have not seen. And how, on any widespread basis beyond the circle of rulers and their bards, could the Welsh imagine Wales before the advent of print and literacy? Nor was there any reason for them to do so. Nationalism is a nineteenth-century creed. It is an identification of people with territory, and sometimes with language, which goes on to argue for an identification of the defined nation with a political state. Such a need, experienced in Europe at a state-nation level from the sixteenth century, becomes an important *cultural* process only with the advent of industrial capitalist societies. People then really do require the bonding provided by a sense of shared nationality. Literacy allows them to communicate and to group together even if they never see each other. Mobility reinforces the need and the senses of a national community. There were countries without maps but no nations, in this sense, without railways.

It is anachronistic to try to read our post-eighteenth-century idea of nationality backwards into societies based on tribal loyalties or organised around the central, divine, authority of the monarchy or possessing a fundamentally different idea of the natural order of life. Except in the most shallow sense it is meaningless to equate a nationalist desire for unity through a state-nation in the twentieth century with the existence of Wales through the centuries, i.e. simply to equate nationality with nationalism. These remarks clearly apply beyond Wales. Until the nineteenth century, except for an élite, there was no use for a widespread, embracing concept like 'nation'. Loyalties and organising principles were based on more immediate concerns for most people.

The history of the Welsh, then, is mostly about the view from below. Through all the centuries lauded or wailed over by later Welsh patriotic sentiment, the luckiest Welsh were those who managed to keep out of the way of anyone powerful enough to afford the menace of a political will. From civilising Romans intent on orderly exploitation of a slave-based Empire, through raiding Vikings eager for regular plunder and on to Anglo-Normans who proved as insistent on settlement in Wales as the Saxons they, in turn, had displaced, war or accommodating diplomacy may have been statecraft and high politics, but for most people mere survival was the toughest skill to wield against brute existence.

They did not share the élite's aspirations. They had a language of course but they were not literate in it – and when they finally were it was the Bible they were set to read. They had rulers, foreign and native, but no say in government beyond an occasional twitch of disobedience, the fury of a bloody revolt, the chance to join in a gentleman's quarrel with his neighbour. Religions – pagan and Christian, in their different forms – came and went like the tide. And like the sea, religions did have shaping force, but a whole world of customs and culture, folk and pagan, secular and irreligious, was often left behind, isolated, untouched. Indifference, too, was a weapon of survival in a universe of élite power. Neither religion nor politics did much more than scratch the surface of all those secret, stubborn, hidden-from-history Welsh lives.

Until the late eighteenth century and the coming of industry, and for some even beyond that, the circumscribed realities of life on the land or on the sea were *all*-important. The material shape of Welsh lives was what formed their idea of themselves, their possibilities, their horizon of limitations. The sea that hems in three sides of Wales gave food and opened up routes for trade and for invaders. The latter were no more deadly than the civil wars whose stumbling battles were usually less of a threat than plague or recurrent local famine. Crop failure and livestock death were constant factors for centuries in the stone-strewn fields and bare uplands. A tiny population scraped a bare, subsistence living. The hills broke up the country into separate worlds where the illiterate and the semi-literate lived out their brief, immobile lives. You could be Welsh in this world – how could you be anything else – but an abstract idea of the nation, of nationhood, had no real meaning. That was true for a peasantry all over Europe. The paradox of nationalism is that it is a future vision wrapped up in the legitimising clothes of the past, real or mythical: it scarcely matters which.

This is why Owain Glyndŵr, forgotten until the late eighteenth century, could be hailed first as a romantic hero and then in the nineteenth century as a founding father of Welsh nationalism. He justified his revolt against the English Crown by reference to rights enjoyed in the past when the Welsh were the original British. He called on ancient genealogies to prove his claim to be Prince of Wales. The fifteen-year struggle did have an anti-English tap root in a time of severe dislocation, but the revolt was sparked by a personal grievance, fed on the uncertainties of English civil strife, and was never a popular uprising.

Glyndŵr led a group of patricians with a similar list of grievances which they were intent on settling. He may have had a consciousness of all of Wales in the way that fifteenth-century Europe was beginning to nurture nation-states, and this concept was supported by the clerks and gentlemen who aided him in his plans for a Welsh 'parliament' at Machynlleth and a Welsh 'university' to service his rule. He was, though, not averse to including chunks of English territory and English-speakers in his Wales, and his revolt was more a regional conflagration than a national war for 'independence'.

It was, again, typical of what was occurring all over Europe – with or without 'national' characteristics. The latter are an invention of the decades around the start of the nineteenth century when languages, peoples and nations were smartened up, trotted out and made up all over Europe from Scandinavia to the Balkans. The nation was postulated and its objective characteristics retailed. The problem then became one of making a national people to fit into the national box.

In the end it was achieved by mass literacy, schooling, banks, roads and military conscription. Major and minor nations were marshalled into line by governments which needed a holding definition the more democratic procedures spread. Consciousness-raising was vital if the local, distinct worlds were to be united into a 'nation'. This process was as common in small countries with a complicated dependency on a 'mother' state, like Ireland and Wales, as it was in self-governing units whose major characteristic held in common by their peoples was a central government, like France and Italy, and again as in confederations of states and cultures, like Prussia and the USA. It did not, of course, follow that a widely felt, if invented, sense of nationality would always lead to an acceptance of nationalism. Indeed this is precisely what happened in Wales.

By the mid-nineteenth century Wales had become a country with a bare majority who worshipped in a nonconformist church of one denomination or other and a people of whom fifty per cent were working in some form of industry. Both preoccupations – religion and material advancement – remained central to the evolution of nineteenth-century Wales. Mid-century criticisms by education commissioners, allied to vituperative thunderings against the state of civilised life in Wales by English newspapers and other commentators, had underlined the connection between the growing power of nonconformity and the use of the Welsh language. The methodists, in particular, had long frowned upon the rather free and easy manner of traditional Welsh folk culture. Iolo Morganwg, for one, reciprocated their dislike. In 1799 he wrote to a London correspondent, 'North Wales is now as Methodistical as South Wales, and South Wales as Hell.' If this was so, there was no stopping the fire: it has been estimated that, taking the nonconformist groups together, they built a chapel every eight days between 1800 and 1850.

The chapels – and the Sunday Schools and the singing festivals and a host of other associated meetings – spread throughout the new industrialising districts even more than in the countryside. The wealth of the industrial districts provided a firm foundation for all this building and for a wealth of periodical literature to match. The chapels were breeding grounds of democratic procedures and of eloquence. They never, the Established Church apart, brought everyone into the fold but they did undoubtedly set the tone of public life and behaviour in Wales, as certainly as did the Roman Catholic Church in Ireland, for fifty years after the middle of the century.

This nonconformist nation became, after the criticisms of the 1840s, conscious of its own growth in eighteenth-century Wales. They too were, in fact, a new offshoot and they, too, required a sense of themselves as a predestined, natural force. They took over the paraphernalia of Welsh patriotism – from eisteddfodau to leeks and daffodils – and added the ingredients of hymnology, respectability and the common people as Hero. The last in the line from princes to poets would be the 'gwerin' – the folk. The Welsh peasant, and to an extent the miner and the quarryman and the tinplater, were idealised as cultured, pious and equipped for modern life.

The indigenous population of Wales was growing at a pace throughout the nineteenth century. Their voice was to be heard through the new democratic procedures of enfranchisement at parliamentary and local level. The politics of this Welsh-speaking, nonconformist Wales – opposed to landowners and Anglicans, in favour of disestablishment of the Church, teetotalism and sabbatarianism – was inevitably radical. The radicalism, though, was not predominantly nationalist. Alliances were made with comparable social groups in England. Wales was, unlike Ireland, benefiting from attachment to England's economy. Welsh politicians, generally, did exercise control after the 1870s. Wales was seen, by the Welsh, as an integral part of the Empire of Nations. The Welsh could be, then, Welsh by origins, language, territory and religion *and* British in politics, social aspirations and links. Except for a few nationalist patriots there was no contradiction in any of this.

In 1886 the Welsh Baptist Union sent a mission to Brittany to investigate the work needed there on behalf of a people who had 'a high claim on the attention' of their 'more fortunate relatives on this side of the channel'. Their spokesman explained:

> The ancient traditions of the chronicles of Brittany, and the old traditions of the country which have floated down the streams of centuries, are rich in references to the racial identity of the Bretons and the Welsh, and the sympathy which dominated them, until in due course of time, owing to a wide channel intervening and various events conspiring to separate them, they became estranged to one another. And now the Brythons of Wales, who have been quickened by the benign influences of the Protestant Reformation, Nonconformist revivals, Sunday-school teaching, and advantages derived from connection with England, are to be contrasted and not compared with the Brythons of France, who have not yet been vivified by such potent influences.

So distinct had the Welsh 'Brythons' become that eisteddfodic prizes were awarded for essays on Welshman who had risen to distinction overseas – 'at home' was now taken for granted. The Protestant Welsh had been so steeped in a literal Biblical tradition that they could, and often did, amidst villages and churches named Saron, Nazareth and Bethania, imagine themselves akin to the Israelites of the Lord. It was a manifest sign of the modern mantle of destiny, for, by 1909 'Welshmen' proclaimed the *South Wales Daily News* 'are everywhere. In every corner of the world they are to be found taking leading places. Even in the Land of the Pharoahs, under the shadow of the Pyramids, they are in the van of progress'. Lists of engineers, bankers, merchants, doctors, soldiers, clerks, scientists and architects followed – even the Bishop of Khartoum was from Glamorgan.

Not that one had to trek so far to bring the Welsh virtues to bear, not even with John Hughes of the Cyfarthfa iron-works to the Ukraine, for John Vaughan of Dowlais iron-works had made Middlesborough the greatest iron and steel town in Britain as surely as the Guests and Crawshays had come into Wales to transform Merthyr a century before. The Welsh dominated Cleveland where they held the skilled and managerial positions, as they did in Pennsylvania. John Vaughan was three times made mayor of his English fief which, by 1896, had a thriving Welsh society whose inaugural meeting was exhorted to further endeavour by Dr John Rhŷs, Celtic philologist and principal of that Welsh Balliol – Jesus College, Oxford. He emphasised how much had changed since

1870 when 'it was very common to hear in a certain class of Welshmen's public speeches a bitter complaint as to the sacrifice it meant for a man to own himself a Cymro.... Now it was seldom heard ... the grievance had disappeared.'

How had this happened? John Rhŷs was convinced in the signs of progress all around him, in so many spheres of activity, that 'under proper leadership a people endowed with the elasticity of the Celts could achieve almost anything'. From this ethnic platform the Welsh needed to invade Oxbridge, the Civil Service and all areas where 'the great Anglo-Celtic Empire extends its influence'.

Or, as O.M. Edwards, Balliol Scholar and Fellow of Lincoln College, Oxford, put it in the preface to his 1901 popular history of Wales: '[after the downfall of the princes and the gentry] a lower subject class became prominent ... and feebly imitating' but 'this class, with stronger thought and increasing material wealth, rules Wales today'. No leadership could have achieved so much without a dedicated army behind it. In the nonconformist bourgeois mythology of pre-1914 Wales, the leaders could appeal to the image of the God-fearing, Liberal-voting, thrifty sons of the soil / collier / slate quarryman / metalworker who had inherited the Welsh past, a past which was incarnate in the national institutions of Wales – eisteddfod, university, museum (from 1907) – and in the leadership of preachers and politicians. All ranks of the army were in love with this image, with the use they had found for 'Wales'.

Naturally it was the 'little corporal' himself, David Lloyd George, the first Welshman to attain cabinet office since the seventeenth century, the man who would lead the British Empire of Nations in the First World War, the man designated by Lenin in 1918 as the most formidable bourgeois politician in all of Europe, who delivered this fictive representation of reality, past and present, most resoundingly. The ambiguity and ambivalence of nineteenth-century Wales are nowhere better encapsulated than in the emotive, yet deeply self-conscious, career of David Lloyd George, who milked the invented tradition of Wales for all its political worth during a lifetime that was, in part, shaped by all this Welsh self-preening.

Today, his statue, a study in frozen vigour, shakes a bunched fist at the National Museum of Wales in the capital city of Cardiff. It is neither a gesture of anger nor contempt nor dismissiveness, for all that his back is turned on Iolo Morganwg's eisteddfod stones in the park behind him. It is merely another gesture. His contemporaries had a Wales of gestures and symbols to share. Lloyd George became one of them – depicted in press and cartoons as another Merlin or Arthur come to deliver up the future. His generation was probably the last to hold, together, an uninhibited sense that the Welsh past gave them a real unity. However, they were also the last Welsh generation to see themselves as the heirs to a rich and promising future. The past for them was not just a key to unlock understanding, it was an excuse to celebrate their arrival as a people of achievement. In the years just before the First World War Lloyd George became the heroic incarnation of those social and cultural characteristics which the Welsh chose to proclaim as national. The Welsh were, as an advanced modernising country, possessed of an acute self-consciousness in language and religion. Their use of history, at that time, was neither humble nor inward looking. In life, Lloyd George did not turn his back on its myths nor shake a fist at its marmoreal pride.

In 1909 he addressed, as its President, the Baptist Union which met that year in Treorchy in the Rhondda. There was nowhere more redolent of the new, emerging Wales – urban, secular and, quite quickly, English-speaking. Lloyd George spoke, with utter conviction and confidence, of the different Wales which he represented. Religion was its mainspring for 'the chapels of Wales were the colleges of the common people' and the Welsh were grounded in great literature – 'the masterpieces of the Book of Job, the high literature of Isaiah and the eloquent epistles of Paul' – that equipped them for the twentieth century. He went on:

> Nonconformity was the first power to do that for Wales.... It taught them perseverance, it taught them organisation, and the importance of permanent work – work that had no flash about it, work that brought no immediate fruit, but work that meant patience and long waiting.
>
> It was nonconformity that taught Wales her politics.... And what had been added unto the people of Wales? First, the democracy of Wales had won their self-respect, they had also won their independence. They stood like men ... the Welsh nation was going forward, ever forward; not following the flesh pots in the land of bondage, but turning its back on these to steadfastly follow the cloud by day and the pillar of fire by night ... forward, ever forward, fighting the sons of Amalek. Many of us have ascended the summit of Pisgah and there from afar have gained a glimpse of the Promised Land. How many of us will reach it I know not but in my opinion we are rapidly approaching it, and the people of Wales can sing 'Bryniau Canaan ddont i'r golwg' [The hills of Canaan are in sight].

1909 was a year for visions in Wales. David Lloyd George, as reforming Chancellor of the Exchequer, could still visit his radical wrath on his old enemies, Tories and landowners, but he could have joined with them in the rather aristocratic National Pageant of Wales presented that summer in the grounds of Cardiff Castle. The aristocracy and gentry of Wales were, indeed, the stars of the pageant but the organisers were at pains to stress the 5,000 participants who framed the picture for the Marchioness of Bute as Dame Wales, and to describe 'Owen Glyndŵr' – played by 'such a loyal and notable Welsh soldier as Viscount Tredegar, who more than fifty years ago rode into "the Valley of Death" in the immortal charge of the Light Brigade at Balaclava' – as 'the famous rebel warrior who led his own people so successfully against the English in the fourteenth and fifteenth centuries'. In episode after episode the 'great events' and 'heroes' of Welsh history were acted out until the climax – which here was the crowning of the 'Welsh' Henry Tudor after the Battle of Bosworth, and the Act of Union between England and Wales delivered by his son Henry VIII in 1536. The national anthem of Wales was sung just before 'God save the King'. There was, for the time, nothing contradictory in these contradictions.

The historian of the pageant was the author Owen Rhoscomyl, whose *The Flame Bearers of Welsh History* testifies to his sacral drive. As Captain Owen Vaughan he had proved a hero in the Boer War which Lloyd George had so vehemently opposed. The divisor of opinion within Wales over that war was less representative of Welsh 'pacifism' than was subsequently claimed and undoubtedly of lesser importance than the sense of community conjured up by 'history':

> This National Pageant of Wales ... is the first function of its kind which is fully and voluntarily representative of an entire nation ... the first pageant ... wherein all classes of the community have lent their services with such loyal patriotism....
>
> And not only do ... notable leaders of society assume the roles of great historic personages in this pageant, but by a happy coincidence scarcely possible outside the pale of the Principality, the parts they play are those of their own famous ancestors. For example, we find Lord Mostyn of Mostyn Hall impersonating the gallant Richard ap Howel of Mostyn, from whom he is directly descended, and to whom Harry Tudor presented his sword ... on the bloody field of Bosworth.... A thousand years earlier, a still remoter ancestor of the Mostyns lived in the person of Princess Tegaingl, the grandmother of King Arthur

the Great. The head of the senior branch of that royal line today
is Sir Piers Mostyn of Talacre. His daughter takes the part of
Tegaingl....

Then when we see half a thousand of the crack football players of the Principality careering wildly across the field, as did the
wild tribesmen they represent that time they were led, half
naked, by Ivor Bach, and won Cardiff Castle from its mail-clad
Norman defenders – then do we recall the fact that, on the
mimic battle grounds of the national sport, Wales leads the three
kingdoms today, and that her youths are still as stout of heart
and strong of limb as they were when they followed Harry of
Monmouth to Agincourt, and smote with British swords and
bows of British yew the flower of the chivalry of France.

This overblown Edwardian fantasy had a purpose beyond giving
ladies and gentlemen the excuse to parade in silks and chain-mail.
It implicitly defined Wales as a nation because it presented a
continuous tradition; it suggested that Wales had joined a British
polity to its own advantage without ever losing a 'Welsh identity';
it assumed, in fact, that the Wales which had been invented in the
course of the nineteenth century was essential to an understanding
of the modern Wales in which they lived, and it offered up this
Wales as a common ground on which all interests and classes
within society could come together.

In 1915 David Lloyd George, then Minister of Munitions in the
wartime government and soon to be the first Welsh Prime Minister
of the British Empire, went to Cardiff to unveil the statues
commissioned before the war he was 'to win'. They were unveiled
on the first floor of the City Hall that now stands next to the
National Museum. As the oil painting of the scene reveals, the
benign, frock-coated Lloyd George stood surrounded by the landed,
industrial, academic, bureaucratic and, in 1915, military élite of
Wales. And the statues, cold and white and Pageant-inspired – paid
for by D.A. Thomas, Rhondda coal owner and Liberal MP for
Cardiff – are of the historical élite of the Welsh nation: St David
who founded the British church in Wales before St Augustine
came from Rome to Canterbury in the sixth century; Buddug or
Boadicea who repelled the Romans at London; Llewellyn, Prince
of Gwynedd and last independent Prince of Wales, who was killed
in 1282; Owain Glyndŵr, the fifteenth-century rebel whose revolt
briefly promised an independent Wales; and Henry Tudor, whose
acceptance of a British dimension would prove as dubious for
Welsh nationalists in the 1920s as Lloyd George's own. But not in
1915. Why *had* this heady historical brew been made?

It was, ultimately, the product of a late nineteenth-century middle-class need to identify itself and its nineteenth-century origins with the quintessence of Welsh history as they defined it. This ideal was then superimposed upon the present. It was disseminated in schools and books at a popular level and given the seal of academic approval in the university colleges. The Pageant of 1909 was echoed, more formally, two years later in Lloyd George's own Caernarfon. Here was stage-managed the investiture of Edward, Prince of Wales, in a rich ceremony of dedication and loyalty. This patriotic event could be seen, like that of Charles in 1969, as a plot to dupe the 'masses'. In this scenario the chief Welsh politicians 'deliver up' the nation to English/British domination and, in due course, are suitably rewarded with titular baubles – Lloyd George becomes the Earl of Dwyfor and George Thomas emerges as Viscount Tonypandy. Setting aside, as a counter-argument, the real political services rendered by these two, the situation *is* more complex. Neither event defused radical politics in Wales – after 1969 Plaid Cymru grew in influence and the miners' unions began their five-year campaign – and that of 1911 has a more diffuse significance, symbolised directly by the linking of the Bishop of Asaph, A.G. Edwards, and the scourge of the Established Church, Lloyd George, in its design and execution.

Neither Liberal politics nor the nonconformist religion, and certainly not the idea of Labour as a *separate* force, could hold together the concept of Wales as an indivisible community, as a nation of natural origins and organic growth. History alone could do this, provided, that is, history could present the outcome of the present as an inevitable progression and one that was not inimical to the concept of a Welsh nation. In its early twentieth-century direction and aspirations, that Welsh nation was middle-class. The late nineteenth century had seen in Britain as a whole an enormous increase in white-collar professions and in the distinguishing characteristics of a middle class – villas, servants, amateur sports, spa holidays. In Wales, whose economy and society were undergoing sea-changes that threatened the less 'traditional' way of life, these middle-class groups required both a justification of their own privileged position and a vision of the past that would promise a connected future. Religion was increasingly outdistanced in this secularising world. Education was a more useful channel for élite doctrines and for a 'designed' concept of Welsh patriotism.

No one designed it more than the great educationalist and populariser, O.M. Edwards (1858-1920), who returned to Wales from an assured career as an Oxford don. He had served briefly as a Liberal MP but found his vocation in editing a series of popular, academic and children's magazines in both Welsh and English. This, allied to his role from 1907 as Chief Inspector of Schools in Wales, gave him an extraordinary influence in the permeation of Welsh culture through society. Within schools he urged the national appropriateness of vocational, rather than academic, training for most Welsh children and, as so many of his contemporaries did, welcomed the new material wealth of Wales inasmuch as it did not give rise to complete social disruption. Allied to a tender nostalgia for an idealised rural past was a hard-headed attempt to provide institutions to safeguard 'Wales'. It was not 'Britain' or 'the monarchy' or 'the empire' which was the threat. The concluding passages of his *Wales – a continuous popular history*, published at the beginning of the twentieth century, are an eloquent summation of the pageant concept of history:

> The effects [in 1900] of the industrial revolution are apparent everywhere. By the mountain dingles and on the edges of the moorlands ruined cottages peep out of a wilderness of ash and willow, and flowers run wild, and the solitude deepens every year in glens once full of children who were born heirs to health and contented poverty. From North Wales the human stream flows continuously to the slate quarries of Arvon and Merioneth, to the coal mines of the lower Dee, and to swell the great Welsh population of Liverpool. From every part of Wales the peasant trudges to the valleys among the Glamorgan and Monmouth hills or to the great seaports on the South Wales coast all teeming with people. Coal and steel and tinplate, of world-wide reputation, have given energy to the labour once bestowed indolently on peat and sheep and homespun. While the population of the central shires is stationary or declining, that of Glamorgan and Monmouth has increased fivefold within sixty years.... Cardiff stands second among the ports of the kingdom, and third among the ports of the world.
>
> Trained by their self-education in religious and literary matters, enfranchised when the new wealth gave them political independence, the Welsh people were peculiarly adapted for local government....
>
> The year 1894, which gave a measure of local government to the Welsh ratepayer, also brought the University of Wales. However strong the Welsh claim to self-government has been, the desire for becoming capable of self-government has been stronger. The development of education has at least kept pace with the growth of wealth and of political power ... the University College of Wales at Aberystwyth [was established] in

1879. In 1883 the University College of South Wales was established at Cardiff and in 1884 the University College of North
Wales at Bangor. In 1889 and the following years the system of
intermediate [grammar] schools between the primary schools
and the colleges was organised [and] at the installation of the
Prince of Wales as Chancellor of the University every class was
represented at Aberystwyth, united in welcoming the realisation
of the dream of so many centuries....

The development of Wales has been twofold – in national
intensity and in the expansion of imperial sympathy. From
Cressy to Agincourt to Albuera and Inkerman its ... sons have
been where the surge of the advancing British wave has beaten
fiercest. To the cause of capital it has given a Lord Overstone,
to the cause of labour a Robert Owen....

The life of Wales, in the intense conservatism of its unbroken
continuity, has not been selfish. The desire to give has been as
strong as the desire to retain.... [The Welshman's] conservative
desire for independence is strong enough to send him to almost
superhuman toil in inhospitable Patagonia, and to maintain
Welsh newspapers and magazines, full of old world poetry and
half-legendary history, among the modern and practical organs
of opinion of the United States.... The first period of Welsh
history ends with the poet's lament for its fallen princes; the
second ends with the poet's vision of a future of more self-
conscious life and of greater service. The motto of Wales is to
be that of its prince – 'Ich dien'.

The nationality of Wales was thereby justified in terms of its being
an historic community no longer bypassed by modern imperial
Britain but capable of playing its own, refined part. This, and the
great celebratory Pageant of the first decade of the twentieth
century, were the end-products of a self-confident Wales, as democratic and nonconformist as it was cultured and ordered. Tories
and working-men were invited to participate in this particular feast.
The latter, especially, were required guests the more the ties of
political and religious association frayed. This did not happen over-
whelmingly before 1914 but the signs were acute enough for nation
and community to be invoked at almost every public opportunity.
Rural disturbances, such as the tithe riots of the early 1890s, were
dismissed as anachronistic aberrations, whilst massive industrial
strife was misinterpreted. The three-year lock-out in the Penrhyn
Quarry at Bethesda was consistently depicted as a struggle between
the ordinary, native people (quarrymen) and an insensitive alien
owner (Lord Penrhyn) who wished to crush the traditional (Welsh)
rights and customs of his otherwise docile work force. Liberal MPs
like Lloyd George could sympathise with the cause when expressed

in these terms but the real struggle was about the quarry work-force's idea of themselves as independent craftsmen. They were being proletarianised, and the idea of a proletariat was one that could not be accommodated within the idea of a nation of 'un-broken continuity'.

In Edwardian England the great cities were blamed for destroy-ing the yeoman ideal of English history, dissipating rural 'stock' into half-men, like E.M. Forster's Leonard Bast in *Howards End*, or corrupting them into the 'ill-bred' louts of countless social analyses. To an extent the nineteenth-century industrial districts of England were excused this social Darwinian probe and, to the extent that urban Wales was industrial rather than metropolitan, so was the emerging industrial working-class of Wales. The strikes in the southern coalfield in the 1870s, and the six-month lock-out of 1898, were taken by Liberal Wales as legitimate demands for wages and for an industrial structure (conciliation boards and trade unions) within the existing framework. Any evidence to the contrary – and especially the community upheaval in the Tonypandy riots of 1910 – was ignored or explained as more induced aberrant behaviour patterns, social and political. What was *not* acceptable was an alter-native ideology or a different construction of Welsh reality. Worse than anything was the pretension to independent thought that was also independent of established institutions.

A Place in the South of Wales

'Tonypandy', Grant said ... 'is a place in the South of Wales....
If you go to South Wales you will hear that, in 1910, the
Government used troops to shoot down Welsh miners who were
striking for their rights. You'll probably hear that Winston
Churchill, who was Home Secretary at the time, was responsible. South Wales, you will be told, will never forget Tonypandy!'
    Carradine had dropped his flippant air.
    'And it wasn't a bit like that?'
    'The actual facts are these. The rougher section of the
Rhondda valley crowd had got quite out of hand. Shops were
being looted and property destroyed. The Chief Constable of
Glamorgan sent a request to the Home Office for troops to
protect the lieges.... But Churchill was so horrified at the possibility of the troops coming face to face with a crowd of rioters
and having to fire on them that he stopped the movement of the
troops and sent instead a body of plain, solid Metropolitan
Police, armed with nothing but their rolled-up mackintoshes.
The troops were kept in reserve, and all contact with the rioters
was made by unarmed London police. The only bloodshed in
the whole affair was a bloody nose or two.... That was
Tonypandy. That is the shooting-down by troops that Wales
will never forget.... It is a completely untrue story grown to
legend while the men who knew it to be untrue looked on and
said nothing.'
    'Yes. That's very interesting; very. History as it is made.'
    'Yes. History.'
    'Give me research. After all, the truth of anything at all
doesn't lie in someone's account of it. It lies in all the small facts
of the time. An advertisement in a paper. The sale of a house.
The price of a ring.'
                    Josephine Tey, *The Daughter of Time*

In 1951, the year Josephine Tey's detective novel first appeared, I
became aware for the first time of 'the legend of Tonypandy'. As
part of a generation dazzled by celluloid vistas at least four times a
week, the revelation came in what we called a picture house –
nobody who ate 'dinner' instead of 'lunch' ever went to 'a cinema'
instead of 'the pictures'. On that night, sandwiched between the 'B'
feature and 'the big picture', was a Movietone newsreel whose
cheery, hectoring tones wrapped up an account of the return of the
triumphant Conservative leader, Winston Churchill, to No. 10
Downing Street as Prime Minister of Britain. And Wales. And
Tonypandy. And after six years of enforced absence in which, as
I was constantly told at home in tones of gratitude and pride, a

majority Labour government had introduced a Health Service which had, amongst other things, given *me* orange juice. The other things were personalised, too. Labour had also, I was told, ended the manner in which a grandmother had once had to choose 'eye glasses' in a squinting process of trial and error from a shop's counter; would prevent the early deaths from TB that had killed my parents' friends; and, above all, was what the war, so near to us then, was really about – a chance for a future for all of us that was not degraded by want and poverty.

These feelings, it seems, were widespread in the Plaza, for when Churchill came on the screen as restored PM there was a spontaneous eruption of rage. The smiling PM waved to us, and we booed and booed and booed. Catcalls and feet stamping preceded flying objects until the house lights went on. The main feature was delayed but we cheered and cheered and cheered. The ogre was banished. At least from the screen in Tonypandy.

In the General Election of 1950 Churchill had come in person to Cardiff to campaign. His speech, without provocation of any kind, raised the issue of his distant involvement in Tonypandy in 1910. He told what he called 'the true story of Tonypandy' in the hope that it would 'replace in Welsh villages the cruel lie with which they have been fed all these long years'. It was, basically, the text on which Josephine Tey's dialogue rested. Clearly, to us in that picture house, it had failed to persuade. In a sense I have been asking the question 'Why?' ever since.

Churchill was right about the manner in which other events had been conflated into the 'cruel lie' about Tonypandy. Nobody was shot in the mid-Rhondda though this was constantly alleged, in fact and fiction, in the 1930s. Two men were shot by troops in Llanelli in 1911 towards the end of the Rail Strike of that year (and several others were blown up by an ammunition truck), sparking off a riot there. In 1911, too, Tredegar, where the fourteen-year-old butcher's boy Aneurin Bevan witnessed the affray, was the scene of shop-smashing that had, in part, an anti-Jewish element attached to its violence. Tonypandy did not stand alone. Even in strictly industrial terms its unofficial strike had been preceded by an equally gargantuan disruption in the adjacent Cynon Valley when 11,000 miners employed by the Powell Duffryn Company came out, in a dispute over wages and customary concessions, that lasted from 20 October 1910 to January 1911. Riots and attacks on blacklegs, communal disorder and troop involvement were all direct parallels with Tonypandy. Yet it was, and is, the latter which caught public attention and came to be symbolic of a society in crisis and a world turning upside-down.

Why was this? In part because Churchill was wrong to claim 'no bloodshed'. Apart from deaths prematurely induced by the ten months' struggle, one man died as a result of head wounds after the clash with police on 8 November. The jury, after being advised that 'if they found that his injuries were caused by a policeman's truncheon' they would also have to decide if 'the police were justified in the action they had taken in using force to repel force for the purpose of preventing disorder', not surprisingly decided that it was not, in the case of the bachelor collier Samuel Rays, 'sufficiently clear' how the injuries 'caused by some blunt instrument' had been received. In his death this unknown forty-year-old became a martyr. He, too, symbolised what others felt. It was the scale of things – the clash of Capital and Labour, the role of government and, above all else, the total involvement of a whole community in an affair that, especially on the night of 8 November 1910, wrote the name Tonypandy into the commonplace book of twentieth-century British history. That was the reverberating echo I had heard in the early 1950s.

There are, of course, more fashionable places to have been born in than Tonypandy, despite its historical glamour. Even the Welsh name Ton-y-pandy – referring to the site of a fulling mill before the coal rush of the 1850s – sounds on English lips more like a broken-down Italian tenor than a Rhondda mining town. Not that it is really a town, but nor should it be called a village either. The boundaries of somewhere like Tonypandy are indefinable. Those who have lived there will tell you, within a street's length or span where Tonypandy 'proper' began and Llwynypia ended, or where Clydach Vale swoops down to end in the 'grander precincts' of De Winton and Dunraven Street or when you have left Tonypandy and entered Penygraig. This intense delineation of territory is nothing to do with council boundaries, political wards or ancient land grants. It is certainly not to do with a separating, physical sense of place since all of mid-Rhondda, and, by extension, large tracts of all the coal mining valleys in South Wales blur indistinguishably the one into the other. What it means is that no one ever actually came from 'the Valleys'. They came from those segments of individual and local experience, geographically de-limited by mutual consent, through which the wider bonding summarised by a term like the Valleys is given reality. Otherwise it remains an abstraction, almost a cliché. So, 'Where do you come from?' – once as insistent a query in place-conscious Wales as its follow up, 'What do you do *now*?' – is defined exactly as a locality whose parameters are known by those who need to know them. Tonypandy was, and might have remained, simply a framework for experiencing social identity. It became a country of the mind. The aspects were twinned.

In common with almost anywhere else in South Wales there were, as I grew up there in the immediate aftermath of the Second World War, the usual shelves of terraced housing undulating across the mountain slopes in lines imitative of the coal-thickened river. There were still colliers in black-face trooping home from shift-work to wash in the tin baths that hung on nails outside back kitchen doors; rectangular, beige account books, their ledgered pages backed by the dull sheen of blue carbon and valued for their record of the Co-op 'divi', still substituted for bank books; fleets of maroon double deckers stuffed the flatter streets like removable wafer fillings on days when some drinking or political club, or Sunday School or British Legion – you did not need to be a member! – decided to take us to the seaside. And on the mountains above our houses the surface ruins of collieries, abandoned since the 1920s, kept their machines and intricate buildings intact enough to serve us as cavernous adventure playgrounds whose jade-green feeder pools glinted more inviting and much more dangerous than the ones Lex Barker's Tarzan swam across in the crocodile-infested Picturedome. From a back-bedroom window I could see allotments, chickens, a seventeenth-century farmhouse, the Vesuvian waste of the coal tip and the railway line which carried only coal on the high level line from the Cambrian colliery where my grandfather worked. Sometimes the snow, drifting and falling from the hills, would cover everything, even the wire-mesh fencing, but never enough to stop the black, steaming train or the wave of its driver.

Now the colliery, racked by one last fateful explosion that killed thirty-one men in 1965, is dead, and in that same year my grandfather, wracked by that news, died too. Behind our street incongruous red-bricked semi-detacheds mark the mountain off with their neat lines, and the mountain's open space is fenced and divided. Where the tip sprawled over half the mountain, the contours are levelled to an astro-turf green and a new comprehensive school has for today's children replaced the demolished relics of pit life. Even the road system has, at last, bypassed Tonypandy.

The density of relationships between place and people, between my linear time and its curving compass of reference, touched me then and has never stopped amazing me as South Wales moves further and further away from its shaping culture. Perhaps this is the common fate of industrial leftovers everywhere. To live through the fag-end of such experience is to carry with you the unusable vigour of a textured life you know intimately, and uselessly. This eerie, almost feverish, shiver of unfulfilment, of being irredeemably marked by a process of living which mocks by its inescapable grandeur and spurns because of its evanescence, is there in Lancashire mill-towns, in the debris of rust and nails and barracks in North-Welsh quarries, and in the sifted coal dust lying in a carpet around the meccano-like coal-breakers of the Pennsylvanian anthracite field. Nostalgia is the joyous betrayal of what is also a real sense of loss. The two embrace to deceive us. Between these two poles, of potential and a dying away, some places, for a moment, are required to represent matters that are given significance by moving through and beyond them. Tonypandy was such a place. 1910 such a time.

The most eloquent testimony to this is the manner in which the name of this obscure place litters the index pages of countless British history textbooks (take 'Tonypandy' out and their actual dedication to English history is more honestly naked). The references are usually inaccurate but, in themselves, speak for Tonypandy's representative role. It is there, even more strikingly in plays, novels and poetry. By the 1930s it was being invoked as emblematic of working-class resistance and struggle in the face of murderous troops in Lewis Jones' epic novel *Cwmardy* (1937) and, with an equally cavalier alteration of facts, but reversing Jones' interpretation to show defeat and folly, in Richard Llewellyn's *How Green Was My Valley* (1939). In a more symbolic sense still, invoking the place as a crucible for the pariahdom of a rootless proletariat, Tonypandy figures as a vantage point for the death of what 'once was Wales' in Saunders Lewis' savage denunciation of industrialised humanity, 'The Deluge', 1939:

> ... *to stand on the corner in Tonypandy*
> *And look up the valley and down the valley*
> *On the flotsam of the wreckage of men in the slough of despair*
> *Men and tips standing, a dump of one purpose with man.*

The transferred despair – from poet to people – is a running thread in the work of another nationalist poet, J. Kitchener Davies:

You went down to Tonypandy for the Strike and the General Strike,
for the jazz carnivals and the football of strikers and police
for the soup kitchens and the cobbling....
And there you were like Canute on the shore
or like Atlas in a coal pit
with your shoulder under the rocks holding back a fall
or with your arms outstretched between the crag and the sea
shouting 'Hey! Hey!'
in the path of the lunatic Gadarene swine.
    The Sound of the Wind that is Blowing (1952)

This incantatory melancholy is present in Idris Davies' collection, entitled *Tonypandy* and published in 1945, though it is, in that year of reforms, tinged with expectation. The ambiguity of response to the meaning of Tonypandy was brushed aside in Alexander Cordell's 1977 novel, *This Sweet and Bitter Earth*, which disconcertingly mixes an impressive local colour with historical pastiche to proclaim the vibrant importance of what happened in 1910. The mix of myth and history is, though, what gives Tonypandy its potency – it looms more insistently in the imagination the more it recedes in the public consciousness. The myth can surface with a straight face to establish an historical mood reference, as it does in Alice Ellis Thomas' ironic comedy of upper-class Anglo-Welsh manners, set appropriately enough in North Wales, *The Sin Eaters* (1978), or it can be used for intriguing dramatic purpose, as in Alun Richards' play, *The Victuallers' Ball* (1969), where a public event is purloined for 'individual' use by a character who wears his claimed participation in the Tonypandy riots of 1910 like a tin medal on his puffed-up chest.

The claim is, of course, for an acknowledged bit-part in a European drama that made Tonypandy, in Kenneth O. Morgan's words, 'a folk symbol'. And makes it reverberate still through the scale of its passions and the importance of its main actors. The local cast was impressive: David Alfred Thomas, Liberal MP for Cardiff from 1909, chief instigator of the mighty Cambrian Combine group of pits in mid-Rhondda and later, in Lloyd George's wartime government, Food Controller as Lord Rhondda; William Abraham, a Labour MP since 1909 but Liberal member for Rhondda since 1885, President of the South Wales Miners' Federation from its inception in 1898, and known by his bardic name, Mabon, and much grieved by the rejection of his conciliatory policies and the denunciation of 'my friend, D.A. Thomas'; Noah Ablett, Noah Rees, W.H. Mainwaring, Will John, John Hopla – Rhondda labour leaders who variously combined a fervour for 'syndicalism' (workers' control to be achieved through the direct action of democratically organised unions) with the politics of the ballot box (Mainwaring and John would become Rhondda MPs). Then add the assembled forces of imported police under the orders of local coal officials, infantry and cavalry and over twelve thousand colliers and their families out on strike until starved back after almost a year's embattled struggle. No wonder John Morgan set out to write a libretto for his opera *Mabon* based on Tonypandy:

> The scale of that drama in 1910-11 ... was epic. There is a tendency to suppose that because Wales is a small country, then its conflicts are small. In this case, at issue was a balance of power within the State between labour and capital. There were a quarter of a million Welsh colliers. The coal they hewed sustained the largest navy the world had seen. British soldiers were involved in the upheaval. Men died. Nowhere else in Europe was there such a startling revelation of the new political order of the century. Therefore to convey this scale the opera will need as large a chorus as is feasible. It cannot be a chamber work.

Certainly not when the 'villain' of the piece, forever protesting his innocence before the howling rage of the mob-like chorus, is none other then an imported star artiste – Winston Spencer Leonard Churchill, MP, then Liberal Home Secretary. It is as if through his person the constellation of events continued to radiate around Tonypandy. Did he send the troops to crush the strikers or not? The question boomed on and on to indict his role as a bellicose Conservative cabinet minister in the General Strike of 1926; to be raised by Atlee in 1940, in private naturally, who wondered whether the Labour Party could support Churchill's emergence as Prime Minister because of the coupling of his name with that of Tonypandy; and, again, as late as 1978 when Prime Minister James Callaghan, during a routine question in the House of Commons over miners' pay, informed Churchill's namesake and grandson that South Wales would never forget the 'vendetta' his grandfather had waged against the miners in Tonypandy. For those who collect 'small facts' about great men *this* issue has been *the* issue. It has been surprisingly contentious since the facts are readily ascertainable.

This is partly because Churchill chose to bedevil the matter with his own false assertions. This was unnecessary since the troops were, on the whole, used circumspectly and, besides, as Home Secretary, if he considered life and property endangered he had the right to use them. Nonetheless it was not true, as the people of Tonypandy had remembered in 1951, that 'the troops were kept in the background'. They did come and they were used. Churchill's self-defence rested on the confusion he fostered (in his own mind?) between his desire for settlement and the actual consequence of his actions.

Churchill was reluctant to accede to the somewhat intemperate demands of the local magistracy and judiciary who had been sending out distress signals as early as 2 November 1910. They were anxious for a military presence to overawe the miners on strike in both the Cynon and Rhondda Valleys (in separate disputes). He was concerned to avoid any unseemly provocation. To this end, early on the 8th of November 1910 Churchill halted the movement of infantry into South Wales by countermanding the War Office's agreement with the Chief Constable of Glamorgan. Instead he sent metropolitan police to help out in the wake of the clash between strikers and local police on the night of 7 November. However, he did allow the cavalry to proceed to 'the district' (i.e. to Cardiff) and when further disturbances occurred on the night of 8 November instructed his designated military commander, General Macready, to proceed to the Rhondda (and to the Cynon Valley) with troops. During the day of 9 November members of two squadrons of the 18th Hussars were patrolling the valleys north of Pontypridd and the Lancashire Fusiliers were billeted in Llwynypia. Four other regimental companies were within a thirty-mile radius so that the troops, as well as well over 1,000 police, were, in essence, an army of occupation. A substantial force of troops and police remained until well into 1911. The strike finally ended in August 1911.

The troops ensured that all mass demonstrations against blackleg labour would be controlled and thereby rendered ineffective. On a number of occasions the troops did more than support the police – who bore the brunt of the fighting in late November 1910, March and July 1911 – for they *did* come into direct contact with the strikers. Bayonets were used to sharp purpose. It was troops, too, who saw to it that trials of rioters, strikers and trade union leaders would be successfully prosecuted in the court at Pontypridd in 1911. Their presence prevented the mass picketing which the leaders of the strikers had seen as their only real hope of an early victory. The defeat suffered by the men of the Cambrian Combine was, in the eyes of the local community, attached directly to the state intervention authorised by Churchill.

This is really what has given the frenetic events in Tonypandy in November 1910 their breath of historical life. It is why Churchill could not simply ignore what had happened. Noah Ablett reminded a packed meeting in Tonypandy in 1912 that they knew only too well what happened when they set out to challenge the organised power of the State. It was in Tonypandy in 1919 that *The Miners' Next Step*, a pamphlet quickly denounced by *The Times* itself, was published by Ablett and his 'unofficial reformers'. The pamphlet, vigorous in style and content, set up arguments against trade union bureaucracy, against nationalisation of the mines, and against a passive, representational parliamentarianism, and stirred men's minds far beyond South Wales. Academic analyses of the exact nature, and weakness, of the industrial unionist tactics and syndicalist strategy miss the resonance the pamphlet had in its plea for locally rooted, democratic structures of power. Their own union, they felt, could be an institutional means to success, through the work place and its lodges, by virtue of its immense size and potential power.

The working out of the subsequent struggles in South Wales, and elsewhere, was to be more labyrinthine than they would have wished. Nonetheless what the 'progressive men' in the coalfield had spotted in the generalised discontent of 1910-11, made more specific in Tonypandy than anywhere else, was the manner in which an industrial dispute had not only revealed the interests of the State but had also forced a community to redefine itself *against* the dominant public culture that was, alone, acceptable to Edwardian Wales. The events in Tonypandy were also evidence of a fractured society in which certain voices could be heard in no other way.

The crisis had occurred within the framework of conventional labour relations. The crowd's response, in both strike and riots, was that of an already industrialised and urbanised society, but on the night of 8 November 1910, and to an extent thereafter, they chose as targets of their discontent features that were symbolic of a community allegedly both democratic and a natural focus of their own being. Forced, via the catalyst of the strike, to reassess their own status they ended by commenting on their relationship to a community defined for them in a graphic code of selective destruction that was strictly incomprehensible to those whose idea of the community was now threatened by an ugly, intrusive reality. Churchill writing to King George V on 10 November 1910 gave the commonsense explanation of the 'insensate action of the rioters in wrecking shops in the town of Tonypandy, against which they had not the slightest cause for animosity, when they had been foiled in their attacks upon the colliery'. This type of 'history as it is made', to quote Josephine Tey, delivered with simple motives and attended by moral judgments, cannot survive the revealing detail which comes from looking into 'the small facts of the time'.

Tonypandy has to be understood, first, within the context of a South Wales coalfield whose labour relations were becoming increasingly acrimonious in the years before 1914. The early exploitation of the central steam coal area from the 1860s had led to a rapid development which was dependent on a huge labour force. Their wages were the single biggest charge on the industry. The seams grew more and more difficult to work in a highly faulted coalfield. 'Abnormal places' – working in water, working coal that contained too much stone, or any factor that denied 'productive' work and hence lowered piecework wages – were more frequent and local disputes were fractious. Productivity continued to fall even as total production and numbers employed rose in the years to 1913.

Agitation for a guaranteed minimum wage was associated not only with the grievance over 'abnormal places' but with hours of work (an Eight-hour Act was passed in 1908) and demands, by some men, for a more militant, centralised union to challenge the owners. The South Wales Miners' Federation had been formed in 1898. It remained a loose-knit, valley-based association, dominated by professional (white-collar) miners' agents. The shape of things to come, in the 1930s especially, could be seen, on the other hand, in the early formation of coal combines, grouping pits and their assorted interests together, that was advocated by the most 'advanced' capitalist in the coalfield, D.A. Thomas. The Cambrian Combine Strike brought all these forces together and served as a catalyst for something more.

The origins of the dispute lay in the refusal of men in the Ely pit of the Naval Colliery to work a new seam at the price per ton offered by management. The seam, experimentally worked for over a year, contained a lot of stone which, the men alleged, meant they would be unable to earn a living wage if management did not increase allowances for 'dead', or unproductive, work. Failure to agree led to the dismissal of not only the eighty men directly affected but also the locking out of all eight hundred men in the Ely pit from 1 September 1910.

The Ely pit was a part of that Cambrian Combine which D.A. Thomas had put together on the basis of the Cambrian Collieries in Clydach Vale inherited from his father. In 1906 he took control of the Glamorgan Coal Co Ltd in Llwynypia (with three pits) and in 1908 of the Naval Colliery Company Ltd (with four pits, including the Ely) in Penygraig and Tonypandy. By 1910 he had the Britannic Merthyr Coal Co, in Gilfach Goch over the mountain from the central township of Tonypandy and, in toto, the employ of some 19,000 men in the mid-Rhondda area.

From 5 September the men in the other Naval pits struck unofficially and, on 1 November, after a coalfield-wide ballot that promised financial aid only, the rest of the Cambrian men, against the wishes of the Executive Council of the SWMF and the local Rhondda miners' agents, also came out in support of the Ely men. The conduct of the dispute was to stay for the ten months of the strike firmly in the hands of the Cambrian Combine Joint Committee made up of representatives from all the separate pit lodges.

From the first few days the mood of the strikers was clear: the stoppage, if it were to be effective, would require a swift resolution that would be dependent on the non-importation of 'blackleg' labour and the prevention of colliery officials from attending to the pumping and ventilating machinery on the surface which would keep the pits free from flooding. Extra police, from outside the district, had been drafted into the area (142 of them) under the personal command of the Chief Constable, Captain Lionel Lindsay. They were concentrated at the Glamorgan Colliery, Llwynypia, so that when on Monday 7 November bands of men summoned by bugle and marching behind the Tonypandy Fife band at 4am in the morning, proceeded from colliery to colliery preventing all officials, engine-men and stokers (sometimes forcibly) from working, they met with little opposition from the thinly dispersed police. Fires were raked, boilers and ventilating fans stopped. At the Cambrian Colliery in Clydach Vale officials were stoned out of the electric power-house built in 1905 at a cost of £25,000. Mounted police were subjected to foot rushes and pelted with various missiles as the angry crowd, taking with them blacklegs dressed in white shirts with cards proclaiming 'Take a Warning' pinned to them, marched through high winds and drenching rain.

At the end of the afternoon only the Glamorgan Colliery remained inviolate: here waited the police and between fifty and sixty officials and craftsmen under the guidance of the general manager of the Cambrian Combine, Leonard Llewellyn. There were, underground, over three hundred horses brought in during the previous week from other pits. The pits to which the horses had been deliberately transferred were especially liable to flooding and the animals were to be the focus of much public and royal concern. To deal with the danger an electrically operated pumping plant, supplied by a large generator, had been installed in the yard. From 9pm the strikers mounted a huge demonstration outside the colliery yard which, around 10.30, turned more serious and finally erupted in a series of fierce clashes with the police that only petered out around 1 am.

The following day, Tuesday, Lindsay's request to the War Office for troops was blocked by Churchill, at least to the extent of halting them in Swindon and only sending seventy mounted police and two hundred Metropolitans on foot. The men, who had assembled on the Athletic Ground, Tonypandy, after being paid off by the Combine, received this news, relayed by Daniel Lleufer Thomas, the stipendiary magistrate, in silence and, shortly after, marched in force to the Glamorgan Colliery where, about 5pm, a crowd remained behind to demonstrate. They were estimated at between seven and nine thousand strong. Stoning of the power-house occurred and led to a number of baton charges by the 120-strong police (18 of whom were mounted). Intense close-quarter fighting followed.

So much, in brief outline, is not in question, but what now led to the riot against the shopkeepers has long been the point at issue. Historians, though pointing out his bias as a pro-coal-owner reporter, have generally accepted the account of David Evans in his contemporary volume, *Labour Strife in the South Wales Coalfield, 1910-11*, which attributes clear, if unworthy, motives to the strikers in their destruction of shops in Tonypandy. Evans, in lurid prose, describes the repulse of the demonstrators by a gallant band of police, the consequent dispersal of the crowd and how, frustrated and angry, they wreaked unjustified revenge on unprotected shopkeepers. This is the umbilical cord between the strike and its handicapped child, the riot. If Evans, bias apart, is wrong in crucial detail, however, then the riot requires another and deeper interpretation whose starting point must be a literary exegesis of a work whose logic and style are inseparable from the 'legend of Tonypandy':

> Captain Lindsay ... ordered the mounted men ... to clear the main road with their truncheons in the direction of Tonypandy and a body of the foot constables to operate simultaneously in the direction of Llwynypia. The mob offered a stubborn resistance;

the police had to fight almost every inch of their way; but after a prolonged effort succeeded in driving the rioters some distance away from the entrance of the colliery. No sooner, however, had the police returned to the colliery than the mob recovered most of the positions from which they had been driven, and charge after charge followed in quick succession....

At last they committed the fate of the fight to one last desperate effort to crush the spirit of the mob and make another rally by it unlikely. This was at about 7 o'clock when the cavalry asked for the previous night ... were detraining at Cardiff, and when the Metropolitans were still on their way to Pontypridd. With a dervish yell and batons drawn they dashed out between 80 and 90 strong from the colliers' yard and cut a way clean through the densely packed mob. Their first purpose was to split up the crowd.... Moving forward [in different directions] in solid bodies of two files they slowly but steadily drove the rioters ahead of them. Constantly the two sides were in furious combat.... The agony cries of the injured, the sharp hissing clash of baton against pick handle and other weapons, the sickening thud of skull blows, and the howling of a mob maddened with rage is better imagined than described.... The end of it was the complete rout of the mob; and the secured safety for the night of the power station at the Glamorgan Colliery. When the rioters had been driven in the Llwynypia direction as far as the Taff Vale railway bridge – a distance of about a quarter of a mile – and in the Tonypandy direction also for about a similar distance from the colliery, the two sections of police doubled back; to their starting point.... Immediately after the repulse of the attack on the Glamorgan Colliery came the sack of Tonypandy....

In their flight from Llwynypia and under the impression that the victorious police were still at their heels, the rioters, desperate at the defeat of their plans to take the colliery, gave vent to their rage by smashing the windows of every shop that came within their reach. Near Penygraig road they halted and realising that they were no longer being pursued by the police they returned to Pandy Square. Then the looting began. Shop after shop was raided and pillaged.... For immediate duty there were only five local constables available. These men did good work, and did much execution with their truncheons, but against such odds their efforts to disperse the rioters failed and for nearly two hours the town was completely in the hands of the mob.

The essential presupposition, in a passage which intermingles 'crowd', 'mob' and 'rioters' in a way that imagines *and* describes, is that the demonstrators were intent on possessing the colliery physically. Foiled in this, the rest of their behaviour is straightforwardly explicable.

There is no evidence that supports these contentions. The only resolution passed by a mass meeting on 1 November had been to stop any official, from Leonard Llewellyn down, from entering colliery premises. On Monday 7 November their actions to this end were, with the one exception, successful as those at work were persuaded, sometimes peacefully some times not, to leave so that fires could be raked. At Clydach Vale where, in the Cambrian Colliery, there was also an electrical power station, the power-house had been stoned 'for some hours' but it only stopped working when those inside decided to leave. They were frog-marched to their homes with a warning. The colliery, though still picketed, was not captured as such.

Nor is there much difference to be discerned in the initial demonstration before the heavily guarded Glamorgan Colliery later that day. The crowd of men, women and youths who had gathered in bitterly cold, blowing weather that was punctuated by heavy rain and showers of hail, were bunched on the steep hill-side overlooking the main colliery entrance or gathered in the road below at the gate. Union Jacks were being waved and all were in good humour.

It was only when Leonard Llewellyn came to the entrance now guarded by a double line of thirty police, with reserves just inside the yard, that the mood changed. The general manager's words of jocular greeting were greeted with hostility and he was jostled. Earlier forays by youths against the police cordon had caused minor scuffles after which Will John, secretary of the Cambrian Combine Committee, had appealed for peaceful persuasion of the enginemen and advised the crowd 'that the police were there for the preservation of order and for the protection of property'. However, the police now drew their truncheons to charge the crowd, who, still in large numbers at 10.30pm overpowered the police and made them retreat inside the yard to the shelter of the colliery offices. These were heavily stoned. *The Western Mail*, a harsh pro-coal-owner newspaper, reported:

> The apparent calm which had distinguished the crowd in the earlier part of the evening disappeared, and after the first truncheon charge by the police upon the appearance of Mr Llewellyn there was a continued period of wild disorder.

Even David Evans is forced to write, though he turns retreat into 'defence':

> Had the rioters driven home in force the advantage they gained

when they carried the cordon and compelled the retirement of
the defensive police forces into shelter behind the colliery offices
they might have succeeded in their extreme purpose; but they
were not certain of the strength of the police and did not
proceed more than a few yards into the colliery which, at this
time, owing to the destruction by the mob of the street lamps,
was in a state of cimmerian darkness.

If it is straining credulity to suggest that these cimmerian Morlocks
were not aware of the police strength drafted in since the weekend,
it is patently absurd to speculate that they did not proceed from
fear and darkness if they did indeed have an 'extreme purpose'.
Besides, Evans' account of the night of 7 November is vitiated
because he ignores (as he has to, given his purpose in 1911 of justi-
fying police action in the face of criticism by the military) that it
was the crowd's action which was the retaliatory one and having
succeeded in that limited purpose they withdrew. From 11.30pm,
now reinforced by police from Clydach Vale, baton charges were
made into the crowd. Far from being intimidated there were still
crowds on the small crossroads square in Tonypandy at 1am who,
armed with wooden palings taken from the fences around the
colliery, clashed further with police for almost an hour.

When the strikers assembled on the Athletic Ground the next
day peaceful demonstration was still the policy urged upon them.
Once more they marched through the streets to the colliery where,
at 4pm, they split up but with most of the crowd remaining
outside. Just before 5pm some of the younger men began to stone
the power-house and youths hustled the police cordon. At this
point the men working the engines under Leonard Llewellyn's
direction sent out the message that they could not keep working
under such a barrage – 'This led to the first charge by the mounted
police'. They galloped into the crowd, estimated at around nine
thousand strong, with batons ready. They only returned, battered,
to the yard with the help of some foot constables.

As on the previous night, it was after the police foray that serious
fighting began. The remains of the wooden palings around the
colliery perimeter were pulled down and a barricade, along with
hastily strewn debris, was erected across the road to prevent further
mounted police patrols – again hardly the action of men intent on
storming the colliery. Concentrated stoning of the power-station
brought on more baton charges and hand-to-hand combat just
before 6pm. The workmen's joint committee which had been
meeting in Tonypandy were called to the scene but proved unable

to address the crowd outside the colliery. Towards 7pm the road, about eight yards wide, was completely blocked by people all the quarter mile from the square to the colliery. It was shortly after this that Lindsay divided his men into two groups and charged the crowd.

On the square an unidentified man was addressing those assembled:

> One of the strikers complained that some of his fellow work-men had been simply battered about their heads by the police without any cause whatever, and he urged those around him to form into a peaceable procession and endeavour to march past the police. He added that they were not to molest the police unless the latter interfered. This apparently met with the approval of a large section of the crowd who at once proceeded up the road in the direction of the Glamorgan Colliery premises.

They continued for some distance 'but it was evident that they were driven back, as a few minutes later there was a general stampede, the crowd rushing back crying "The police are coming"'. Those in the back who can have had no physical contact with this particular police rush may then have run through the town but those to the front certainly did not retreat. A large advertisement hoarding near the Thistle Hotel above the square was torn down, as were brick and stone pillars, and the police were engaged as Evans so graphically related. Later, over a hundred people attended the doctor's surgery, many more were injured, one fatality occurred; forty police suffered wounds.

What is clear is that the police charge, though it scattered the crowd, did not drive the demonstrators back into and through the town (many were there already, setting out on their attempted peaceful march) and, crucially, did not clear the colliery entrance for 'as the squads of police marched *through* the huge crowd assembled in the vicinity of the Glamorgan collieries, where the other police guarded the entrance to the colliery yards, huge stones were hurled at them from the embankment and mandril sticks were freely used by the strikers on the main road'.

It is the police who regrouped and returned to the colliers as PC W. Knipe remembered:

> It was really hell. We had a terrible job driving there, driving them back to the Square. Well, we only could get them as far as the Square. On that night, then, that was the night they wrecked all the shops.... And the whole of the time we could do nothing

about it, we could not drive them further than the Square. They drove us back every time. And on this night they ripped down all the hoardings, the boarding that was running from the bottom, by the Thistle Hotel ... right up to the Colliery entrance. Boardings about nine feet high, enclosing the colliery you see. Well they pulled all these and ripped them up in the roadway, so that stopped all traffic and it stopped us.

All contemporary reports agree, as the shopkeepers were later to complain, that there were no police in the town for at least an hour after 8pm, so that Evans' five local constables must have been busy earlier, presumably around 7pm. The Metropolitan police did arrive at Tonypandy railway station (about half a mile down from the square) at 9.30pm but were immediately put back on the train to Llwynypia from where they proceeded first to the colliery and then on to the top end of Tonypandy where they were stoned. When they marched back to the colliery they were 'received with a chorus of groans, stones were thrown, and blows aimed at officers'. One who retaliated against this crowd, still assembled at past 10.30pm, was pulled down and only escaped by wriggling away leaving his helmet and cape behind.

The image of a mob first savagely intent and then terrified by the police into the flight of mad dogs deprived of their prey is no more than a lively journalist's foray into social psychology. On the contrary it was Lleufer Thomas, the magistrate, who had 'taken up residence' near the Glamorgan Colliery since the onset of trouble (presumably in Llewellyn's house *Glyncornel* high in the trees overlooking the Glamorgan Colliery), who sent at 7.45pm, as the police were disengaging from the crowd, a telegram to the Home Office which underlined what had been the coal-owners' and police desire since 6 November, i.e. before any disturbance had occurred: 'Police cannot cope with rioters at Llwynypia, Rhondda Valley. Troops at Cardiff absolutely necessary for further protection.'

When the troops arrived on 9 November under Major-General Macready they did not prove as susceptible to the orders of the local coal-owners and others as had been anticipated. Macready especially was to be extremely sceptical about what he termed the 'coloured' and 'alarmist' reports made by various colliery managers during his period of command. In his memoirs he repeated the views he had submitted to Churchill on 11 November:

> Investigations on the spot convinced me that the original reports regarding the attacks on the mines on November 8th had been exaggerated. What were described as 'desperate attempts' to

sack the power-house at Llwynypia proved to have been an attempt to force the gateway, against which an ample force of police under the Chief Constable was available on the spot, and a good deal of stone throwing by which windows were smashed and machinery might have been injured. The wooden palings round the mine had been pulled down, and had the mob been as numerous or so determined as the reports implied, there was nothing to have prevented them from overrunning the whole premises. That they did not was due less to the action of the police than to the want of leading or inclination to proceed to extremities on the part of the strikers. This fact was further exemplified in the attack on another mine, Clydach Vale, of which highly coloured reports had been received. In this case eight local policemen held the bridge leading to the colliery, while the mob made no effort to move to the right or left and swarm into the colliery enclosure, a very much easier proceeding than forcing the narrow bridge.

There were ten entrances to the pits of the Glamorgan collieries, a fact which lends further credence to the words of a local lodge secretary who, when asked by Lord Brockway (then Fenner Brockway, on his first reporting job outside London) if the men had intended to capture the power house, replied:

> If we had desired to do that we could have wrecked the colliery premises with ease on Saturday [5 November] before the extra police were drafted into the district. We had 10,000 men in our procession each carrying a pickaxe or some similar instrument and we marched past the colliery without throwing a stone, although it was only guarded by thirty police.

It was over the weekend that the extra police arrived as, on the Sunday, Leonard Llewellyn moved from his house, in wooded acres nearby, in order to stay inside the power-house with those he had gathered there. The Glamorgan Colliery was a good place to make a stand if, as early as 4 November, it had been decided to hold one provocative citadel only. It was near Llewellyn's house and it was not as isolated as the only other electrically pumped colliery, the Cambrian, at the top of the precipitous Clydach Vale. Furthermore, unlike the Naval pits in lower Tonypandy, the Taff Vale Railway bisected the colliery yards and any reinforcements could come and go with a mechanical ease denied them elsewhere. It was not particular colliery property which was at risk before 8 November because the Glamorgan pits were not, of course, the only ones in the Combine, but rather the whole idea of the rights of property-ownership which, in fortifying the pits at Llwynypia, Llewellyn and his supporters were thrusting in the face of the strikers.

The aggressive assertion of these rights by the police was the immediate spur to the riot of 8 November, though the crowd was more angry than either fearful or frustrated. The attack now on other property-owners flowed down well-worn grooves. There were, in a sense, two riots. Fighting ceased outside the Colliery at about 7pm and 'thousands of strikers', scattering with their 'staves', rushed through Tonypandy to the station because 'the rumour had got abroad that cavalry would arrive' about 8pm. In this burst down the narrow, winding main street, shop windows were smashed in and some goods taken. Perhaps those who discovered no troops had arrived moved back through the half mile from station to square where they would find the victims of the last, and toughest, bout with the police milling about with the rest of the crowd who had been unable to march up to the colliery. By 7.30 a number of shopkeepers had put up makeshift shutters. These were simply torn down as after 8pm more intensive smashing of shop premises went on, in the wake of the struggle with the police, and continued virtually unabated until after 10pm.

When the riots were over analyses came thick and fast. What caused most disquiet was the apparently wanton attack on shopkeepers. It was this destruction of the social fabric of a new community that had to be explained away so that, in Lleufer Thomas' phrase, 'the good name of South Wales' should not be further besmirched. For General Macready, as for a number of outside commentators since, there was no difficulty:

> The impression conveyed to my mind in regard to the action of the strikers throughout those disturbances, and the motives for rioting, is that the doctrine of extreme socialism preached by a small but energetic section is entirely responsible for the premeditated attempts to destroy property.

The quest is for local, 'hot-headed' ideologues to blame at a time when the official, moderate leadership of the SWMF was being castigated by their own members. Later some of these leaders were to be singled out for retribution but there is no hard evidence for Macready's opinion, whilst there is much that goes counter to it. Thus the meeting of Sunday 6 November which he mentions as an inciter of riot was specifically concerned with the prevention of work and the non-importation of blackleg labour: these remained priorities and both issues were responsible for the future serious disturbances on 21 November 1910 and in March and July 1911. Secondly, the leaders of the workmen's committee were not, primarily, those who had become associated by 1912 with advanced or syndicalist thought; the latter's absorption, in a conscious sense, by more than a handful was the result, not the cause, of the stormy events of 8 November. Thirdly the riots were consistently disowned by those responsible, in any way, for the conduct of the strike, even by the most advanced lodge, the Cambrian itself, whose committee resolved: 'that we ... condemn and deplore the damage done to property in this place'.

These unexceptional sentiments were, in varying degrees, endorsed by the varied troupe of British socialists who trekked to the Rhondda after that Tuesday night. The riots were, they felt, justified because of the ill-treatment meted out by owners and police, yet also blown out of all proportion and, indeed, unnecessary. The emphasis was on the need for political organisation and on the alleged paucity of damage. The *Plebs Magazine*, which, through men such as Noah Ablett, had close links with many involved in the dispute, summed up this trend of thought, albeit in a hodge-podge of detail that mixed up separate incidents, in its editorial for December 1910:

> In the narrow streets of ... Tonypandy, closely packed with men who could not get to the fighting [at the colliery] some shop windows were broken, and goods damaged. After a severe and prolonged struggle, the unorganised miners were dispersed by the police who, exulting in their victory, committed outrages.... Non-combatants, hundreds of yards away, were truncheoned at sight. Men and women coming out of the street cars were brutally knocked down.... From now on the strikers organised themselves. Conflicts with the police were avoided as far as possible.

Others who had no wish to justify the riots, nonetheless also reduced the matter in size. T. Mardy Jones, miners' agent and future Labour MP for Pontypridd, was reminded of his days at Ruskin College and the University students' japes at Oxford:

> [Besides the rioters were] a gang of about 150, chiefly youths and men let loose from the public house.... This gang ... appeared to be more of a spontaneous outburst at the outset than an organised gang of wreckers.... It was not until some time later that the looting began. Many of the miners who were eyewitnesses of the same cried 'Shame' on the rioters, but they could offer no effective resistance. The great mass of miners

resent the outrage strongly, and deprecate deeply the serious loss of property and business sustained by the local tradesmen, many of whom the miners knew to be their best friends.

Keir Hardie, first Socialist MP in Wales for Merthyr (1900-15), agreed with these specific points and added a new note: 'The window smashing [at Tonypandy] was the work of a very few men, not one hundred all told, and many of these were strangers who had been drinking most of the day in the public houses and were in no way connected with the strikers.' Four Rhondda clergymen declared that the riots were the work of 'a small gang of half-drunken, irresponsible persons, many ... from outside the affected district ... the mad outbreak of 150'. Even the local tradespeople defended the good name of 'the main body of the strikers' and 'the better class of colliers' against 'a gang of irresponsible persons'.

At which point this verbal diminution of a crowd in its thousands and the banishing of the events of the nights of 7 and 8 November outside the Glamorgan Colliery seems inextricably related to what was the apparently unacceptable thought that a very large number of people had been actively involved in the destruction of Tonypandy's commercial life. Instead a tirade of arraignment is directed against the outcast groups of youths, drunks and strangers. Youths there certainly were (around fourteen per cent of the entire mining work-force in the coalfield was under sixteen years of age) but those same youths who stoned the Glamorgan Colliery were also rescued from the clutches of police by 'young men of apparently from twenty to thirty years of age'. Men in drink there were, too, though the fact that the magistrate had closed the pubs early (at dusk) might have kept some from being drunk, whilst the bulk of the crowd had been at the mass meeting or on the streets for hours anyway. The accusation against 'strangers', like that against youths, seems common to the aftermath of most riots as a way of pinning guilt to those with no real stake in what is considered the day-to-day reality of local life; but the strangers can have been few at most and of the meagre number of seventeen who were tried in 1911 for their part in the riots, all were from mid-Rhondda, five of them women.

Women had been involved in the fracas all along. On 7 November they were out on the streets in Penygraig, Llwynypia and Clydach Vale as early as the men and led the cheering as action was taken against non-unionists and, later, the police. That night, outside the Glamorgan Colliery, women gathered up loose stones in aprons and buckets and acted as ammunition carriers for the men whom they were urging on. Lleufer Thomas had pressed that women and children keep indoors when he relayed the Home Secretary's message to the strikers on the afternoon of 8 November, but they were certainly out in numbers again that night.

The crowd acted, too, with a measure of control and of local knowledge remarkable for so many drunken strangers. They began by knocking in the shop window of T. Pascoe Jenkins JP, the senior magistrate of the Rhondda valley and resident of thirty years standing; amidst scenes of widespread wreckage they scrupulously avoided one iota of damage to a particular chemist's shop despite the fact that all other chemists were prime targets: this was the shop of Clydach Vale-born Willie Llewellyn, an ex-rugby international who had played in the Welsh team that had defeated the otherwise invincible All Blacks from New Zealand in 1905. Other grievances were so direct that J. Owen Jones, a Tonypandy draper whose shop was gutted, inserted a notice dated 10 November in the local paper in which he offered £50 reward to the Cambrian Combine Committee to be given to any named charity 'if a certain statement attributed to me can be proven'.

An eye-witness who was a boy in 1910 described how he and a friend observed the start of the riot from a side-road above the square:

> They started smashing the windows ... they smashed this shop here, J.O. Jones, a millinery shop that was on the other corner.... We saw that being smashed and then next door to the millinery J.O. Jones, there was a shop and they smashed the window there.... On the other side here, there was Richards the Chemist ... they smashed that. And they smashed the windows of these three small shops here, one was a green-grocer, the other one was fancy goods and the other one was a barber's shop, and I knew the name of the barber quite well, it was Salter, because we used to think it swanky to go to Salter's to have a hair cut, you see. They smashed Richards the Chemist, then there was the boot shop next door to it ... and next to that was Watkins the flannel merchant ... they smashed that and they stole the shoes out of [the] boots, flannel out of Watkins and greengrocery, well they only picked up there. Well next to that there was a few steps up and there was a dentist and one or two private houses. Well, they didn't smash. We didn't see anything that happened below the bridge because ... we were afraid to go down there in front of the crowd.... Oh, there was a huge crowd.

The crowd was not organised but it knew what to do in the

euphoria of release that followed the catalytic police action. It shared both special grievances and communal assumptions about the direction and legitimacy of its action. For the editor of the Rhondda's newspaper the riots, instigated and carried out by thoughtless youths and women from further afield 'the mania for loot strong upon them', meant that 'a notional obloquy has come upon Wales through the roughness of the times'. 'Tonypandy' he wailed 'is no longer an unknown township.... The pity of it all is that Tonypandy has to bear the brunt of the defamation and for years the ill repute will stick to it.'

No such qualm disturbed the majority of the local population who were more in tune with the brash topsy-turviness of their real world of false appearances. The music hall, so well-patronised by coalfield society, was doing its unconscious best to offer ironic reflection. That Tuesday night the management of the Hippodrome Theatre closed because of the trouble, though not before customers were given tickets for later readmission to see the comedy pantomime *Wrecked*. At the Theatre Royal, close by, 'despite the tumult raging within almost a stone's throw' remarked a singularly oblique critic, the packed audience watched *The Still Alarm*, an American drama in which there was a 'special engine house scene introducing the beautifully trained horses'. Patrons were advised to watch for the forthcoming attraction 'The Gay Gordons'.

Illusion aped reality over the mountain, in Ferndale, where those busy avoiding the riot that night could have watched, in anticipation of the real thing, W.J. Churchill's *Happy Valley Minstrels* – 'the troupe which is undoubtedly the finest that has visited the district for some time'. They began their programme with 'Come Away to the Silvery Moon' and ended with 'the grand military finale' – 'The Dark Town Grenadiers' – to roars of laughter. And if this is not enough to substantiate Oscar Wilde's dictum about life imitating art, the Workmen's Hall in Ferndale was producing in the following week *The Girl Who Took the Wrong Turning* (presumably she turned right at Porth and was in Tonypandy Square with 'the mania of loot upon her').

Nor were portents confined to the garish music hall. Acute Rhonddaite semiologists might have noticed that in February 1910 at the Ynyshir Workmen's Hall in lower Rhondda, where Noah Ablett was checkweigher, Saron Choral Society had performed G.F. Root's sacred cantata 'David the Shepherd Boy'. The part of Goliath was taken by Police Sergeant Mitchell.

In a place addicted to the escapism of theatricality, the art of gesture could invade the streets whether in the contemptuous spillage of foodstuffs and apparel on to the roads in place of theft or in the joy of disrespectful, self-glorying parody 'rendered heartily' by young men and women in the streets of Tonypandy a week or so after the riots to a well-known tune:

Every nice girl loves a collier
In the Rhondda valley war
Every nice girl loves a striker
And you know what strikers are
In Tonypandy they're very handy
With their sticks and their stones and boot
Walking down the street with Jane
Breaking every window pane
That's loot! Pom pom. That's loot!

And the music hall was not the only source of parody. In the third week of that cold, dramatic November, colliers' wives, their babies cocooned in shawls, paraded around the streets with a 'dummy' collier (doubtless a trophy from the night of 8 November), and sang, to a hymn tune:

At Cambrian pits – look up this way
Colliers will work for three bob a day.
If colliers grumble, Leonard will say,
Pick up your tools and clear away.

The jubilant defiance which turned the riots into a festival of disorder had its roots in the nature of mid-Rhondda. Its development dates from the latter end of the nineteenth century when, in rapid succession, pits were sunk by the Naval Colliery Company and opened for production – the Pandy pit in 1879, the Ely and Nantgwyn in 1892, and the Anthony in 1910. The number of men at work rose from 800 in 1896 to 2,640 by 1908. At the other end of the raw village of Tonypandy, with its straggle of wooden huts, stone cottages and a few shops, the Glamorgan Colliery Company were opening up pits No 4 and No 5 in 1873 at Llwynypia, with No 6 to follow in 1876, whilst in Clydach Vale, branching off from the main valley bottom, Samuel Thomas, father of D.A. Thomas, had two pits working by the year of his death, 1879, and there were three in production by 1900. The amalgamation of the pits in mid-Rhondda into the Cambrian Combine gave the group over fifty per cent of the total coal production in Rhondda by the First World

War and made it, with its subsidiary shipping and patent-fuel interests in Britain, France and Scandinavia, one of the two 'most complete self-contained organisations in the coal trade of the world.'

In 1875 the main Tonypandy road running alongside the river, not yet an oil-silk black, was mostly bordered on its western side by small stone cottages, but as the area boomed after 1890 the street, given its position below the slopes that loomed over it, became the only likely area for a commercial high street in a ribbon development. Undulating terraces of houses were now strung out on the steep hillsides above the main road of Dunraven Street where was built by 1900 an imposing grey stone police station set slightly off the road and flanked by a double-flight of steps like a sawn-off French chateau. Other required amenities followed – the Tonypandy and Trealaw Free Library established in 1899 by local businessmen, and the red-bricked Judge's Hall, the gift of a large landowner. It could hold 1,500 and contained both library and billiard hall. It was opened in 1909 by HRH Princess Louise who, since it was situated conveniently near the railway station, could have avoided the town itself, though this was now enlivened by the Empire Theatre of Varieties, also opened in 1909.

The following year the enterprising Will Stone's electric biograph was enlivening the Theatre Royal, erected in 1892, whilst at the Hippodrome the electric bioscope was projecting its flickering images twice nightly. Boxing booths, portable theatres, and travelling fairs on a field behind the square, all added to the raucous glitter of a spectating world which was undermining the more sober pursuits of nonconformist Wales. For the more energetically inclined – brass-bands, choral-singing and rugby apart – and for paying customers only, J. Owen Jones, draper, launched out in early 1910 when he formally opened, just above Tonypandy Square, the Pavilion, which housed 'the express roller-skating rink'.

Later that year Big Bill Haywood, the American Union leader, would thunder at the mid-Rhondda miners from the stage of the Theatre Royal on behalf of the Industrial Workers of the World; police would be housed in J. Owen Jones' skating rink and Lleufer Thomas would issue a nervously requested notice to the effect that the draper had no choice in the matter (in December gales the tin roof blew off and the police shifted to the Hippodrome); and in 1912 an intricate debate led by Noah Ablett would proceed on the virtues of nationalisation versus workers' control before a full house in the Judge's Hall.

Between 1901 and 1911 the total population of Rhondda increased by 34.3 per cent from 113,735 to 152,781 (this was thrice the average increase for England and Wales) and the 1911 figure was undoubtedly lower than it would have been in 1910 since the Cambrian strike had witnessed a temporary exodus from the mid-Rhondda district. Its estimated population was 38,819 in 1910, when there were 7,116 inhabited houses in the area.

Housing needs had been met by private speculative building – in 1909 the number of houses in mid-Rhondda was 6,868 – which did not, despite its basic patterning and haste, adequately house a population whose birth rate was outstripping the death rate, whose colliers married in their early twenties at the peak of their earning capacity and where many lived in single rooms or cellar dwellings. Many houses were too expensive or too large for some families and the Urban District Authority, in being since 1894, had not made any housing provision themselves. Houses would vary from four-roomed cottages to more substantial three up and three down terraces. The pits had spawned a rash of houses, shops, chapels and pubs whose only saving architectural grace was that they had to conform, in local materials of slate and pennant sandstone with red and yellow brick for the recent constructions, to the limiting physical configuration of a twisting valley whose bed was hemmed in by clumps of steep hillsides on which the orgy of house-building had to proceed.

A London reporter washed down to Tonypandy in the wake of the strike described the scene with the same transfixed horror as Charles Dickens had viewed Preston for his Southern readers in the 1850s and George Orwell, with the same audience in mind, the industrial North in the 1930s. How, after all, could you comprehend Tonypandy without knowing that it lay

> in a narrow winding valley confined by squat, denuded hills upon whose bleak sides tower huge mounds of rock and rubbish excavated from the numerous coal pits. The river, sometimes almost dry, sometimes rushing down in tempestuous flood, but always pestilential with all manner of garbage and offal, is crossed and re-crossed by the railway over which, all day and all night, roll the never-ending coal trains on their way to the distant sea-port. The high road, where it may, runs its course alongside the odorous river, but for the greater part of its length it has to hug the steep slopes of the cheerless hills.... Long rows of steep gardens rise sheer from the road-side to a line of small stone-built four-roomed cottages. A paved alleyway at the rear, the length of the terrace, gives access to the houses, and from

this narrow alley another series of gardens continue the ascent to a similar row of cots, and so the terraces rear themselves until the topmost is reached from which the roadway, the pits, the railway and the river are seen in panoramic array. Each alley has one waterspout, common to all the homes in that row. The two tiny back rooms are darkened by the overhanging gardens of the higher terrace, and the houses are so low that a man must stoop before entering.

Effluent poured into the river from works and houses so that in the summer the high, rich smell of decayed matter and slaughtered meat must have been pungent indeed. Nevertheless the prevailing grimness of the environment was alleviated, in turn, by the very social capital which had brought it into being, as a whirligig of sounds, smells and sights caught up a population barely a generation (and often not that) away from the land.

Rhys Davies, the novelist, remembered Clydach Vale before 1910 in his evocative autobiography, *Print of a Hare's Foot*:

In the last decade of Victoria's reign my optimistic father had opened a grocery shop in the centre of the vale's long main road and called it, for some far-fetched reason, Royal Stores. With several other shops, it stood opposite the Central, a massive pub of angry-red brick and dour stone.... A two-horse brake, its floor covered with straw in the winter, stopped outside the Central at fixed times, plying from and to Tonypandy railway station with as many as eight passengers....

Within sight of my father's shop were two non-conformist chapels, Noddfa and Libanus (there were five others up and down the vale), also St Thomas's church (English), a police station with cells for violent Saturday night men and rioters in strike time, and the Marxian Club (not called 'Marxist'). A doctor's surgery sent a warning smell out to the pavement night and day. There was a shop for locally slaughtered meat and one for ironmongery, flower-seed packets and punishment willow canes; also Ada Lloyd's shop for fruit and vegetables and, in her parlour behind hanging bunches of bananas, spiritualist seances; also a shop for sweets and ice cream kept by an Italian couple ... also Evans the Boot, selling what his nickname implied; and Eynon's for moleskin pit trousers, singlets, buttons, American oil cloth, and 1s 11$^{3}/_{4}$ d per yard Welsh flannel out of which shirts and other distressing garments were made.

... Fish and Penclawdd cockles arrived twice a week in a seaside smelling donkey cart, and the Crier with handbell stopped almost as regularly outside the Central to bawl announcement of some coming event....

We lived for years behind and above our busy shop; a living-

room, pantry and scullery behind, three bedrooms above, It was
a 'credit' shop and a history of family fortunes. On a lectern
desk panelled with a frosted glass screen lay an enormous black
ledger, six inches thick, a double page for each customer. Its
chronicle of strike-time debts was my mother's bible and bane....

The shop smelled of wholesome things. Golden sawdust
thrown fresh every morning on the swept floor between the two
long parallel counters ... an odorous coffee-grinding machine,
mounds of yellow Canadian and pallid Caerphilly cheese, rosy
cuts of ham and bacon, wide slabs of butter cut by wire for the
scales, and bladders of lard. Behind the counter over which my
mother presided stretched wall fixtures stacked with crimson
packets of tea, blue satchels of sugar, vari-coloured bags of rice,
dried fruit and peas.... Soaps gave their own clean smell, especially the favoured kind which arrived in long bars and, cut into
segments, was used both for scrubbing houses and washing pit-
dirt from colliers' backs and fronts. Slabs of rich cake lay in a
glass case.... [There were] biscuit tins ... packets of Ringers
tobacco, black chewing shag, spices, almonds and dried herbs....

Every Aladdin's cave had to have a statutory Uncle Ebenezer of
course. From May 1909 the mid-Rhondda grocers decided,
secretly and by a mutual indemnification pact, to operate a 'black
list' system of credit for known customers. Nor did they prove
more generous with their own employees, as they decided in the
summer of 1908 to end the common practice of giving Christmas
'boxes' (i.e. gifts). These primary concerns apart, however, it was
the tradesmen who were initially, and predominantly, concerned to
instil a sense of community without whose social mediation their
own role, in a society pulled together only for profits and work
from coal, would be barren. It was the outward sign of a civilised
respectability that they most valued. They reacted rather stiffly,
through their Chamber of Trade, to 'young people wandering
around and desecrating the Sunday' and 'thought the playing of
gramophones on a Sunday was quite a disgrace to the locality',
with which the Free Church Council, itself worried about the
'prevalence of boxing contests' in Tonypandy, doubtless
concurred.

Other desired improvements were not quite so restrictive: they
were to the fore in having a public drinking fountain put up in the
square; constantly urged better electric lighting in the main street
(especially after the riots, when they requested it be kept on all
night); suggested in the summer days that 'small boys be employed
to collect manure from the roads during the day'; and provided a
deputation to the council to urge 'provision of public lavatories for

both sexes in the district, more especially for ladies'.

At the beginning of 1910 these midwives of modernity had cause to congratulate themselves on their past endeavours and future possibilities when the Mid-Rhondda Horse Show Association, formed in 1905 to assist the Fire Brigade, gave a banquet in honour of its retiring President, Leonard Llewellyn. The toast was 'The Trade of the District' to which its proposer, local landowner William Morgan of Maes-yr-haf, said:

> If they looked back upon the history of Tonypandy for the past eighteen months, they could honestly say that no other district in the Rhondda could show such great development, and much of that was due to one of the most public spirited bodies in the country – the Mid-Rhondda Chamber of Trade.... He hoped that the present movement for Incorporation would be successful, and that they would have the control of the police, reduce their rates, and place Tonypandy in the front of Rhondda townships.

Councillor D.C. Evans, in response, had no doubt that leaders on both sides of the coal industry would prove conciliatory in the current negotiations, whilst J. Owen Jones, the chairman of the Mid-Rhondda Chamber of Trade declared, to great applause, that the tradesmen's earlier fears of loss of trade after the formation of the Cambrian Combine had now been exchanged for 'hopes of a good time in store'. Unfortunately, the president of the Horse Show for 1910, none other than D.A. Thomas, was not present to praise his predecessor so Alderman Richard Lewis JP did it, extolling Leonard Llewellyn as a man who had 'realised the claims and duties of true citizenship'. Looking around him he saw the sons of men who had started in business with him at Tonypandy forty years ago, and the sons were better than their fathers. The future of mid-Rhondda, socially, need not be in danger at all when they had such sons taking their part in the social welfare of the district. After touching upon the past managers of the Glamorgan Colliery, the speaker said that Mr Llewellyn was a noble successor of that noble line.

Leonard Llewellyn was generous, too, in his hospitality and the availability of his animals, even if the ingrate General Macready, who refused invitations to his officers and himself to dine, did describe him as 'a forceful, autocratic man ... who, by his rough and ready methods, was apt to drive those working for him to a state of desperation'. The Chief Constable, Lionel Lindsay, had no such qualms, as his cryptic diary entries for 1911 reveal:

April 3rd – Dined at Llewellyn's with officers of the Somersets.
April 11th – Dined with Llewellyn and officers of the Somersets.
July 6th – Office in morning.
Meeting ... re-arrangements in the Strike Area.
Pageant in [Cardiff] Castle Grounds in afternoon. I
was ... on Leonard Llewellyn's Piebald. The children
looked lovely.

When Lindsay wrote that the 12,000 strikers and their families had
been out of work for over eight months and were being starved into
submission. Public sympathy had focussed more closely on the
plight of the three to four hundred horses who were supposedly at
risk in November 1910 and of whose safety Llewellyn had assured
government and king after the arrival of the military. Llewellyn had
been photographed holding a black cat he had bought up from the
mine and the strikers, whose offer to allow the horses to be brought
up under their supervision he had refused, now devised a bitter
language of their own: whenever Llewellyn's name was mentioned
at meetings they set up a chorus of miaows; when they marched to
Pontypridd in December to hear charges of intimidation against
Gilfach miners they carried a white banner decorated with a lean
black cat and inscribed with the legend 'Hungry as L...'; whilst in
February 1911 when the first set of charges were brought against
John Hopla, checkweigher at Glamorgan colliery, they followed a
wooden hobby-horse. Those charged, and sentenced or fined, wore
their summonses in their caps during the march, whilst others
shepherded a black and white retriever carrying a card that said
'Leonard's pet' or held notices asking 'What about the horses?'

Llewellyn answered that question in March 1911 when he and
his assistant manager were presented with medals at the annual
dinner of the Polo and Riding Society at the Hotel Metropole,
London, for their bravery in rescuing the horses from drowning.
Llewellyn, referring to the 'temporary mental aberration of the
men', said that 'as a Welshman he very much regretted that such
a thing should have happened in Wales'. Then in May 1911 the
Countess of Bective gave out RSPCA medals for the same service
of 'heroism in rescuing pit ponies' and Llewellyn presented his
black cat to a London newspaperman. It had been a rough, but
hardly downward, journey from the day in January 1910 when he
had been hailed as 'the pioneer of all the important movements that
had tended to the better welfare of the Rhondda in general'. That
was the occasion when he was re-elected President of the Mid-
Rhondda Chamber of Trade for the year of 1910. The speaker was

the retiring Chairman, J. Owen Jones, draper, stockist for cotton, linen and wool goods on Tonypandy Square.

Drapers were the great hold-all emporia for everything, other than foods and ironmongery, in places like the Rhondda. 1910 was not a good year for them in Tonypandy. J. Owen Jones had announced his winter clearance sale in late January as 'big purchases with a small purse'. He pleaded and warned in a judicious mix – 'owing to the absence of draper's weather during autumn and winter, his stock in all departments' was 'exceptionally heavy' whilst 'the serious condition of the cotton market' meant that 'except for a few days in 1904, cotton has not been so dear for 35 years' so that customers should 'secure their wants in this sale'. Alas, and despite the portent of a seismic shock that lasted for twelve seconds in mid-Rhondda in February and shook the railway signal-box 'as if by lightning' so that it set going all the bells, J. Owen Jones at his summer sale of all-round reductions explained that his price cuts were 'much greater than usual, owing to my stock being considerably heavier, the death of his Majesty King Edward VII and the exceptional weather [i.e. prolonged rain] we have had for the greater part of the summer'. On 8 November the people of mid-Rhondda finally took the hint.

The persistent rain, on the other hand, may have added to the trade of J.W. Richards, a dispenser of poor relief on the Pontypridd Board of Guardians who carved the meat in the Llwynypia workhouse on Christmas Day 1909, but was usually a dispenser of spectacles and medicaments. On the side of his shop on Tonypandy Square was painted a large advertisement: 'Kurakold – Richards' Unrivalled Remedy at 1/- and 2/9 a bottle – a quick and permanent cure for all disorders of chest and lungs.'

Doctors were few, and attached to the collieries. Chemists were quicker, easier and cheaper. They were, with their bright displays of coloured bottles and chemicals, the equivalent of the nineteenth-century peasant's healers, charmers and travelling quacks. There was in the Rhondda every aid to a full bionic life. By post could come 'artificial legs, surgical boots, deformity stock – hands, arms, artificial arms from 7/6'. Less drastic cases could settle for vegetable pills to purify the blood', 'effervesant salts', 'Thompson's Electric Life Drops for the cure of nervous Debility' which 'act so quickly on a weak and shattered condition that health is speedily restored', or the *sans pareil* Burdock's pills from Swansea, 'one of the oldest and best medicines having been more than sixty years before the public for purifying the foulest blood, and removing every disease of the stomach, liver and kidneys. Cures scurvy and scrofula, sores, eruption of the skin and all diseases arising from an impure state of the blood', whilst for the young, worm lozenges whose 'effect upon weak, delicate children (often given up as incurable) is like magic'.

Such ardent advertising knew its potential consumers. In 1905, the year the new £25,000 electric-power house was installed at the Cambrian Collieries, Clydach Vale, 33 men and boys were blown up in the Cambrian No 1 pit, and two months later, not five miles down the valley at Wattstown, 119 were killed underground. Clydach Vale and Llwynypia had in 1909 the highest birth rate in a Rhondda where illegitimacy was rocketing way above the British average. There were in 1909 throughout the valley only 130 deaths of children under twelve months old per every 1,000 live births, whereas the average for 1899 to 1908 had been 190 per 1,000; but this can have been scant consolation, even given a greater degree of resignation than now conceivable in industrial societies, for the parents of the 724 children from a 1909 total of 5,557.

Colliers died of 'pulmonary consumption' or 'phthisis' at eleven times the rate of any other occupation. The coroner's table of investigated deaths for the years 1897 to 1900 shows a low rate of death for those succumbing to alcoholism, strain [sic], hernias, homicide and injudicious feeding [sic] and rises through convulsions, heart disease, burns, drowning and being run over by carts, trains and trams until it reveals that over a third to a half of these deaths are from routine accidents in the pits. Those colliers who greeted Dai Watts Morgan, the second miners' agent for Rhondda, in the summer of 1910 with shouts of 'What price are flowers Mr Morgan?' had their equivalents on 8 November in those who threw Studley's fruit and vegetable produce all over the road on Tonypandy Square underneath two hand-painted signs that read, in tandem, 'Studleys – Fruit Merchant' and 'Wreaths to Order'.

During the months that led up to the strike the repeated complaint of the men working for the Combine was that management was endangering life in their drive for profits to feed their over-capitalised concerns. The chaotic bargain system of payment for various work done underground (other than hewing), from setting up props to packing waste stone away in a difficult stall, was over-reliant on the verbal contract of collier and foreman, whilst the latter could find his allowances to the men squeezed by a margin-conscious management. Colliers doing similar work in different seams or pits could find an enormous discrepancy in wages.

At the Ely pit before the dismissal of the men on the Bute seam in September there had been some disquieting accidents, from the death of five men in a pit cage crash in August 1909 to the crushing of a collier underneath the fall of an inadequately propped section of coal in 1910. Both cases for compensation brought to the courts were dismissed by the coroner as accidents caused by thoughtless workmen, though the Naval Lodge Committee alleged management's deliberate negligence. The Committee called for courts of inquiry composed of men 'who know the miner's life as it affects him from within' and claimed that South Wales coal owners 'in order to create big dividends at the expense of the most cheapened labour are constantly employing men as colliers who are without knowledge or experience of any aspect or feature of the miner's life and work'. D.A. Thomas had that same month stressed the independence he gave to his managers and, exulting in the jibe that with the creation of the Cambrian Combine he had bought 'a few sucked oranges', countered that 'he did not mind if there were a few more sucked oranges about. With Mr Llewellyn to look after them, they were prepared to go on dealing in sucked oranges and Cambrian marmalade.'

As the industrial crisis deepened in mid-Rhondda, local clergy and tradesmen made representations to both sides in the industry. This alliance was not surprising since, apart from the fact that eleven Welsh clergymen held shares in the Cambrian Combine, the Free Church Council's Welsh Federation had been active in September 1910 in agitating against the government's attempt to repeal the 1677 Sunday Observance Act. This would have opened certain shops legally but closed down the large number of shops who were opening illegally and to the detriment of the leisure of shop assistants whose hours of work, from 60 to 100 a week, were way beyond the colliers, who now had the protection of the 1908 Eight-hour act. It was argued that shop assistants in South Wales were particularly overworked, with late openings on Saturdays and even deliveries on Sunday mornings. Certainly the hours of closing agreed by mid-Rhondda grocers to meet the Shop Hours Act were hardly early ones at 7pm and 7.30pm for three nights, 1pm Thursday, and 8 and 11pm on Friday and Saturday respectively.

Traders, like it or not, were centrally involved in these industrial troubles. At the end of October 1910 the Ely pit men had been out for two months and distress was already severe in the Penygraig area. The Mid-Rhondda Chamber of Trade publicly congratulated itself on having given £30 to the distress fund; the Penygraig local

Chamber of Trade pledged financial and moral aid to the work-men in their struggle for improved conditions, and simultaneously sent a successful deputation to Glamorgan County Council to plead for a local police station since the one in Tonypandy was all of three-quarters a mile away and advantage was taken 'by young powerful men of the disorderly class'. When the final offer hatched between the SWMF executive and the owners was rejected unani-mously by the local men in late October it was the plight of the traders that was the first concern of the community's glue-maker, the local newspaper:

> We deplore the result [of the vote] because an industrial struggle of this magnitude brings in its train, not only complete dis-organisation of the trade of the district ... but also the suffering [of] those who are no part to the dispute.... But apart from mere sentiment, a strike at this period of the year, when trade is look-ing up and tradesmen are laying in large stores in preparation for a brisk demand, means the withdrawal of a huge sum of money from active circulation in the district, with the conse-quent paralysis of those trades and industries which depend upon the coal trade for stability.

Matters did not improve when a mass meeting of the strikers greeted Leonard Llewellyn's offer on behalf of the Cambrian Combine directors of £100 a week to the distress fund so long as the strike lasted with cries of 'Let him keep it' and 'Let his money perish with him'. It was the irrecoverable nature of lost profits that worried the commercial élite of mid-Rhondda, and it was not only profits lost from trade. During 1909, spurred on by the Housing Act of that year, the Mid-Rhondda Trades and Labour Council had begun to collect evidence of the housing conditions in their district. A conference was held with other areas in upper Rhondda in early 1910 and representations eventually made to the UDC concerning overcrowding, insanitary conditions, subletting, high rents and the practice of some tradespeople in compelling tenants to buy in their shops. The Medical Officer of Health was asked to investigate the allegations, which he assessed in a Special Report presented in July 1911. This accepted the general complaints of poor living conditions and asserted that the worst situation so far as sanitation and overcrowding were concerned was to be found in Clydach Vale, Llwynypia, Tonypandy and upper Trealaw. Dr J.D. Jenkins agreed that 'key money', or the highest bidder having pref-erence in obtaining tenancy, was common, as was arbitrary raising of rent when one set of tenants moved out and another in, and:

There are ... cases in respect of whom the inspectors are informed that houses are only obtainable on certain conditions, such as an undertaking or promise on the part of the incoming tenant to purchase goods such as furniture or groceries from the owners. Some house-owners, again, object to tenants with many children, while some provision merchants are said to prefer tenants with large families, because every additional child helps to swell the bill for provisions.

Consequently the summer of 1911 saw a degree of suffering amongst tradesmen – one who owned half a dozen houses had lost £40 in rent, whilst his weekly shop takings were down from £90 to £25. Another estimated losses at around £800, with a drop of £160 a week. The doleful reporter concluded:

A gentleman who is in a big way of business and who owns a very large number of houses and shops estimated his loss well over £1,000. In normal times he received in rental £2,000 a year but his receipts had dropped to about £30 a fortnight. He paid a glowing tribute to the honesty of some of his tenants. 'I have some tenants' he said 'who deserve the highest praise. Some of those who have secured work are paying me honourably and there are others who are sacrificing their hard-earned savings rather than go into debt.' He regretted to say there were others who were quite unscrupulous. After having secured work elsewhere they had left the district surreptitiously and had sent him back the keys by post without giving away clues as to their present whereabouts.

On Tuesday 8 November, all through the day their whereabouts were clear. Most of the men (the exceptions were the Naval Colliery workers) had only been paid off that week so they had, to that extent, money in their pockets, though none, of course, to spend on inessentials. They were already deprived – not yet, absolutely, of the wherewithal to live, but rather, relatively, of the ability to enjoy consumption of those conspicuous goods that were the hallmark and sole justification of this high-wage society, from Saturday-night shaves and barbered hair to women's hats and the white muffler scarves that no collier dandy could be without. The shops in Tonypandy were not looted for food. They were wrecked by men and women who knew closely the intricate and inseparable local factors that made up the skein of socio-economic connections which enwrapped their community. They knew, further, who aspired to control everything through this basic lever. The riots were not planned in advance, which is what bothered so many, yet they were not merely the spontaneous response to the kaleido-scopic incidents of those two strife-torn nights, for they were structured both in the sense that the crowd acted in concert and also in that the damage they wreaked was a deliberate assault on the civil order of a world that had been made for them.

From early on the Tuesday thousands of men had strolled or paraded, in groups large and small, through the packed face-to-face streets that stood in tiers above the river bed, crisscrossed by sheer hill roads, un-made-up and covered with loose stones, that debouched on to the main road below. They discussed the fighting of the Monday night, they sang popular music-hall ditties or strode along behind amateur fife bands to the engaging sound of concertinas. In the morning a tailor's dummy had been commandeered from a shop and was now held aloft in his finery as a mascot. A baker's van which stopped on a call in a back street lost all his bread, perhaps in reprisal for the firm's prominent advertisement earlier in the week that they had reduced the size of their farmhouse family loaf to meet the requirements of strikers' families. When the riots broke out that night those who had anticipated a simple industrial struggle misread the signs. The correspondent of *The Western Mail* wrote in disbelief: 'Even drapers' establishments were smashed open and wearing apparel, as well as drapers' goods of all descriptions, was looted unceremoniously.'

The crowd who stoned windows after 8pm did so to a stop and start pattern of whistling, so that 'the absence of the police and other important events' were 'notified by members of the apparently inoffensive crowd to the aggressors'. Dummies and finery, silks and top hats, were thrown on to the road in contempt or worn in mockery. Jars of sweets, cigarettes, pans of ice cream and packets of tobacco were scattered around and raided by children. Sixty-three shops were damaged, and some were completely ransacked, including the twinned draper shops of Mr and Mrs Phillips. Mrs Phillips told an outraged reporter for the drapers' profession:

> People were seen inside the counter handing goods out. They were afterwards walking on the Square wearing various articles of clothing which had been stolen and asking each other how they looked. They were not a bit ashamed, and they actually had the audacity to see how things fitted them in the shop itself. They were in the shop somewhere about three hours and women were as bad as men.... Everything was done openly and the din was something horrible.

One outfitter was completely denuded of its extensive stock of mufflers. At 10pm, although the recently arrived Metropolitan police were housed in the skating rink 100 yards away, Haydn Jones' drapery, already 'smashed to atoms' was now further infested as 'collars, straw hats, braces and caps were passed from hand to hand openly in the street and exchanges were indulged in between the looters'.

These were revolutionary acts, albeit without a play to frame them, nor was Lionel James of *The Times*, who arrived two weeks after this world-turned-upside-down had reverted to the stability of a war of attrition, so far wrong when he despatched the news that though 'quiet ... knots of sullen men are parading the streets, and the mouth of every alley way is blocked with idle miners. It is just the same oppressive atmosphere that one experienced in the streets of Odessa and Sevastopol during the unrest in Russia in the winter of 1904. It is extraordinary to find it here in the British Isles.'

The riots were not a momentary aberration. Similar incidents, though smaller in scale naturally, are peppered through late 1910 and into 1911, with a chemist's shop in Porth and a grocer's in Clydach Vale being attacked on 9 November. The conventions of social behaviour continued to be flouted, to the dismay of more responsible society. In April 1911 when renegotiated terms were again put to the men (and massively rejected), those who voted by secret ballot walked about with the unused portion of the ballot paper stuck in their coat 'publicising to the world at large how they voted' and rendering 'the ballot nothing short of a travesty'.

There were shifts at ballot box level, too. Leonard Llewellyn had resigned his seat for Clydach Vale for business reasons in September 1910. By 1912 all three local councillors for the ward were Labour representatives – William Abraham MP was reelected as usual in December 1910 though in a poll whose reduction was entirely due to his loss of votes; more significantly he, and the Welsh national anthem he customarily invoked, were both booed at an eve of poll meeting. The four ILP and two SDP branches in the Rhondda had contemplated running a candidate against him and, despite the fact that finances forced their withdrawal, urged all socialists to 'abstain from voting and working in this mock election for Mabon as a protest against his industrial and political action'. From 1911 there was an independent labour organisation established and the unofficial reform movement in the SWMF found itself a solid base in a mid-Rhondda from where in 1912 *The Miners' Next Step* trumpeted recall of MPs, reorganisation and reform as the platform to wider action. The Trades and Labour

Council had pressed for local Labour councillors to give an account of their stewardship twice a year at public meetings, 'with the aim of nursing the electors in the importance of having Labour men in our Councils', two years before the articulation of ideologies and plans of action in that famous pamphlet tilted, from a real strength, at the amorphous hegemony of a society whose public face had been more vulgarly marked on the night of the riots.

However the earthquake, even if it had set all the bells ringing, did not bring the temple down. On the 1911 Rhondda UDC, out of a total of 30 seats, 11 were held by Labour men, 4 by nominees of the coalowners, 4 by representatives of the building trade, 3 by shopkeepers, 2 by doctors, 2 by clergy, 2 by publicans and brewers, and 2 by independents. At the 1912 elections Labour representation increased to 14 but only 9 of these were avowed socialists.

Those who were brought before the courts for intimidating non-unionists or for theft were imprisoned or fined and treated to the magistrates' line in moral homilies. Thomas Richards, fined £1 because he had stolen coal from a truck in the Glamorgan colliery yard to light a fire for his three children and wife, was told that strikers had been warned of 'the gravity of such offences'; William Morgan who stole clothes from an outfitters to pawn and was given three weeks for his pains was informed that his theft was 'an extremely mean one'; and a fifteen-year-old caught pawning goods taken from J.R. Evans, draper, on the night of 8 November was fined £2, bound over for a year and made to attend regularly the Sunday School which had not seen him since the strike began. Will John and John Hopla who had spearheaded the Combine Strike were singled out for twelve-month sentences (later reduced to eight) for their part in the last disturbances of 1911.

With blame apportioned as far as could be done legally, and the strikers back in work on the price-list they had spurned in October 1910, the management applied salt to smarting wounds. They issued strict orders that the men, out for almost a year, should handle most carefully all horses since the latter's long lay-off would have softened them. A haulier who was dismissed for alleged disobedience and for hitting a farrier in the course of this was summoned for assault, where Lleufer Thomas, extending his all-encompassing brief, remarked that 'it was absolutely essential that discipline should be maintained at the colliery by the officials'. The haulier was sent down for six weeks. At the Cambrian Colliery offices current rent and back rent for houses not owned by the company itself were deducted from pay without the employees' consent. These were the bitter fruits of defeat, whilst for those policemen who had distinguished themselves in action came the rewards of promotion as three inspectors became superintendents and seven sergeants were made inspector. They put something into the district, too: a paternity case was brought by a Clydach waitress deprived of her wedding ring and delivered of a male child born on 29 August 1911; and Inspector (formerly Sergeant) James Davies of Mumbles near Swansea who 'stands 6 ft 2 in in height and has a physique of commanding appearance', was now to be utilised in Tonypandy.

Before Christmas 1911 those traders whose advertisements had noticeably diminished in the course of the year now severally announced 'Tonypandy's Great Shopping Week'. For fathers and mothers, they pronounced 'Santa Claus is undoubtedly the shop-keeper and Tonypandy tradesmen are doing their best to attract them'; 'Young men looking at the windows of Messrs Jones and Evans, outfitters, Tonypandy, cannot fail to notice something to their taste.... Their range of mufflers is claimed to be the *finest* in the Valley'; 'The chemists generally seem to have almost forgotten that they ever were chemists and have apparently entered into a league with Santa Claus with the idea of supplying everyone with a present of some description.'

For Will John, Henry Hopla and John Hopla who were doing hard labour it was not so easy to forget. John Hopla died a broken man in his early twenties, shortly after his release. The 'organic community' could not survive the rending of its temple veils any more than the 'organic' Welsh nation could evolve through time-less characteristics.

What had occurred in Tonypandy in November 1910 was, in many minds, a very un-Welsh state of affairs. Clearly something was rotten in the 'state of Tonypandy'. When Rhys Davies reflected on the matter in his popular survey volume *My Wales*, in 1937, he decided that the civic disturbances of his boyhood must have been the work of a 'section of the industrialised race ... composed of ... rootless ruffians and barbarous *aliens*, particularly Irishmen who were ... bored with the monotony of work'. If only they had all remained in the bosom of those nonconformist chapels which 'preserved the Welsh spirit' and 'offered the ancient Welsh foods ["spiritual and artistic tendencies"] in abundance to thou-sands of souls who might have been utterly ruined and corrupted in the brutal "new towns" then there would have been no "sack of Tonypandy" by a "slavering and barbaric-eyed ... enraged mob".'

After Tonypandy, action had to he taken on the secular front to redress spiritual decline. Daniel Lleufer Thomas intervened in matters great and small. In 1913 he rejected a defence lawyer's plea that the 'indecent postcards' his client (a local barber) exhibited were regarded as 'art' in London, Rome and Paris, by remarking that 'what would appeal to the artistic mind in Paris would not have the same influence in Tonypandy'. By 1917, when he was heading Lloyd George's Commission into Industrial Unrest, Lleufer Thomas could spell out his long-held conviction that 'civilisation' was dissipating with 'Welshness'. It was the disintegration of the latter, as defined by loss of language, spirituality and ethnicity, that underlay the more mundane reflections of the Commission:

> The Rhondda has an abundance of cinemas and music halls, but not a single theatre. Owing to the absence of municipal centres and centralised institutions, the development of the civic spirit and the sense of social solidarity – what we may in short call the community sense – is seriously retarded.

The nature of the community represented by places like Tonypandy, 'its Welshness' and its development were, inescapably, questions that required political answers. Who and what would 'control' Tonypandy were matters no one could divorce from the issue of 'ownership' and the full process of democratic argument. *The Miners' Next Step* with its no-leadership proposals was a conscious attempt to find an organisational framework in which the collectivity of action and sacrifice expressed in 1910 and 1911 would not be either controlled, except by its own volition, or dissipated.

The working class of mid-Rhondda in 1910, in their anticipation of the more generalised struggles of the 1920s and 1930s, stand for the working-class of South Wales. More than this, as with those who 'rose' against ironmasters and the state in Merthyr in 1831, they give a particular moment and place a typicality that echoes far beyond their time or their country. They were asking a series of questions, through their industrial strife and its connected social crisis, which could only be answered by defining a different community in a new Wales.

It was this process of change which Arthur Horner, first Communist President of the South Wales Miners' Federation in 1936, sought to encapsulate in a phrase in 1946 – 'I am a Welshman who speaks with an international accent.' A year later, as General Secretary of the National Union of Mineworkers, he would welcome the nationalisation of the coal industry that swept aside the coal-owners. In that combination of local roots (Wales) and political idealism (Communism) and in settling for an administrative bureaucracy once spurned (pragmatic reformism), Horner's career was an individual example of where that definition of a new Wales ended. It was not a neat solution to the problem but it was one, as Horner knew, whose origins lay 'in a place in the South of Wales' and what it had meant when he had walked, as a sixteen-year-old, through the night and over the mountains from Merthyr Tydfil to Tonypandy when news of the troops' arrival had been heard:

> When I reached Tonypandy the rioting had been going on all through the night ... I saw in action ... the vicious alliance of the Government and the coalowners, backed by police and armed troops, against miners who asked no more than a wage little over starvation level. I never forgot that lesson.

Tonypandy in 1910 was the tip of a Welsh iceberg.

Colour Wales Green

The finest sight of Nature is a crowded street.
Jimmy Breslin, New York columnist, 1996

The worse thing that happened after the First World War as far as those who had 'produced' Wales were concerned was that the clothes no longer seemed to fit. Industrial Wales, by the early 1920s, was becoming a monster. The Welsh Frankenstein had not only a bodily strength which was 'useful' for the nation, it had a growing self-consciousness which was becoming a nuisance. Popular culture and popular politics were being fused into a new identity which was, in significant ways, defining itself *against* an established concept of Welshness. If Wales was not a thing but a process, then a working class which was itself in the process of formation would inevitably clash with a national settlement whose terms were not negotiable.

As long as proletarian disruption was limited to unruly behaviour in drink or to physical violence or even riotous strikes, it was, however regrettable, not considered a threat either to the social order or to the national framework of that order. The law, religion, education and the discipline of the economy could be invoked as short- or long-term solutions. When these forces were challenged *politically*, as was clearly happening from the early twentieth century, alarm bells sounded. Explanations were sought. In particular the argument, from a wide range of concerned Welshmen, was that industrialisation, and its companion, anglicisation, had undermined the being, values and virtue of Wales. For some this became an absolute justification for 'de-industrialisation'. Others, more importantly, since the effects of the action have been more profound and long-lasting, looked for subtler ways to reverse the process.

In 1921, a three-month lock-out in the British coalfields marked the effective end of the 'revolutionary' phase which industrial unrest had seemed to promise for a decade. For South Wales it was, with hindsight, the beginning of the inter-war years of mass unemployment and industrial defeat. At the time 1921 looked more pivotal than pendular. This was especially so for those who tried to analyse the broader social and cultural forces that had made the coalfield what it was. Two very different views from informed, but detached, observers were set out that year. Both are remarkable.

The first was that of the Ministry of Health's Regional Survey Committee on South Wales. They based themselves, to an extent,

138

on the government's 1917 Commission of Enquiry into Industrial Unrest, and developed the theme of social degeneration and national dilution:

> The anthracite miners [of West Wales] are mostly Welsh-speaking, and they cling to manners and customs which are characteristic of the Cymric race. They have not been influenced to any considerable extent by the immigration of people other than those from the Welsh-speaking counties in the immediate vicinity. The eastern portions of the coalfield on the other hand, have been invaded to a very large extent by emigrants from all parts of the United Kingdom, with even a sprinkling from beyond the seas.
>
> This great influx of a more or less alien population ... accounts to some extent for the acceptance by South Wales miners of economic and social theories and policies which would appear to cut across Welsh tradition [i.e. socialism and syndicalism].
>
> Of the total population enumerated in Glamorgan and Monmouthshire in 1911, only 65.13 and 63.5 per cent respectively were returned as having been born in the country where they resided [and] about one fifth of the total population of Glamorgan and one fourth of that of Monmouthshire were English-born or born outside Wales.
>
> The immigrants are often not of a very desirable character. They comprise a considerable proportion of more or less irresponsible people of disorderly habits who do not at first make desirable citizens and who give a bad name to the particular locality in which they settle.

Alleged racial/linguistic features are thereby the motivating factors behind behaviour patterns which are not only 'disorderly' but also cut across, in their subsequent polities, 'Welsh tradition', for as the 1917 Enquiry had emphasised to its own satisfaction: 'Until some fifteen to twenty years ago, the native inhabitants had ... shown a marked capacity for stamping their own impress on all newcomers, and communicating to them a large measure of their own characteristics; of more recent years the process of assimilation has been unable to keep pace with the continuing influx of immigrants.'

This was indeed a reiterated concern. Others noted the anxiety but did not see the changes as undesirable. One such was Sir Alfred Zimmern, briefly Professor of International Politics at the University College of Wales, Aberystwyth, after the First World War. In May 1921 Zimmern went to Jesus College, Oxford, to address the Cambrian Society on his 'Impressions of Wales'. Zimmern was harsh and perceptive. 'The Wales of today is not a community. There is not one Wales; there are three.... There is Welsh Wales; there is industrial, or, as I sometimes think of it, American Wales; and there is upper-class or English Wales. These three represent different types and different traditions. They are moving in different directions, and, if they all three survive, they are not likely to re-unite.'

What followed was the reverse of patronising timidity:

> Of American Wales, the Wales of the coalfield and the industrial working-class ... let me only say ... for the benefit of those who are apt to sneer at South Wales as a 'storm centre', what a joy it has been to pass even a too fleeting and infrequent week-end among men and women who really care for ideas and love the search for truth. There can be few audiences in the world, even in Jewry, so alert and intelligent as a gathering in a Welsh mining village. Judged by the keenness and receptivity of the products, the mine (or is it the Socialist Sunday School?) can compare favourably with State and rate-aided institutions. I do not blame the editors of the *Plebs Magazine* [for independent working-class education] and their followers for a certain exclusiveness on which they pride themselves in holding their light aloof from the University; but that the University should mean so little to the coalfield, that it should even display, on occasion, a deliberate preference for the unlettered, if titled, capitalist over the zealous and lettered proletarian is surely an ironical comment on the meaning of the word University.... I know intellectual earnestness and integrity when I see them, and I have passed no happier or more uplifting hours in Wales than in the company of men whom, precisely because of their search for truth, the faint hearts of the academic world have ignored and neglected....
> It is more than material light and heat that Wales may yet win from her coalfield.

That was, by 1921, exactly what was feared. There were crude, repressive measures adopted – police, courts, troops – to check popular manifestations of 'disorderly habits' but those who had thought more deeply about 'the matter of Wales' were concerned to switch the intellectual direction of 'American Wales' and, when that failed, to welcome the destruction of its material foundation.

The prime condition for stability was considered to be the reassertion of a 'balanced' Welsh life. This meant above all a culture based on rural life. The image of that life rather than its reality was the essential factor; it could be held up as a prior, and superior, culture and thus act as a control on the present. Until the 1930s few seriously suggested an actual substitution of industry by an agrarian civilisation but the key features could be transplanted.

And if, as Thomas Jones, secretary to and intimate of successive Prime Ministers from 1916 to 1931, suggested, looking back from the vantage point of 1951, taming and civilising by 'religion and tradition' were not working efficiently in South Wales even before 1914, then what, in an increasingly secular and non-traditional society, would?

No one phrased the problem more acutely, or more often, than Daniel Lleufer Thomas (1863-1940). He was one of a generation of country-born Welshmen who became luminaries in their own land after a sojourn in Oxford. Along with O.M. Edwards and John Morris-Jones (1864-1929, Professor of Welsh at Bangor) he helped found the Dafydd ap Gwilym Society in 1886 and pursued, as they did, its ideals of nationhood when he served as a public figure in Wales. From 1909 to 1933 he was the Stipendiary Magistrate for the central coalfield of the area of Pontypridd and Rhondda. He headed the Enquiry of 1917. He helped found and in 1911 was the first President of the Welsh School of Social Service, which was designed to introduce Christian precepts into society in industrial and rural Wales, especially so far as adolescents were concerned. Lleufer Thomas had begun his public career with high hopes in those confident 1890s when the success of 'Welshness' was trumpeted. And nowhere more so than in the investigation of the question of the Welsh countryside over which Lleufer Thomas presided as Secretary.

The great problem through the nineteenth century had been that of the land. The divide in Welsh society was depicted as between anglicised, absentee landlords and Welsh tenant farmers. The latter, buoyed up by professional men in Welsh market towns, had integrated their economic grievances with religious and political separatism. Radicalism was rooted in the Welsh countryside. The political representation won at all levels by this body of related interests secured a monument to itself in the shape of the Commission of Enquiry into the Land Question. From 1893 to 1896 nine distinguished public men questioned informants all over Wales. Their multi-volumed report, and its digest compiled by the Secretary, Daniel Lleufer Thomas, reviewed matters that were virtually settled, at least by the 1890s. The content was archival material from the outset. And yet the mere existence of the report in such bulk declares its importance as a therapeutic gesture.

Public, official Wales which had spawned the Commission knew that the relative decline in the economic importance of the land was as nothing compared to the land's cultural, almost spiritual, function in the lives of the Welsh. The golden boy of Welsh politics, Tom Ellis, MP for Merioneth and Liberal Chief Whip in the Commons, was an impassioned witness for the prosecution before the Commission he had played a large part in establishing. He was certain that there was 'finer ore for the making of Welsh national wealth in its peasant and cottage homes ... than in its rocks and hills'. The countryside was the sustaining spirit even as the mineral exploitation of Wales proceeded. Only the land could guarantee the national humanity of the new industrialising districts.

The Land Commission's Secretary could reassure Tom Ellis by referring to the Rhondda where a population of 1,000 in 1851 had multiplied one hundredfold by 1896, and was still rising:

> It might have been expected that in the Rhondda Valley, which is practically entirely given up to the coal industry, a cosmopolitan population, possessing no particular characteristics of a racial kind, might have been found; that is not the case; speaking broadly, the characteristics of *Welsh* life, its Nonconformist development, the habitual use of the *Welsh* language, and the prevalence of a *Welsh* type of character are as marked as in the rural districts of Wales.

All was well, then, if the features of life in the Golden West, whence Daniel Lleufer Thomas came, could be rooted forever in the East. Those Welsh characteristics were seen by 1911, when the Rhondda's population was over 150,000, as already swamped. In 1913 Lleufer Thomas addressed the School of Social Service's annual meeting on the concern he now felt for the consequences of the process of wealth-making which had given his Wales such national hubris, politically, culturally, nationally, just twenty years before.

> While the change in methods of production known as the Industrial Revolution appeared much later in Wales, it has consequently been compressed within a shorter period of time. The transition from the simple life of the country to the more complex one of the town or industrial community has for Welshmen involved a more complete break with the past; ... the process of urbanisation in the industrial districts has been more rapid than in any part of England.... A mixed crowd, drawn from all parts of the country, and it may be from several nationalities, pour into the districts.... There is a pathetic lack of leaders, men of strong moral character to set up, by the example of their own lives, a high standard of conduct ... throughout most of the industrial districts.... There is going on a steady transition from one language to another. Some parts are gradually, others rapidly, being Anglicised.

That was the description. Within two years, in 1915, he addressed the National Eisteddfod to warn of its implications:

> Owing partly to the influx into Wales of a large non-Welsh element, and partly to other causes, the ideal of nationality and of religion would seem in danger of being repudiated in some of the industrial districts in favour of an illusory ideal of a cosmopolitan, and perhaps to some extent materialistic, brotherhood.

These cries became more anguished the less influence they exerted. For a time there was a real battle. South Wales seemed determined to subvert all that was regarded as traditional in Wales. No matter how much it was to be deplored, neither the divisive nature of class-based politics nor the downfall of a formally organised religion like nonconformity could seriously be questioned in this society after 1918. Anglicisation was no longer the acceptable face of bilingualism: it was an insidious destroyer of the world still contained within the Welsh language – perhaps, some began to argue, *only* contained within that tongue. The statistics did not make for comfortable reading. It was true that as early as 1900 less than half the population contained in Wales could speak Welsh, but those who considered the matter pointed out that the total number of Welsh-speakers was still rising in 1911. By 1921, that fateful year, both the percentage decline (to thirty-seven per cent) and the absolute decline, were irrefutable evidence of a crisis for the language that made the matter a political issue.

For a section of the Welsh middle class, this linguistic or cultural threat was directly connected to a material decline and a loss in political influence which neither 'British' Liberalism or Labourism (let alone 'cosmopolitan' socialism) could redress. The establishment of the Welsh Nationalist Party in 1925 was an outcrop of the double crisis which a middle class intent on succouring its Welsh identity was undergoing. It did not begin to translate this anxiety into formal, effective political channels until the 1950s, which is why Plaid Cymru can be depicted before the Second World War as a political party in name but a cultural 'group' in essence. If the idea of a Welsh nation expressed through its language and literature as a rooted civilisation was the positive side of the group's leading intellectuals, the negative pole was the industrial, anglicised world which had to be nullified if 'Wales' was to survive. South Wales was the prime example of the destruction of Welsh civilisation and history.

As far as language was concerned Saunders Lewis, leading exponent of nationalist ideology in the inter-war period as President of

Plaid Cymru 1926-39, was quite explicit even against the 'softer' approach of party members. As the 1931 census revealed a further drop in the percentage of Welsh speakers, Lewis thundered:

> Even in the Nationalist Party itself I fear that there are some who do not yet realise that a 'bilingual Wales' is something to be feared and avoided, that the decrease in the number of monoglot Welsh speakers is a tragedy, and that a Welsh-only Wales is alone consistent with the aims and the philosophy of Welsh nationalism.... We cannot therefore aim at anything less than to annihilate English in Wales.... It is bad, and wholly bad, that English is spoken in Wales. It must be deleted from the land called Wales: *delenda est Carthago.*

In the service of this ideal Lewis and other leading nationalists developed attitudes to contemporary European affairs that their enemies labelled fascist but which were in fact a compound of social authoritarianism (tinged with Roman Catholicism) and a yearning for 'strong-man' leadership. However naive and ineffective the nationalists of the 1930s were as political figures, their cultural views could be nurtured within the wider society of Wales. They were clear, too, that only a dismantling of the industry (and democracy?) of South Wales could provide a basis for their vision of the Welsh future. In as much as the savagery of the Depression was a way towards complete 'de-industrialisation' it offered a possibility for the kind of economic change envisaged, for, as the nationalists' chief spokesman on agriculture wrote in 1937: 'Placing the people back on the land is not only appropriate, but is essential if the Welsh nation is to live ... a nation with its roots in the country and the soil.'

No matter how sophisticated the economic analysis of a D.J. Davies, in favour of 'small capitalism' and co-operative ventures, Saunders Lewis' clarity was uncompromising. 'Christianity' he argued in 1938 'is as essential to the Nationalist Party as is anti-Christian materialism to Marxism.' And where, in Wales, was 'Marxism' rooted? In the coalfield of the Southern belt which, as he had insisted in 1934, must 'for the sake of the moral health of Wales and for the moral and physical welfare of its population ... be de-industrialised'.

The ferocity of this strain of thought did not win Plaid Cymru many direct adherents. Yet its logic could be broken down into an ideal kept 'for best' and a more pragmatic approach to power-broking. This is the route Plaid Cymru adopted, with increasing success from the early 1960s to 1979, after 1945. It is the reason why Saunders Lewis 'withdrew' from active politics after the war. His earlier political intransigence led those 'cultural' nationalists he so despised to reject his party and his solutions down to 1939. What they shared in common with him was a class perspective on the 'Welsh' crisis after 1921 that also based itself on a theory of national decline. Whatever else it was, it was scarcely liberal. On the contrary the struggle to control Wales continued at a pace as economic and social deprivation deepened.

The thirties have been laundered in the post-war liberal mind with such effect that their image now reeks of passivity and pity. So far as Wales is concerned this lugubrious half-truth has been, perhaps, overemphasised at the expense of a sustaining humour and collective struggle. What has been ignored even more, however, is the positive, hand-wringing delight some took in the economic and social wretchedness of the inter-war years. These were, in some minds, the years of come-uppance for the industrial South. Misery was deserved. Guilt was apportioned. Blame was fixed. Best of all was the fact that the swelling discord of alternative politics and culture which was so feared between 1910 and 1926 had been either stilled or marginalised.

The images needed to control a changing Wales were superseded by the reality of the cost of the 1930s. Mass unemployment damped down more spirits than the incessant rain. It was long-term, in double figures and structural. The workforce in coal-mining alone was halved in a decade. In twenty years almost 450,000 people migrated out of South Wales. All the switches directing a society's basic energies had been thrown into reverse. South Wales became a case-study, and no one liked this more than the social pathologists whose advice had been rejected.

In 1942 Dr Eli Ginzberg, an American sociologist who had spent some time investigating the condition of South Wales in the 1930s, published his considered reflections in New York. The title of this book, which examined the social deprivation and institutional response in Wales, was *Grass on the Slag Heaps*. The colour green would serve a number of writers intent on deriving social morality from an intellectual paint-box. Ginzberg concluded:

> It is difficult to help people who will not help themselves, and many of the tragedies that befell the Welsh during the postwar decades can be traced to their own shortcomings and to the shortcomings of their allies, the trade union movement and the Labor [sic] party. The failure of the Welsh to help themselves must in part be explained by their inability to do so. As early as

1934 Lord Portal called attention to the fact that the leaders of South Wales were noticeably inept, a result of the fact that the most virile and able people had migrated. This kindly interpretation of the ineptitude of Welsh leaders cannot, however, explain and surely cannot justify such stupid practices as sending trade union leaders to Parliament as a reward for faithful services to the Federation.

Ginzberg's book came complete with a preface by the man who had, in his long career, invested most in the theory and practice of leadership. Thomas Jones (1870-1955), arch-organiser of educationalists, philanthropists and the guilty rich, was a Welshman whose distress at the material downfall of his country after 1918 was only matched by his conviction that the necessary redress was the prerogative of a leadership equipped with the traditional weapons of national faith. The opportunity, wrestled for and lost immediately before and after the Great War, had returned with the destruction of proletarian pretension to political superiority in the maw of the Depression. The proletariat had, in this view, been unable to do any more than destroy a community. They lacked, as he said in 1933, 'standards and authorities':

> Standing over against the miners' home life in the old days were two authorities – the minister of religion and the employer of labour, and for both there was usually a real respect. The miner was contented because his responsibilities were limited and clearly defined. What was asked of him he did.

Confronted by strikes, riots and a plain disregard for both religious passivity and employee deference, Tom Jones, and a like-minded group of public men, could only await their turn. They had long urged greater provision of 'objective' education for working men by the University of Wales through a system of classes. They had supported, from 1908, the establishment of a South Wales Workers' Educational Association. In the 1930s, with increasing success, these bodies did fill the vacuum left by the collapse of independent working-class education. The latter, institutionalised since 1912 in the 'Marxist' Central Labour College and its offshoot of 'Plebs League' classes in the coalfield, could no longer be supported by the much reduced wealth and confidence of the Miners' Federation. The Central Labour College closed forever in 1929. Tom Jones' non-sectarian working-man's college in distant Harlech, to provide training for the 'leaders' of the 'unemployed centres' in South Wales, opened in 1927. The miners did not officially support this venture until well after the Second World War but they had no real counter to it.

From 1930 Tom Jones, as secretary of the Pilgrim Trust, acted as dispenser-in-chief of aid to the stricken Valleys. Educational facilities through the WEA were keenly promoted. In 1932 Percy Watkins who had been a university bureaucrat, then Secretary of the Welsh Department of the Board of Education, became, at Jones's behest, head of the Welsh section of the National Council of Social Service. Nine major educational settlements were established in South Wales between 1927 and 1937. They functioned at the intersection between social service, educational provision and public guidance.

Percy Watkins in his memoir of 1942, *A Welshman Remembers,* expressed a puzzled, somewhat irritated, attitude to the reception of these attempts to restore 'standards' and 'authority':

> It is a strange thing that these honest efforts of ours to bring cultural opportunities within the reach of the unemployed in the days of their helplessness and hopelessness did not receive the encouragement and support that might have been especially expected from the political side of the Labour movement and from the trade unions. The former preferred to regard the motives of our movement as nothing more than an attempt to provide 'dope'.

This 'dope' was not intended to incorporate working-class militancy (patchy anyway) or their institutions (much battered) in the revived national-liberal consensus which had nurtured the coterie grouped round Tom Jones. Its short-term strategies would have been, in the 1930s, ineffective against the root-and-branch development of socialist politics and union solidarity. Where these were challenged directly it was by the repressive measures of victimisation, company unions, mass unemployment and equally mass policing. And these all ultimately failed. In the long term the inevitable acceptance of this political reality was made palatable for the disinherited by the installation of 'Labourism' as an administrative necessity for a basically unreconstructed economy and society.

The objection to the 'dope' was partly a residual mistrust of those who had elevated 'community' above 'class' and, instinctively, a gut understanding that what was on offer as 'cultural opportunity' was a window on to the supposedly superior understanding and behaviour required for social health. The imbalance caused to 'Wales' by the coalfield had passed through the fever of social disturbance into the lassitude of social collapse. As Tom Jones was to reflect, things had been far better arranged in North Wales where the 'social structure was ... balanced between agriculture, industry and well-to-do visitors from Liverpool, Manchester and the Midlands'. One alternative, then, was to present the qualities of an élite, expressed through unrepresentative institutions, irrespective of their detachment from any popular base. Behind it lay the correct assumption that the pressures for individual well-being and social mobility would, in due course, translate the mutuality of these one-class communities into institutional forms 'better' served by administering politicians than visionary class warriors. Then, once again, the functionary class bred to serve such a society from the 1860s would come into their own. The grammar schools, pride and joy of 'Labour' Wales, are an instance of the correctness of their assessment.

The 1889 Intermediate Education Act laid down a system of secondary education for Wales that was in advance of England through its early, and relatively generous, provision of places. Control of these schools by local education authorities ensured that the demands of parents for social attainment via education would, largely, be fulfilled. Until the 1940s this only affected a minority. The knock-on effects in shaping Welsh society were to be considerable but they did not seem to have great influence on the essential issues in contention in the coalfield before the Second World War. Some public figures in Welsh life had, nonetheless, been long concerned with the direction of educational policies which produced leaders and teachers instead of maintaining a cohesive community. O.M. Edwards, Chief Inspector for Education in Wales since 1907, attempted to add the ingredient of Edwardian national idealism about an organic Welsh community. The weight of social pressures from below and a democratic reflection of these aspirations prevented his innate cultural conservatism from shaping the curricula and potential of Welsh schools, but after the war a philosophy of Labourism, enshrined in local councils, was readily adapted to incorporate elements of this strategy. The Wales that emerged as 'red' and Labour in 1945 was, even in its strongholds, not fully capable of turning its defensive, community politics into an aggressive weapon. Caught up in its own anchored development it failed, except in the case of some individuals and instances, to break free from the concept of a world that was said to require government, leadership and control.

The reality of Welsh life was the renegotiation of a settlement whereby, in political terms, Liberalism shaded into Labourism and the latter 'agreed' to be bound by a social and cultural consensus that was addicted to merit as a measuring stick and national sentiment as a common inheritance. Neither communism, left-wing socialism nor nationalism were able to contend politically because they did not see the Depression years as a fall from grace. Those who did were more in tune with popular conceptions. They strove to deliver, in whatever institutional form they could devise, gratification of individuals and families despite the communal collapse. In doing so they suggested, implicitly or explicitly, that something *could* be done. The meaning of the rise and fall of the coalfield society as a collective society was thus undermined from within by a policy of piecemeal accommodation and overlaid by a mythology whose potency derived from its universality as a parable. The most important 'document', in terms of its power and its sociological interest, ever written about South Wales was, naturally enough, a piece of fiction which still haunts the popular mind with its accusations of guilt and redemption.

It was in 1939, at the end of those two decades of out-migration which had bled Wales at the rate of 20,000 people a year, that Huw Morgan first told us that he, too, was leaving. He put, in an amazingly capacious 'little blue cloth' that his mother used 'to tie around her hair', his best suit, a pair of socks and two shirts, and left the Valley forever. Or so Richard Llewellyn (1906-83) began his best-selling saga *How Green Was My Valley*. The book has never since been out of print. It has been translated into thirteen languages, transferred twice to the small screen and made into an Oscar-winning Irish-American-Welsh extravaganza in 1940 by John Ford. It presents, quite simply, the best-known image of Wales in the world. It is a Wales its hero leaves in the first sentence. He leaves because *his* Wales has gone (politically, socially, linguistically and racially) out of control.

The novel is a key document for two reasons. First, its enormous world-wide popularity clearly owes its success to a genre of glamorised nostalgia but, even more so, to the moral fable about humanity which is at the heart of the narrative. Secondly, its equally enormous popularity within Wales derives from an ability to incorporate a mythology of Valleys' life – chapels, sex on the mountain, choirs, pit disasters, slag heaps, rugby football, boxing and the ubiquitous 'Mam' – with a skilled, and dismissive, analysis of the meaning of these myths. *How Green Was My Valley* turned the drama of coalfield history into a romance that dripped with realism and moralism. It remains the most well-known and well-read book ever written by a Welshman, or anyone else, about Wales. It requires close consideration.

The storyline is a simple one. Huw's first person narration takes us, in a sequence of almost uninterrupted flashback, from the late nineteenth century to just before the First World War. Authenticity is irrelevant here; the war receives no mention, for example, whilst the minimum wage struggle is mixed in with earlier disputes over the sliding scale. The sole references to present time refer to the slag heap that, with a creaking symbolism, is threatening to bury Huw's home. Brothers and sisters, and their spouses, father and mother, and one or two close family associates are the pegs on which Huw's recollections are hung. The device of the time-shift, our knowledge that their lives have been, and that all Huw relates has no longer any tangible existence, is used to great effect because, in this manner, only the past has any real meaning in the novel. In a rhetorical coda, at the very end, Huw defiantly voices the emotions he has been playing on:

> Thirty years ago, but as fresh, and as near as Now.... An age of goodness I knew, and badness too, mind, but more of good than bad, I will swear. At least we knew good food, and good work, and goodness in men and women.
>
> But you have gone now, all of you, that were so beautiful when you were quick with life. Yet not gone, for you are still a living truth inside my mind. So how are you dead, my brothers and sisters, and all of you, when you live with me as surely as I live myself?...
>
> Are my friends all dead, then, and their voices a glory in my ears? No, and I will stand to say no, and no, again. In blood, I say no....
>
> Did my father die under the coal? But, God in heaven, he is down there now, dancing in the street with Davy's red jersey over his coat, and coming, in a moment, to smoke his pipe in the front room and pat my mother's hand....
>
> Is he dead? For if he is, then I am dead, and we are dead, and all of sense a mockery.
>
> How green was my valley, then, and the Valley of them that have gone.

The passage is complex. Undoubtedly, they are all dead, so the present of the Valley society is worthless, 'a mockery'; on the other hand, their existence, in the past, and our ability to recall it, can invest the present with meaning if we absorb the lessons that were ignored when the Valley was still 'green'. The book's universal popularity lies in its view of the connection of industrialisation and 'Nature', in its distaste for a society no longer related organically to natural rhythms of life. No wonder that the great myth-maker of the American West, John Ford, should make a film of it, for it is brimming with images of familial self-sufficiency, of simple pleasures ('There was nothing to do outside at night, except chapel or choir.... But even so, we always found plenty to do until bed-time, for if we were not studying or reading, then we were making something out in the back, or over the mountain singing some-where. I can remember no time when there was not plenty to he done'), of a frontier existence, uncontaminated by a mechanised world. The original settlement (Gilfach Goch) has been built around the first migrant workers, who possess all the advantages of an idyllic rural life with the bonus of industrial prosperity thrown in. The place is an Eden, a South Wales Utopia, in which the Valley, the Mountain, the Hill, and the Town are each capitalised and compartmentalised. The Valley is a haven between the Mountain's barrier and the Town's threat, a separate civilisation:

> As soon as the whistle went [the women] put chairs outside their front doors and sat there waiting till the men came up the Hill and home. Then as the men came up to their front doors they threw their wages, sovereign by sovereign, into the shining laps, fathers first and sons or lodgers in a line behind. My mother often had forty of them, with my father and five brothers work-ing. And up and down the street you would hear them singing and laughing and in among it all the pelting jingle of gold. A good day was Saturday, then, indeed....
>
> We always had hams in the kitchen ... all the year round, and not just one ham but a dozen at a time. Two whole pigs hang-ing up in one kitchen, ready to be sliced for anybody who walked through the door, known or stranger....
>
> There was always a baron of beef and a shoulder or leg of lamb on the dishes by my father. In front of him were the chick-ens, either boiled or roast, or ducks, or turkey or goose, whatever was the time of the year. Then potatoes, mashed, boiled and roast, and cabbage and cauliflower, or peas or beans and some-times when the weather was good, all of them together.

Hard cash, then, not the 'falsity' of paper money, and with colliers earning, in fiction anyway, around £6 a week in the 1880s, lots of it; add to this a veritable cornucopia of wholesome food, described again and again in the course of the book, and kept perpetually before us by that cunningly placed, reverberating adverb 'always', and you have a contented, 'natural' way of life on a communal pattern. The fact that the community has not been artificially created is stressed. Mr Gruffydd, the minister with a social conscience, explains to Huw why the chapel deacons have publicly chastised an unmarried mother:

> You may realise, Huw ... that the men of the Valleys have built their houses and brought up their families without help from others, without a word from the Government. Their lives have been ordered from birth by the Bible. From it they took their instructions. They had no other guidance, and no other law. If it has produced hypocrites and pharisees, the fault is in the human race.... Our fathers upheld good conduct and rightful dealing by strictness, and it is in Man Adam to be slippery, and many are as slimy as the adder. The wonder is to me that the men of the Valley are as they are, and not barbarians all.

The stern but cohesive morality of the community is, then, based on fundamentalist religious precepts allied to self-discipline. The backbone here provided is that of individual rectitude and self-reliance. When, and if, the codified laws of outside civilisation intrude, then not only natural justice will have to go, for there is a clear, but unstated, link between the fruits of prosperity and happiness and their concomitant, the pure, simple life. And in its turn, solely for the sake of clarifying its symbolism, this open honesty of purpose is equated with Welshness. Thus, when Huw's father hits Elias, the grocer, the Welshman who has turned thief and profiteer, he is warned:

> 'I will have the English law on you.'
> 'Well' said my father 'you have had a bit of Welsh law, tonight, for a change.'

At school Huw is persecuted for speaking Welsh by a Welsh schoolmaster ashamed of his own nationality; later he beats the man senseless when he finds a young girl being treated as he had been. Throughout, Huw's first person narration employs grammatical inversion of normal English usage in order to suggest a Welsh linguistic pattern. The upholding of Welshness is not important in itself (i.e. for real, historical reasons), but because it stands as representative of a pristine state, unsullied by the modern world – another link with the myth of the American Adam, starting afresh in the New World, whether as farmer, trapper, scout or cowboy, but always released from the chains of a cramping European heritage. Immigration means impurity of the blood, an invasion spearheaded by industrial greed and urban mores; it involves the alteration of society. A revival meeting is held:

> Wickedness was creeping into the Valley without halt or check. Thieves were there, and vagabonds, and drunkards by the score, and even bad women.
>
> 'Before you are much older' [Mr Gruffydd] shouted ... 'you will have policemen here to stay. A magistrate next. Then perhaps even a jail. And the counterparts of those things are hunger and want, and misery and idleness. The night is coming. Watch and pray.'
> 'Amen' said the people, soft and deep.

Shortly after this, a child, Dilys Pritchard, is sexually assaulted and killed. The minister forms the men into 'the Vigilants'. They know where to go:

> Around each public house and all round the three rows of houses where the half-breed Welsh, Irish and English were living, the men took a stand, almost elbow to elbow, so that none could go in or out....
>
> Up to the rows of houses where the dross of the colliers lived. These people did the jobs that colliers would never do, and they were allowed to live and breed because the owners would not spend money on plant when their services were to be had so much the cheaper. For a pittance, they carried slag and muck, they acted as scavengers, and as they worked, so they lived. Even their children were put to work at eight and nine years of age so that more money could come into the home. They lived most of them only to drink. Their homes were bestial sties, where even beasts would rebel if put there to live, for beasts have clean ways with them and they will show their disgust quick enough, but these people were long past such good feeling. They were a living disgust.

All these are questioned until the hapless Idris Atkinson is singled out and given by the Vigilants to Dilys' outraged father and brothers, who take him off to perpetrate their own outrages. This evil, subhuman lumpenproletariat is treated in the language used by Edwardian novelists about the urban working classes, only here the condemnation is supposed to be coming from respectable, God-fearing working men who are, of course, a 'pure' race since 'the dross' is not Welsh: 'One by one, they came and went, all of them quiet and in fear, and some Irish, some Scotch, some English, and some inter-breed Welsh.'

As the novel proceeds we realise the community is threatened by the taint of alien blood as well as the disruption of alien ways. The women hold the families together, in good and bad times; they are respectable, put in charge of the household, level-headed, purveyors of muted sex. We hear of women working at the pits but they are so outside consideration that we never meet any: 'I will not allow my sister to be treated like a pit-woman,' Ianto said; 'Shut up and behave yourself,' Owen said, 'You are talking like the women at the pits.' Despite difficulties the family unity is maintained, and the unity of the community is cemented in the chapel and in its finest collective expression, the choir, that eventually sings before Queen Victoria herself. Why, then, does the community, ultimately, fail to hold together?

The straightforward answer seems to be that greed destroys it; too many men, employers and employees, unwilling to moderate their appetites for money. However, the actual working out of this aspect of the tale is far more complex and subtle. From its refusal to be schematic derives its persuasiveness. Gwilym, Huw's father, becomes a checkweigher when the book starts; the men strike and lose. Gwilym, their representative, regrets the suffering *and* understands the owners' viewpoint: 'Our wages must come down. They are not getting the price for coal that they used to, so they cannot afford to pay the wages they did. We must be fair too.'

Nonetheless, his checkweigher's hut is removed so that he has to work in the rain and cold. His sons are angry but he refuses to let them 'make my case a plank for your politics'. When Davy, the son who 'wants Socialism', calls the men together for a mass meeting, his father puts the case that is, in fact, the novel's – an acknowledgement of injustice, a desire to see this rectified but a rejection of any action beyond conciliatory dealings:

> You are right in what you want, but you are wrong in your ways of getting it. Force is no good to you until you have tried reason. And reason wants patience. And if patience wants a tight belt, then tight belt it should have. You cannot ask the help of God with hate in your hearts, and without that help you will get nothing. It is no use to say you will all go together in a Union if you have no notion what the Union is to do. Get better wages? You will have better wages or as good as can be got without a Union. The owners are not all savages, but they will not give you whatever you want just because there are a lot of you and you use threats. Reason and civilised dealing are your best weapons.

In rejecting this advice the men are turning their backs on the old ways. For the meaning of the novel, the result has to be disaster. The Valley grows blacker and the slag heap larger. Huw asks why 'ugliness and hate and foolishness' have come to the Valley:

> 'Bad thoughts and greediness, Huw,' my father said 'Want all, take all, and give nothing.... You will have everything from the ground if you will ask the right way. But you will have nothing if not. Those poor men ... are all after something they will never get. They will never get it because their way of asking is wrong. All things come from God, my son.'

The father dismisses the inter-valley Union that Davy helps organise, dismisses the men's demands as unreasonable and their unanimity as akin to that of monkeys. He becomes the 'Superintendent' of the pit, second in command to the manager. The men's resentment of the course of their former leader is dealt with (and dismissed) in a key scene in which Huw's mother goes, secretly, to a mountainside mass meeting to berate them for their accusations and to tell them her husband has only had the just rewards of hard work – 'He has done nothing against you and he never would'. Later, and without any intervening explanation Gwilym is again in receipt of their confidence. Ambiguity, ambivalence, even downright confusion, characterise the treatment of Union action. Father and sons express the two good aspects of Union demands in a society teetering on the brink of change; the father's way, being that of the 'good society', is right in the last analysis; the sons offer a hope of modulating the change, however slight their chances. Gwilym has to quarrel with his sons because of their lack of patience and they, with him, through his failure to see some differences in attitude are needed. Then, the best parts of each are brought together by Mr Gruffydd, the Christian activist, who is not afraid to tell the local owner that not all pay as well as he does:

> 'You manage your own colliery. But others are managed by paid servants with the owners interested only in the profits. Rich, lazy lordlings and greedy shareholders are our enemies.'
> 'And middle-men' said Davy.

It is Mr Gruffydd who makes the father see the justness of the demand for a 'fair living standard' as a minimum and who brings Gwilym and his socialist sons back together. They can all unite against those who are not the producers of wealth. With the disturbance of the former 'natural balance' (and the sole reason advanced for this is the lowering of wages with the influx of outsiders), the sense of spirituality has been lost. The profiteering from coal is the enemy to be fought in the shape of financial manipulators. Unions have to be 'civilian regiments to fight in the cause of the people' since the sources of control have become remote. Mr Gruffydd is presented as the spokesman of reasoned militancy:

> 'Your enemy is usury. And the usurer takes no heed of men, or their lives, or their dependents' lives....'
> He went through the history of the Valley and spoke to them of the steady fall in wages, and their willingness to work for less and less, while others who had nothing to do with coal, but handled only paper, or owned the land above the workings, took more and more.
> 'You must fight', he said. 'Fight. Fight now.'
> 'Tell us what to do', men were shouting. 'Show us a way.'
> 'Elect men to Parliament', Mr Gruffydd told them.
> 'Gain for yourselves representation ... approach the chief men in the coal trade and in the Government. Do all things with order.'

Eventually the men, after a weakening strike, obtain, along with a cut in their potential earnings, a minimum wage. All this takes place before the disturbances (based on the mid-Rhondda troubles of 1910-11) with which the novel ends and which, in reality, preceded the 1912 Minimum Wage Strike. The reversal of order is all part of a necessary confusion; it stems from Llewellyn's need to make the men's case a fair one, and to see that they receive some justice without introducing the complexities of the actual situation in which the feverish disorder of 1910-11 led on to the national demands of 1912. The men's case can thus be simplified into what is legitimate and what is not, further separated by the different manner of their framing. The spoilation of the Green Valley and the destruction of its community may be reduced, thereby, to a homily on extremism, as reasonable methods of redressing grievances are spurned.

Conditions worsen in the pits; the owners, no longer local men, became more intransigent. One by one the heirs to the Valley, Gwilym's sons, leave – Ivor dies in a pit accident; Owen and the younger Gwilym go to America; Ianto to a works in Germany; Davy to New Zealand. Huw, of course, is leaving as the book begins. Salvation, now, only lies in flight – precisely the solution of those novelists in the mid-nineteenth century who, following Carlyle, agonised over the 'Condition of England Question' in the first throes of industrialisation, and rejected trades unions as irrelevancies or positive evils.

The meetings of the men became disorderly, occasions to air general disgruntlement. Huw, now a carpenter, regrets, as his father had done earlier, their stupidity in the mass, their decision to come out on strike again. A stranger comes and addresses them on Marx and Hegel:

> I listened to him for minutes, but there was too much noise about me to hear all he said for the men were arguing among themselves and in places there were fights. Red revolution and anarchy was what the speaker wanted, with a red flag to fly over all, and everybody equal....
> It was pain to me that men could be so blind, but it was greater pain to know that my brothers and Mr Gruffydd, and the brave ones of early days, had all been forgotten in a craziness of thought that made more of the notions of foreigners than the principles of Our Fathers.

Or, as the father had said, long before: 'I am not in favour of anything put up by a lot of old foreigners.... Owain Glyndŵr said all there is to be said for this country hundreds of years ago. Wales for the Welsh. More of him and less of Mr Marx, please.'

So that the meaning of the romance may, at the last, unfold, the novel ends in a way that dispels all the early ambivalence that surrounds the men's struggle for wages. Those concerned only with the lost paradise of the early part have been blind to this, although it is integral to any understanding of the book's motivation. Indeed, it is the supreme lesson preached.

With the men on strike, at the behest of 'foreign' influence, Huw wonders if he, or his father, should try to move the men from their folly:

> 'My son', he said 'your good brothers are from home only through speaking to them, and for them. They warned them enough not to strike. They saw its uselessness, at the last, as I have seen it these years past. Speaking to them now is a waste of breath. They are drunk with unreason. Leave them.'

The wheel has turned full circle; the futility of direct, industrial action is underlined by its constant opponent. The final chapter cobbles together the Tonypandy riots, and other incidents of 1910-11, just as an earlier lock-out is, in fact, a description of the summer of 1926. The father goes from pit to pit inspecting them for safety, soldiers and police are imported, a half-wit is batoned to death, the enraged men try to attack the boiler-house to stop the pumps and thus flood the pit – 'There were strangers among them, who seemed to be giving the orders' – and Huw, with two publicans (ex-boxers and gentle souls), fight through to the boiler-house to assist the police and the manager.

Huw and his father, both still claiming to be unionists, are prepared for the opprobrium of being called scab because they alone are in possession of their senses. So Gwilym risks his life, at the hands of the men, by working for the owners, and underground, 'with his eyes sharp for danger to the livelihood of men'. With Gwilym in the pit, the water rises too fast for the pumps, and Huw calls for volunteers to go down ('while the cattle were shouting ... and leaders ... were being offended'):

> 'You are cutting your own throats,' I said to them. 'If the strike ends tomorrow you will have weeks of waiting while they take water from the levels. More waiting, more idleness, more going without.'
> 'Come closer' somebody shouted, 'and we will cut your throat and send your guts to Churchill.'
> ... Nothing could be done with them.

Gwilym is trapped and dies underground. The story ends on the note of plangent sadness and heartfelt despair that has been in the background throughout because, of course, we have from the first page been looking back. The next thirty years of Huw's life (to 1935) are barely mentioned. They are, in truth, an irrelevance, years of social misery which are a continual, if understated, comment on the tale he tells us. Unemployment, the economic depression that is to devastate the community, and that we know, as we read in 1939, is now to come, can be taken as the curse that lack of contentment and disavowal of the old rationale will bring:

> Why is it, I wonder, that people suffer when there is so little need, when an effort of will and some hard work would bring them from their misery into peace and contentment.... The mark of shoulders rubbing in idleness was coming plain to be seen, all along the walls in the main street, telling of the thousands wasting the rich moments of their lives, with the earth offering them an abundance just beneath their feet, and given free to them, by God. Well, well.

Well, well, in truth! The scenario can only allow removal from the de-natured, de-nationalised masses. Huw and his family die or take themselves off to the (white) Dominions or (white) Patagonia. Two novels later Huw has been *Up Into the Singing Mountain* and *Down Where the Moon is Small*. Finally he comes back to where the

Valley should have been green. We have a surprise in store. It is! And for that reason it can now be almost ignored as the more central, and abiding, question of what to do about 'Wales' surfaces to fill the vacuum. This becomes the obsession of Huw as he tells us his new story (subsidised by the Welsh Arts Council) in Llewellyn's novel *Green Green My Valley Now* (1975).

The message was plugged into the sensibilities of the professional, subsidised Welsh of the 1970s because it had been simmering for half a century. It is conveyed neatly by the maps that adorn the inside covers: the back one is of the Patagonian settlement in Argentina (the acceptable face of nineteenth-century colonialisation for the Welsh) and the front one is of a bottomless Wales which starts around Builth Wells, extends north to the Lleyn peninsula and omits all of industrial South Wales. Huw, now a very rich man, does revisit his old home, about two-thirds into the novel, and is amazed at the sight. He is, in fact as well as in fiction, at Gilfach Goch where the end of the collieries in the early 1970s, did see a massive 'face lift' or grassing-over. The river runs clean. The slag is gone. So is the work and the structure of a communal culture, but Huw is there for the landscape:

> This was not the Valley I had known. From other brains another Valley had been born ... cleaner, happier, greener, than any since the time of my grandfather....
> How green was my Valley, then, yes but green, green my Valley now, all praise and thanks to the Lord God, and his craftsmen, of the gentle pen, and the giant machine.

A territorial redemption had been affected. A *deus ex machina* has rescued people who had created ugliness 'without knowing ... blind in the pits, blind in the kitchen, blind in the pubs, and blind in the pews'. And in the 1970s, still blind as they struck for more money – 'Stupidity on Stupidity, and no end except in another strike.'

For Richard Llewellyn, and in this he remained representative of a professional Welsh class that sighs and pockets the small change, sympathy for the 'masses' is connected to a belief in their submissiveness and, as an alternate, their frenzied folly. The denizens of the Valley are never credited with consciousness of any sort. They are not the agents but the victims of circumstance. Llewellyn's reductionism is, of course, crippling to the structure of his historical imagination – he cannot afford to accommodate the triumph of rebuilding a union in despite of employers' attacks in the 1930s on its very existence; the attainment of a national union of mineworkers;

the long-deferred nationalisation of the industry. The induced disillusion and run-down of the 1950s and 1960s, do not figure any
more than a new generation's struggle in the strikes of 1969 to
1974; land reclamation followed, shamefully, only in the wake of
1966 and Aberfan, the foulest coalfield disaster of them all; alternative employment did not attend spiralling pit closures or reseeded
colliery sites.

Nonetheless Llewelyn's last Welsh novel has a meaning, like his
first, which goes beyond any fictional technicolour. Unlike the first
novel, which treated themes of universal significance, the sequel
has neither the literary gambit of a child's-eye-view nor a sweeping
theme. Its compass is narrow to match the shrunken world of
Wales and the manageable proportion for which its middle class
has settled. The novel's significance lies in the logical manner with
which Huw reacts to life in contemporary Wales. 1939 is carried
forward to 1975 quite easily. It would be encouraging to speculate
that Llewellyn was being a degree or two ironic. The evidence for
such literary sophistication is as thin as Llewelyn's connection to
other visions of Wales was broad. *Green, Green My Valley Now*
makes fully explicit the latent populism of the earlier work, though
this is now tricked out with monetary authoritarianism, imbued
with linguistic shamanism and justified by a snobbish aestheticism
dressed up in national costume. South Wales, though not on the
maps, lurks everywhere, only now, in its decline, it is to be
welcomed as a verdant echo of its aberrant, temporary, past. Its
proletarian universality can have no place in a timeless Welsh
world.

Welsh political nationalism, in its recent guise, would not swallow
Llewelyn whole. But the nationalists of the 1930s, and those who
look for salvation through linguistic grace, sup at the same table. It
was Saunders Lewis who told the unemployed of the coalfield in
1935 that they should spurn government dole in return for 'Welsh
self-help', and that the '[socialist] idealism of South Wales would
lead to evil consequences and moral rottenness'; only 'the Welsh
Nationalist Party ... offered the simple life instead of the Pentecostal
Utopianism that was the curse of the country'.

When Huw Morgan returns to Wales in the 1970s he does so
with the intention of recreating that 'simple life' out of the bounty
of his purse. He had enjoyed that already in 'pure' Patagonia but
now, driven out by military corruption and with his fortunes well
secured, he seeks to buy and restore the ancestral home of his wife
in the heart of Wales. It had been abandoned for thirty years, and

left a hundred years before that when his wife's family had migrated to Patagonia to 'speak their own language, worship as they wanted, and live in freedom, with their own people about them'. No mention here, of course, of the rural distress that forced people overseas. Or of the fact that most of the Patagonian settlers, impelled by economic motives, were from the iron-works and coal-pits of the industrialising South. Even less of the discomfort, evictions, repression and subordination of the Welsh-speaking farm labourer at the hands of the Welsh-speaking tenant farmer. Nothing of the successive attempts to crush unionism and discourage literacy amongst this same class until well into this century. Why should there be? Llewellyn shared in a brand of Welsh history in which all of the past of 'the nation' is transformed into a crusade against slavery from Caractacus onwards, whilst the 'patrimony' (for this brand of national history *is* more about property than people) is lost 'to Romans, Saxons, and the brothers of the Norman bastard, and their sons, and on, until, with time, they called themselves English'.

How can 'Wales' be saved? Self-government is one possibility, with a new 'business' party formed if 'fact and cold reality' can be overcome. More to the point – and in a chilling representation of the actual domestication and privatisation of Welsh public life – 'Wales' can be transformed into a house. Huw solicits help to scour the Welsh countryside for genuine Welsh furniture and antiques. The best canvases of young Welsh artists are purchased. Nothing fake will adorn the Welsh Shangri-La. Nothing reprehensible is occurring, of course, because 'Wales', and its magnificent patrimony, is only being rescued (by those who know and appreciate) from Americans and the ignorance of 'a rabble, each with a union card, and National Insurance, and a squintbox, and radio and some with a car, a washing machine, a mortgage, all of them bound in an idiocy, and no thought for what is to come ... and when the strikes came, or whatever, they are caught, flat, with nothing.'

An old cabinet-maker, discovered in this flurry of artistic preservation, spotlights the fatal ambivalence which contaminates all individual purchase and possession of art – its transmutation to monetary value. Once more Richard Llewellyn hoists on his own unwitting self-righteousness the listening Huw Morgan:

> 'A few years and nothing will be left. Nothing to tell what sort of workmen we were. Or if we had craftsmen in wood, or anything else. It will be another time like the Roman pillage. They took everything ... now it is pillage with money. The

people are too ignorant, too selfish to know. Two beautiful armchairs, see, and tassels on the arms, and look, now, at that brocade, will you? Perfect for looking at the telly. Hours, years of comfort after the day's work, look. Give me that old table in exchange – O, yes, take it, and thank you sir! The poor blind fools don't know the table is worth a couple of hundred times, and more, than the armchairs!'

'If you find anything you know is good, let me know', I said. 'Or buy it. You can trust me. Who's doing the pillaging?'

Who indeed? In the end the Welsh, inveterately demoralised by their crushing past, prove incapable of action. Huw and his new wife, Teleri, jet back to the South Atlantic, but not before she reminds Huw that Welsh is 'a root language of mankind ... English is an old jumble of everything.... The language of the industrial revolution.... A language of the machines. Perfect.'

Those who would colour Wales green have first to dismiss the meaning of the lives of all those who had imagined – in their politics and their struggles as much as in their daily sweat to survive – an alternative Wales. 'Imagining' Wales was the hardest, and most valuable task performed by those who lived in 'American Wales'. It remains their greatest legacy. It required not myth or nostalgia but interpretation.

All Things Betrayed Them

In Cardiff at dawn the sky is moist and grey
And the baronets wake from dreams of commerce,
With commercial Spanish grammar on their tongues;
And the west wind blows from the sorrowful seas,
Carrying Brazilian and French and Egyptian orders,
Echoing the accents of commercial success,
And shaking the tugs in the quay.
Puff, little engine to the valleys at daybreak,
To northward and westward with a voice in the dawn,
And shout to the people that prosperity's coming,
And that coal can be changed into ingots of gold,
And that Cardiff shall be famous when the sun goes down.
. . .
Down the river in the morning flow the empty corn-beef tins,
Down the river in the evening flow the curses of the crowd,
Down the river in the midnight flow the little broken dreams
Down the river through the seasons flow the dregs of all our griefs.
O little crooked shabby river hurrying down to Severn Sea,
Tell the ships of all the oceans of the tragic towns you know,
Of the aimless, hopeless mornings and the patient men who wait
In the streets and on the ridges, in the sun and in the snow.
              Idris Davies, *Gwalia Deserta* (1938)

In retrospect the late 1940s stand out as the last authentic years of that distinctive culture which had been fashioned in South Wales. Its strength had been the fusion of disparate traditions, diverse peoples and clashing ideologies. The net result had not been a new consensus but rather a novel outlook which informed and directed democratic politics, popular culture and even the language of a world intent by the early 1920s on having a say in its own making. The moment was a brief one to savour. Arguably it was effectively ended as an aggressive intention by 1921. In the economic war of attrition that followed the post-war 'stabilisation' of Britain, the miners were forced on to the defensive in ways unforeseen by pre-war conciliators or class-warriors. So far as Wales was concerned, with its mining workforce outnumbering all other occupations by at least four to one, it was a threat to the society itself. The world turned topsy-turvy very quickly.

The South Wales Miners' Federation had seriously considered affiliation in 1921 to the recently formed Red International of Labour Unions. From Moscow Lenin eagerly enquired, 'How many miners are there in England? More than 500,000? How much in South Wales? 25,000?' There were, in cold fact, more like

270,000 coalminers then employed in South Wales. Within the next fifteen years 241 coalmines closed down. The workforce was reduced in the same period of time to less than 130,000, and only rose to just over 140,000 with the onset of war. The 'Fed' which had been so powerful that its influence can be said to have permeated all of the institutional features of South Wales had been so splintered by the six-month lock-out of 1926 that it proved incapable of organising even this drastically reduced complement of men. As late as the mid-1930s only half the men employed in the coal industry in South Wales were paying dues to the union. The rest were either non-unionists through unwillingness or inability to pay or else they were in the rival, company union set up by some employers and a hard core of anti-Federation workers in the wake of 1926. This body – the South Wales Miners' Industrial Union – though relatively small, and confined to a few scattered enclaves, was a running sore which mocked the SWMF's pretension to authority over wages and hours as surely as did the dismal state of the industry itself. Worse, it derided the hopes of those who had seen the industrial muscle of an organised workforce as only the first step to wide-ranging social changes.

Perhaps the most ironic feature of the politics of the coalfield in the 1930s was the formal success achieved within this context. By 1935 the Fed had been restructured and streamlined under the pressure of the shifting balance of economic forces. It now reflected the increasing weight of the relatively unscathed western or anthracite part of the coalfield and the long-term decline of the ravaged central and eastern sections of the steam coalfield. A rank-and-file executive committee directly in touch with working miners replaced the one dominated by 'professional' miners' agents who were formally excluded. In shape and in potential it was the centralised, non-bureaucratic, rooted SWMF which the syndicalist pamphlet *The Miners' Next Step* had trumpeted in 1912. Arthur Horner's election as the first Communist President of the Fed in 1936 was a direct reflection of the changes wrought. And yet, of course, all this happened not in the expanding, triumphant world of working-class power envisaged in 1912 in Tonypandy but in a shrinking industry, amongst a battered workforce and with unemployment – structural and long-term – running into double figures that could, in places, be themselves doubled, and doubled again, like a gambler's losing streak.

It was, in these circumstances, quite remarkable that before the outbreak of the Second World War the SWMF could again boast of a hundred per cent solid organisation. This was not managed by the enforced contributions that men and owners agreed to in 'a closed shop' from 1942 but by the traditional cohesiveness insisted on, sometimes in the face of a recalcitrant minority, by the men themselves in pit after pit. The device of 'show cards' on pit-heads to indicate paid-up dues was turned into a crusade to re-build the Federation. In its own pits the Fed wore down the opposition of its employers. Where the 'scab union' was entrenched with employers' connivance only a concerted campaign of propaganda, strikes and wily negotiation could winkle the rival out. Towards the end of 1935 a series of stay-down strikes erupted in pits where non-unionists and company-unionists were ensconced.

These 'stay-downs' fired the imagination. They were a weapon of repossession. Hundreds of men remained underground in their pits across all the valleys of South Wales in an act of collective defiance that ultimately ensured the demise of company unionism. At the beginning of the year the defiance had been even more that of a whole community. Protest marches were directed against new government regulations that would have reduced unemployment assistance in addition to operating the humiliation of the means test. The ideal of 'popular front' politics became a living reality in South Wales in January and February 1935. Hundreds of thousands of people demonstrated within their valleys. The marches brought together political opponents – especially those Labour Party supporters and Communists who had denounced each other endlessly in the despairing years after 1928 – chapels and churches, men, women and children, in a cry of anger against continued injustice. In Lancashire, in Yorkshire, in Durham, in the old centres of Britain's industrial revolution, the same emotion filled the streets. In South Wales over 300,000 people were estimated to have marched in their own localities on successive weekends in cold, rainy weather in January and February 1935. The so-called National Government was forced to listen. They slapped a standstill order on their regulations. Aneurin Bevan later commented, 'Silent pain evokes no response.'

Nye Bevan himself had been elected to Parliament for Ebbw Vale in 1929. If the Fed had not been in such sore straits in the 1920s it is not inconceivable that the young miners' leader would have found his niche within the union structure. As it was that avenue for leadership was blocked to a number of Bevan's contemporaries, including one of his rivals for the Ebbw Vale candidature, Bryn Roberts, who went off to found NUPE. At the end of the

1930s the irony of the syndicalist 'capture' of the Fed's structure was echoed by the engrossing by the miners of parliamentary seats they had struggled in vain to take before 1920. Bevan then found himself in a Parliament in which thirteen of the fifteen Welsh Labour MPs who held all the coalfield seats were men who had had an official connection with the SWMF itself. The paradox was easy to unravel. The Fed had expanded to fill the gap left by the desertion of the coalfield by other, once-hopeful bodies. Bill Paynter, President of the SWMF (1951-59) and General Secretary of the NUM (1959-69), explained the link between Union, politics and society as he looked back from that other year of struggle, 1972:

> The Miners' Federation Lodges were pillars of the communities because the Miners Institutes and Welfare Halls provided places for the social and cultural activity, and their domination of the local Labour Parties decisively influenced local politics. It is not surprising, therefore, that this kind of background produces a loyalty to the Union so strong and primary that the Union is regarded as a substitute for a political organisation.

That political tandem carried an organised working class capable of representing its society into the post-1945 world. However, it was not Noah Ablett's 'working class militant' that acted as a spearhead. It was, on the contrary, the battle-hardened leadership of a determined, if chastened, working class that now manoeuvred for change through reform. It is indeed the case that at the end of the 1950s disillusion with nationalisation of the coal industry, so warmly greeted by the miners in 1947, had spread beyond minor grumbles to a heartfelt expression of lost opportunity. Nor did the Labour Party's tenure of government between 1945 and 1951, for all its major reforms, seem to have done any more than dent the brass face of capitalism.

The two leading socialists from South Wales lived out the last decade of their active political life in anger and frustration. Aneurin Bevan (b.1897) witnessed Labour's defeat in the 1959 General Election. He died in 1960. Arthur Horner (b.1894) retired as General Secretary of the NUM in 1959. He died in 1969. Since their early political visions came to be tarnished by the corrosive realities of the inter-war years and were tempered by the limitations of a new post-war consensus both men have been placed in the halls of commonsense historiography, i.e., they adjusted and compromised. If this is an accurate tactical assessment, it is more than inadequate as a description of their motivating strategy and of their representative significance for the coalfield society which formed them.

Arthur Lewis Horner was, in the words of Eric Hobsbawm, both 'the ablest leader the British miners have ever had [and] the most brilliant and capable trade union leader of twentieth-century Britain'. The boy-evangelist and boxer who had walked over the hills from Merthyr to Tonypandy in 1910 stayed in the Rhondda Valley to drink in heady draughts of Marxist economics and syndicalist strategies from the brew prepared by his mentor, Noah Ablett (1883-1935), the moving spirit behind the formation of the Marxist-orientated Central Labour College (1912-1928) and main inspiration of what was termed 'Welsh syndicalism'.

By this Ablett meant a mix of direct action and industrial unionism, on the assumption that 'political' ideas, being a superstructure arising out of the economic conditions of society, must lag behind the actual facts. In South Wales conditions were forcing trade unionists to believe that only revolutionary Socialism was possible. Could they, on the face of it, support and organise an industrial union – on a revolutionary basis – for the abolition of capitalism, and at the same time support a political party that did not go in for the abolition of capital? That was in 1910. In 1917 the SWMF agreed to alter their rules so as to include such an abolition as an aim. Ablett's 'syndicalism' was overtaken, in the early 1920s, by the Communist Party's greater capacity for sustained organisation with its coherent theory of state power.

Nonetheless, the influence of 'syndicalism', in its Welsh context, did not perish. With hindsight, Bill Paynter reflected: 'It has often been said of me that I was a miner and trade unionist first and a communist second.... I have to admit that it has a great deal of truth in it.... It was true, too, of Arthur Horner and of most leaders who have lived and worked in the mining valleys of South Wales.'

Certainly one of the reasons for this was the continuing immediacy of the Fed's power and its position. It did not have to wait as a union for a pluralist society to make up its mind and fall in line. As Aneurin Bevan said in the Rhondda in 1938 when the SWMF supported him after his expulsion from the Labour Party for advocating alliances to the left that the executive disliked and feared, the South Wales miners were 'the most class conscious, the most advanced, the most democratic section of the working class'. It was precisely in this spirit that Horner persuaded the conference called in 1944 to turn the federal MFGB into the more centralised

NUM to accept as one of its objects the rule the SWMF had underwritten in 1917:

> That there shall be contained within the Rules what is already in the South Wales Rules – our determination to work 'for the purpose of and with the view to the complete abolition of Capitalism'. We do not think that the Executive explanation that we are out for public ownership of the mining industry is tantamount or equal to the abolition of Capitalism. We cannot accept that Nationalisation of certain industries is the abolition of Capitalism.

Horner's advocacy and acceptance of nationalisation three years later must be seen within this framework of ideas as well as within that of the restricted possibilities whereby a trade union leader worked. Naturally in a society which, as the Government's 1946 Regional Survey clearly tabulated, was still teetering on the edge of deprivation in almost all of its basic amenities – from pre-1914 housing to undercapitalised pits – nationalisation was going to be welcome. But in 1947 it was also considered, especially in South Wales, to be a first step. Horner never abandoned the political faith that societies can be self-making as well as made. He, like South Wales, viewed the world in the 1940s not only from the cautious perspective of inter-war decline but also through the light of the heady possibilities that had marked out his society.

The plasticity of pre-1914 South Wales lay in a more optimistic sense of the future – economic and political – than seemed practical later. Individual and social destinies were there for the moulding. Ablett's role as a lightning conductor of these aspirations was crucial. The catalyst he emphasised was work. Work was the motor, work was the prop, work was the profit lever, work dictated the framework for their lives out of work. Control of the work process could then lead on to control of every other sort of power as the ripples of the pond spread concentrically outwards. Nationalisation in Ablett's view simply inverted the proper process. It was a con trick that substituted state control for private ownership and allowed 'ignorance in Whitehall to sit in judgment on knowledge in the Rhondda'. Ablett coolly instructed a mass audience in mid Rhondda in 1912 as the MFGB sought passage of a bill to nationalise the mines:

> The future does not lie in the direction of bureaucracy. The roadway to emancipation lies in a different direction than the offices of a Minister of Mines. It lies in the democratic organisation, and

eventually control, of the industries by the workers themselves in their organised capacity as trustees for a working class world. No Minister of Mines will lead us to our emancipation. That must be the work of the workers themselves from the bottom upward, and not from the top downward.

Ablett, and those he influenced through a network of education classes, believed that an existing working-class institution like the SWMF, with its root-and-branch structure of lodges and district councils, could be captured and then reorganised (the subtitle of *The Miners' Next Step*) in order to radiate the power that could be felt almost tangibly in the pits, the colliery villages and the eager minds of South Wales. The key to Ablett's conceptualisation of the nature of power was his profound understanding, based in work experience, of the connection between a localism that refused to be parochial and the human energies needed for social change.

It is the same confident ring that can be heard in the title of Aneurin Bevan's only book, *In Place of Fear*. When Bevan published this in 1952 he was the principal exponent of the creed of democratic socialism through Parliament. It was a position he had adapted and refined in the years of economic decline. Bevan, in describing Ablett as a 'leader of great intellectual power and immense influence', was forced to add that 'these dreams of early success did not survive the industrial depression of the twenties'. Since Bevan was also in the quest for power he concentrated on other means of attaining it. It did not take the failure of the General Strike to teach him this. He saw clearly enough that 'the essential argument had been deployed in 1919.... The leaders in 1926 were in no better theoretical position to face it.... To me the events of that time had an eerie character. It was like watching a film unfold that I had already seen made. The currents of history were running strongly against us and in the result we were sucked under.'

However, to exchange direct action ('Why cross the river to fill the pail?' Ablett had asked; Bevan's reply would have been 'Because they've diverted the water!') for the pragmatism of Parliament was not to lose the greater for the smaller, any more than accepting nationalisation in 1947 was considered the final victory: 'It has always been for me a painful spectacle when some Labour spokesman tries to justify a piece of Socialist legislation on exclusively "practical" grounds. There are at least two considerations to be kept in mind when making policy: its applicability to the immediate situation certainly, but also its faithfulness to the general body of principles which make up your philosophy.'

Aneurin Bevan dealt with reality by shuffling dreams. He was the supreme product of his people's social imagination. In a sense his own style of thought and expression turned his life into a living novel. If by fiction we mean an imaginative ordering of experience designed to uncover the real traits of human life, then Aneurin Bevan was his own greatest creation. The word 'rhetoric' is a snide cliché lamely applied to the speeches of a man who was intent on argument and explication not demagoguery and pyrotechnics. His wit was intimate. His expression was lucid. He was the eternal gate-crasher who dared to question the existence of the gates:

> The first function of a political leader is advocacy. It is he who must make articulate the wants, the frustration, and the aspiration of the masses.... A representative person is one who will act in a given situation in much the same way as those he represents would act in that same situation. In short, he must be of their kind [and speak] with the authentic accents of those who elected him. That does not mean he need be provincial.... It does mean he should share their values ... be in touch with their realities.

Aneurin Bevan knew that his South Wales had, in his own lifetime to 1952, walked a tightrope between 'aspirations' and 'realities' that gave its history awesome implications. The politics of his world, so swiftly and intensely brought to a premature fruition, were invested with a vibrating sense of expectation. He knew precisely what he meant when he wrote that 'abstract ideas which ignite [the] mind are those to which ... experience provides a reference'. His formative years had been spent in a Tredegar and, by extension, a South Wales that was buzzing with ideas.

It is this which gives such poignancy to his overall career. It has also made it too easy to ally his political frustration to his physical decline in the context of a more general shrivelling of the ambition and ideals of his society. A concentration on the events (the 'facts') of Bevan's life not only takes the intellect out of his response but, worse, denies the fusion of 'abstract ideas' and 'experience' which Bevan exemplified. Those who interpret Bevan and his society in this way inevitably mistake decline and loss for despair and defeat.

The sophistication of his message has been blurred by the betrayal of the hopes of his generation and by the intermittent failure to depict his coalfield world other than through romance or paraphrase. For its significant shape we have to attend to the word of those politicians who were more concerned to embody it than to administer it, and to those writers who were perfectly attuned to its tortuous ironies.

The literary question was how to discover a form that could embrace a distinctly non-traditional content. Any number of writers tried. Some enjoyed a contemporary reputation. Three of them, two self-taught coalminers who became writers and a university-educated schoolmaster, produced literature whose style worked like a scalpel on the dead-weight of their material. Their common dilemma was how to indicate a collective history that did not exclude the individual but refused to separate that experience from that of the society. Their common solution was to slough off naturalism, whether gritty or romantic, and replace the doomed attempt to document reality with a fictional world whose own reality was a comment on the world it attempted to represent. The art of Aneurin Bevan in reverse.

The poet, Idris Davies (1905-1953), a coalminer until 1926, was often uncertain about his exact role in and attitude towards a society in which he was nonetheless frozen. The novelists Lewis Jones (1897-1939) and Gwyn Thomas (1913-1981), the former a coalminer and leader of the unemployed, the latter an Oxford-trained linguist cum teacher, entertained no such doubts. These three were, in very different ways, crushed by the burden of truth-telling they imposed on themselves.

Idris Davies, born in Rhymney 'to a collier and his wife', walked a tightrope between a burning disgust for the messy despondency of industrial Wales and a firm recognition of the validity of its communal defences. It was only when the latter seemed to be atrophying in the early 1950s that he looked more ardently for a 'national' solution that could offer redress, perhaps through the traditions of history and the tranquillity of a rural life. Of the three writers, only Idris Davies was Welsh-speaking, and this has given him much retrospective interest in the eyes of sympathetic 'nationalist' readers who have argued that his Housman-like, clickity-clacking rhymes prove the impossibility of using the English language to demonstrate the broken-backed nature of his Welsh community. By making both poet and poetry, form and content, simpler than is the case, the subtlety of Idris Davies' choral drama has, until quite recently, been missed.

Critics have now recognised him as a major poet of socialist lyrics. This judgment rests principally on his two collections *Gwalia Deserta* (1938), thirty-six poems which deal with the rise and fall of South Wales, and *The Angry Summer: A Poem of 1926* (1943) which, in fifty poems, takes us through the industrial defiance and defeats of the 1920s. The fact that Idris Davies' father was a colliery engine winding-man, and therefore an aristocrat of labour, may have planted the seeds of incipient 'petit-bourgeois deviation' that some gimlet-eyed analysts have spotted in Davies' wobbling political analysis. Certainly his later verse is vacuous. His gestures become those of the outstretched palm rather than the clenched fist.

Some of the change was wrought by his transformation from a coalminer into a schoolteacher. He became a 'poetic' observer of people and events he had once seen from the inside. His taste of the Rhondda in 1942 came when he was evacuated with his English school and it appears to have come as a shock, perhaps because the packed life of Rhondda was less balanced than his own Rhymney Valley upbringing, perhaps because the latter was now swathed in the memory of a different personal and public past. In the Rhondda he met those he considered 'the narrowest and most vulgar people I have met anywhere' and insisted that he had 'got rid of all my political illusions'.

Although he did hymn the Labour triumph of 1945 as a 'socialist victory' his deepest impulses became a yearning for, almost a dream about, the 'Wales' that had once existed in the West and, as far as the coalfield now attracted his attention, a humanistic cry of 'enough is enough'. The last verse of his 1945 poem 'A Carol for the Coalfield' closes the door on the false rhetoric of the poem's refrain 'That the future shall be greater than the past':

> *Last night the moon was full above the slag heaps and the grave-yards*
> *And the towns among the hills, and a man arose from his dream*
> *And cried out: Let this day be sufficient, and worthy of my people*
> *And let the night winds go on wailing of the future and the past.*

It is a measure of Idris Davies' achievement that we can readily accord the bruised sentiment its full worth. He knew, after all, what had already been endured by 1945. Even so, in terms of the history he had unpicked in his earlier poetry, this was a retreat of the imagination. No longer would he weave public events, official pronouncements and individual dramas in a cunning combination of dramatic monologue and commentary that oscillated from indignation to ironic acceptance. Idris Davies, in two verses, had been able to reveal why A.J. Cook's hold on the miners in 1926 was not cerebral but visceral, and why the more this shiningly brave man was loved the more he was denounced:

> *Here is Arthur J. Cook, a red rose in his lapel,*
> *Astride on a wall, arousing his people,*
> *Now with a fist in the air, now a slap to the knee,*

Almost burning his way to victory!
And tomorrow in all the hostile papers
There will be sneers at Cook and all his capers,
And cowardly scribblers will be busy tonight
Besmirching a warrior with the mud of their spite.
The Angry Summer

The poetry of Idris Davies which proclaimed this emotion for 1926 and all it entailed was also able to assess the society which had become too frozen in the cold 1930s for anything humane, or innocent, or natural to thaw. Idris Davies contemplated a South Wales coalfield that demanded a power of mind to dissect its ambivalent state.

The village of Fochriw grunts among the higher hills;
The dwellings of miners and pigeons and pigs
Cluster around the little grey war memorial.
The sun brings glitter to the long street roofs
And the crawling promontories of slag,
The sun makes the pitwheels to shine,
And praise to the sun, the great unselfish sun,
The sun that shone on Plato's shoulders,
That dazzles with light the Taj Mahal.
The same sun shone on the first mineowner,
On the vigorous builder of this brown village,
And praise be to the impartial sun.
He had no hand in the bruising of valleys,
He had no line in the vigorous builder's plans,
He had no voice in the fixing of wages,
He was the blameless one.
And he smiles on the village this morning.
He smiles on the far-off grave of the vigorous builder,
On the ivied mansion of the first mineowner,
On the pigeon lofts and the Labour Exchange,
And he smiles as only the innocent can.

For Idris Davies the brute indifference of the outside human world could not inspire him with the same passionate anger once his idealised working-class community presented him no public aspect other than a vulgar one. He literally missed out, through physical absence in training college and teaching in England, on the revitalisation of the coalfield's politics that came in the mid-1930s. If he had remained at work in South Wales there can be little doubt that he would have avoided the personification of his theme (in the person of Dai, the miner he addresses in *Tonypandy*, 1945) as a helpless, hopeless recipient of fate. The latter was a wonderful blanket with which to douse the collective embers. Idris Davies was a social poet because there was no other way to indicate the interaction of a people and a history without betraying their lives. After 1926 and the creeping impoverishment of the coalfield, most writers found it more convenient to look for Pavlovian responses as the cause of behaviour.

Apart from Richard Llewellyn who substituted the romance of the forties for the documentary of the thirties right at that decade's end, the most successful purveyor of South Wales realism was Jack Jones. His episodic novel, *Rhondda Roundabout* (1934), was turned into a play which reached the West End stage and no doubt elicited charitable feelings towards those who no longer posed a threat: Jack Jones writes of South Walians who are strong-hearted, good-natured, hard-working people but who have been unluckily afflicted by the Depression and hence are embittered by poverty. The last chapter of *Rhondda Roundabout*, entitled 'May-Day in Heartbreak Valley', has the leading character, Dan Price BA, a young minister, watching a march:

> Stretched out in fours for about a quarter of a mile behind the leaders were the rank and file of Rhondda Communism, many carrying banners on which could be read 'Down with the Means Test' and 'Down' with many other things besides. A platoon here and there sang and there were many women carrying babies who marched at their husbands' sides. A few of those lining the streets tittered now and then as the procession marched by, but Dan saw nothing to laugh at. What he saw were rows of careworn faces, faces which had looked in many directions for help and guidance before becoming bitter and turning to Communism as the last hope.
>
> 'Please, God, help them' he murmured as the last section of fours marched by him, and it may have been that it was then that he decided to continue serving God in the Rhondda.

The appeal of this genre of writing lay in its hand-wringing, heart-rending care, in its simplistic analysis and its implied solution. Philanthropy and guidance can undo the radicalism which springs from bitter, unwarranted poverty. Intellectual decisions, anger, self-consciousness, class consciousness and the education of work itself are shunted to one side. The significance for others of the coalfield saga is reduced to a limited, transitory, almost parochial, misfortune in the eternal pattern of human destiny or, as *The Times*' special correspondent had written to enlighten that paper's readers in 1928: 'The coal valleys bear the marks, psychological as well as physical, of having been the arena for a scramble by everybody, high and low, for quick money. The miner, still intensely religious, especially on Sundays, has lost his light heart and taken to politics.'

The convenience of this diagnosis is that social miseries are unnatural mishaps of the present, so any social and political disquiet can be taken as temporary in its cause, unusual in its incidence. The present becomes a norm, acceptable, natural, and where the distress of any actual, present existence does intervene, the perpetual present can always be located in an eternally stable past that waits to be delivered into the future.

The melodramatic quality of the inter-war history of the mining valleys invited caricature. What it needed was insight. The one writer uniquely equipped to run the fictional gamut from the 1890s to the 1930s was the communist activist Lewis Jones. His second novel, published in 1939 after his death in January of that year, was not round about or suggestive of individual escape. Its title was plural, and defiant: *We Live*. With its predecessor, *Cwmardy* (1937), the novel spans a shifting history which brilliantly evokes the open-endedness of the lives of the people of Cwmardy. Lewis Jones spent all his short life amongst the inhabitants of the Rhondda. He does not back away from their ordinariness nor worry over their 'vulgarity'. Although the ostensible hero of his novels is Len, a sensitive boy whose life as miner, communist and volunteer for the Spanish Civil War, acts to intensify the broader story, his major protagonist is Len's father, Big Jim, whose unconquerable spirit is the foundation for Len's political sacrifice.

In these novels the community's growing consciousness that its only salvation derives from class politics is never just imposed as a diagrammatic overlay. The question of control is raised and answered in a narrative that moves through the events in which people discovered the issues for themselves. We follow the development of characters in their society, from Tonypandy in 1910 to the strikes of the 1920s and into internecine left-wing politics, before the novel reaches the stirring stay-downs and popular unity of the late 1930s.

Lewis Jones had an intimate acquaintance with all these things. He had been born in the mid-Rhondda in 1897, became the youngest-ever chairman of the Cambrian Colliery Lodge at the end of the First World War, went to the Central Labour College, where his two-year stint overlapped with that of Aneurin Bevan, and emerged after 1926 as a dazzlingly gifted platform orator and organiser of the unemployed. Lewis Jones' deeply meditated

Marxist perspective enabled him to probe the immediacy of his own life by placing it within a framework of development. His account of the 1935 marches is, like all his best writing, pregnant with a future that is not forced but which is, because the marchers can feel it themselves, available:

> By this time the head of the demonstration had reached the square, which was dense with people cordoned off to make way for the demonstration to pass through to the assembling field.... For over half an hour the people of Cwmardy poured through the square which was their ancient battle-ground into the field where most of their vital decisions had been taken....
>
> The bands, each with its own vivid and distinctive uniform, were scattered at regular intervals through the length of the demonstration, adding to its vivacity and colour. A bugle sounded, drums rolled once more, the bands took up the refrain, and the procession began to unwind itself from the field [and] marched twelve abreast through the main street, most of whose shop windows still wore shutters as mementoes of past battles.
>
> When the front of the demonstration was two miles advanced, and on the summit of the hill to the east of Cwmardy, people were still pouring from the assembling field. Len lifted his head sharply into the air when he fancied he heard the distant strains of music in the direction left of the demonstration. He turned to Mary and the workman next to her.
>
> 'Can you hear anything?' he asked.
>
> They both looked simultaneously past Len, and he, seeing their amazement, turned his head to look in the same direction. He drew his breath sharply and his perspiring face went a shade whiter. The mountain which separated Cwmardy from the other valleys looked like a gigantic ant-hill, covered with a mass of black, waving bodies.
>
> 'Good God,' the man next to Mary whispered, 'the whole world is on the move.'
>
> Mary did not reply for some time, unable to take her eyes from the scene, although her feet kept automatically moving her forward in time with the band. Then she murmured, 'No, not yet. But the people are beginning to move it now.' She said no more, and even the bands were quiet. The people seemed overwhelmed with the mighty demonstration of their own power, which they could now see so clearly. Their voices suddenly became puny, and articulation was left to their feet, which rattled and sang on the roadways with music more devastating in its strength than all the bands in the world.

Lewis Jones never had to contemplate either the eventual decline of the Communist Party's influence in the post-war world as it signally failed to melt people into Party even in South Wales, or the dribbling away of the collective energies he had actually seen. This does not mean, anymore than it did with Bevan or Horner, that his practical attainments as a political activist were fruitless. In his life and thought he balanced the need to succour life as it was and the need for human dignity that is only possible when such succour becomes a secondary consideration. His role was to embody his interpretation during his lifetime. He was, said his youthful friend and admirer, Gwyn Thomas, 'a high priest of self-expression [who] was constantly hinting at the need to deepen our wisdom, our sophistication; that we must cease to be simple'.

Gwyn Thomas, born the youngest in a family of twelve in the Rhondda, was twenty-two when he watched, spellbound, those gargantuan human processions of 1935. He had become – like 'a cuckoo, an anthropological freak' he said – a student at the universities of Oxford and Madrid. His response, too, was to seize on the meaning of these protests in terms of mass power and revolutionary upsurge. The fact that, like Idris Davies, he was personally able to break away never made any difference to Gwyn Thomas' sense of being umbilically tied to all those things which filled him with the anger for creative energy. His first novel, *Sorrow for Thy Sons*, bristled with fury. It lay in his drawer for about fifty years and was only published in 1986.

It is unlike his later work in several respects. It is told in the third person and moves from the viewpoint of Alf who remains unemployed in the Valley to Hugh, his brother, who returns from college to the Valley; hardly anything of the familiar hyperbolic wit surfaces in a prose that is relatively spare. Characterisation is apt and conventional. At the same time the dialogue, the internalised speeches (in letters and in conversation), as well as the tension between utter hopelessness and determined action signal Gwyn Thomas' interests. In this book Gwyn Thomas deals with the politics of the unemployed and the public occasions of the 1930s in a more direct fashion than he later devised. The outside world is presented, through Hugh's eyes, as sublimely uncaring of the fate of the unemployed. He writes from college to tell Alf of the uselessness of any appeal:

> When I came here first I tried to explain to them about the valleys I came from. I told them exactly why we thought that bailiffs, policemen and preachers were basic elements of that ceaseless, maddening oppression that makes such a sordid, miserable mess of nine out of ten lives that see the light between

the hills of a mining valley. I thought they'd understand. That understanding is part of the intelligence with which we are born and it stays with us until we go to earth, unless in the meantime the zeal of our parents turns us into a bailiff, a policeman or a preacher. But these people didn't understand. They thought I was being smart and witty. They looked pleased at having discovered a fresh talent. They told me they'd have me back to tea again when the weather was not so sultry. As far as I can see at present, these people are the real strength of society. We protest with words. They would answer back with forms of violence that we would never dream of. Even when our hatred of unemployment, want, insecurity and avoidable disease is at its angriest and most violent, we have doubts about how far our anger and violence can go, and how best to direct them. These people have no doubts. Their cause, in their eyes, is sacredly, unquestionably just, and exclusive of all fears and hesitations. Having no doubts, they have rid themselves of the most damnable hindrance known to human activity. It makes them invincibly strong. There is something serene in the completeness of their armoury. It makes me afraid and draws my horns in. It brings me up to the conclusion that I had best look after myself and those who are closest to me, and let the rest of the world go to hell where it rightly belongs.

Hugh's return home does nothing to convince him otherwise. He notes with scepticism the attempts to arrange marches against the new means test regulations. The brothers walk home from a meeting of local politicians:

> On their way down the hill the two brothers said very little. Alf dragged at a cigarette that had broken in his pocket. He held his fingers tightly over a puncture in the paper. Hugh had his hands stuck into his overcoat pockets.
> 'Impossible!' Hugh said.
> 'What is?'
> 'Sixty or seventy thousand people in the streets on Sunday. Stupid optimism.'
> 'The streets are pretty long. There might be room for a couple of thousand more.'
> 'You've got too much faith in the valley dwellers.'
> 'It's you've lost touch. You don't know them like you used to.'
> 'They are not the same as they used to be. I remember a fire in their eyes strong enough to drive the rainstorms from the pavement. Where is it gone?... The old militancy is dead. The brains of men and women don't produce militancy. It's the speed at which life is lived at does that. When the coalowners made a riot out of profit making, the workers lived in a riot of

178

dissipation or revolt. When the oppressors slackened their tempo, so did the workers.'

'The oppression remains unchanged. It never slackens.'

'Changed in quality then. For so many people unemployment is the end of the world. Why should they struggle to change a world they think is going to end? It's a slow grinding agony, Alf. First it drives you to thoughts of terrorism. But the oppression of the Labour Exchange is so subtle, so persuasive, and man's got such an urge to be as the cattle are, that thought gives way to a quiet, starving, surprised sort of tolerance, an existence that has no interest, no value, no responsibilities.'

It is the turning point of 1935 which brings the novel towards its conclusion. Hugh will, in the final sentence, leave the valley but not before its quaking indignation has changed his mind, and lit up the minds of others. The sensation of a world-in-the-balance is conveyed by Gwyn Thomas, too. Hugh Evans will not be representative of 'the people' in the manner of Lewis Jones' sacrificial hero, Len Roberts, but the moment echoes beyond 1935 for Gwyn Thomas:

Sunday
'See then,' said Alf, stretching out his hand towards the other side of the valley. Hugh followed Alf's fingers. Down the mountain road Alf was pointing at the thousands of men, women and children, with brass band and banners, who were marching eight deep, well marshalled and singing....

The people in front of Hugh and Alf began to move. The brothers fell into step. A young boy, the son of one of the limping men, walked by Alf's side, playing a harmonica as broad as his face. The boy had a loose, undisciplined mouth and drivelled a good deal but the music he produced was sprightly. He worked on three tunes, a Welsh folk-song re-set on a rhythm basis; a tune of the American Civil War, and an anthem of the international class war. At intervals the boy's father turned round with a handkerchief in his hand and wiped the boy's mouth.

Hugh looked once more at the vast body of demonstrators who were advancing down the mountain road half a mile away. They were now approaching the bed of the valley, making for the point where their road converged with that along which Hugh's contingent was marching.

'It's significant' he said. 'Watching this is like listening to great music, only greater, much greater. Wonderful people! When they can come on to the streets at a few days' notice with ranks as firm and as solid as these, there's nothing they can't achieve. I'll never forget this moment. Here is the final answer

to all that goddam poetic loneliness I've fed on like a swine ever
since I grew to full height. Fifty thousand of the oppressed
banding together against a common injury. Strong faces. Strong
bodies marching. Strong voices singing. Strong wills....'

Silence, except for the sound of the feet and the boy's
harmonica. Hugh noticed that a lot of feet made stopping
sounds as they reached the floor as if the soles were leaving the
uppers. The sky was darkening for rain. Hugh could see no
more than three or four men who had brought raincoats. He
heard one man say he didn't care a damn if it did rain. The rain
would make people think even more than they were thinking
already, and their thoughts would flow with the rainwater into
channels of active and desperate resistance.

If Gwyn Thomas had continued to write in this mode, if indeed he
had published this novel in the 1930s, he would now be considered
one of the major proletarian writers in Britain this century. As it
was he fell silent, though not inactive, for another ten years and
first came to public notice in 1946. He was rightly regarded in
Socialist Britain as a 'voice from the Valleys' but the exuberant
comic vein which he tapped in the 1950s for increasingly grotesque
effect caused him to be misread by many. His essential intentions
as a writer had not altered. What he had crafted was a unique style
– a style of malicious obliquity, with which he was able to interpret
a history. He did not now wail over what might have been or just
celebrate what had occurred. Gwyn Thomas became the supreme
stylist of all those things that both signalled and betrayed the South
Wales coalfield as a culture.

It was not weak wills or linguistic loss or poor leadership to
which he directed our attention but the crushing material deprivation that made surviving by being inhuman into a virtue. Instead
of describing the historical protests that had repudiated this form
of subtle enslavement he concentrated on the insignificant, petty
details of life that marked the passage of these people's lives more
regularly and more glumly than any sudden burst of light. Then he
assembled a narrative 'voice' which was really a choral commentary on the relationship between the mundane basis of life and the
philosophies, religion, ambitions and ideologies that sought to
shape attitudes. His theme was hypocrisy, betrayal, absurdity,
courage, and, above all, intellect. His characters, stripped thread-
bare in numbing poverty and left on a refuse heap of broken
humanity, are, by that very fact, in life as in fiction, free to see and
to talk, with coruscating satire, of the follies of the world. They are
the witnesses of one of the greatest tragedies in Welsh history.

What gave his early writing such intensity (six books published between 1946 and 1952) and gave his own voice, in conversation, such thrilling passion, was his intellectuality. He wrote and talked about working-class life in Wales with deliberate verve and humour ('I think my humour shows the way in which the intellect of the Welsh working class might have developed their world') in order to assimilate their experience into his own. Unlike any other writer of his generation on these themes, what he recounted was not community warmth or political solidarity or sentimental hearts or family sacrifice or individual release or even the heroic submission to a manual labour that killed you bit-by-bit so that you might live piece-by-piece. His writing, and the history of South Wales, would be much more readily forgettable if it did recount such things. *The New York Times* said of his early work that it was about 'scarecrows on a refuse tip'. The grimness of the image was exact but Gwyn Thomas' desire was to reveal the wonder of what these twentieth-century equivalents of Baudelaire's rag-pickers had discovered for themselves. His subject was, he once said, 'the underlying threnody – the intellectual climate discovered by them.'

Between 1946 and 1949 he published *Where Did I Put My Pity? – Folktales from the Modern Welsh*, *The Dark Philosophers*, *The Alone to the Alone* and *All Things Betray Thee* (the latter two published under different titles in the United States). The first three books are set in the 1930s; only the last deals with public upheavals – ostensibly, a revolt of ironworkers in Merthyr in the 1830s – but it, too, is really an operatic reflection on the nature of human commitment and betrayal. Raymond Williams called it 'a remarkable creative achievement', something which applies to all of Gwyn Thomas' writing during his first great burst of energy. His appropriate form was a string of tragi-comic fables that cannot really be called 'novels' any more than his late 'plays' were really performable. Their puzzle is the enigma that has now shrouded the historical meaning of the coalfield itself. The code can be broken by letting go of prior assumptions about depth of characterisation, plots serving as more than washing-lines for hanging the narrative, and conclusions being justly resolved by development.

In October 1950 he replied to an unexpected fan letter and gift from the New York poet and playwright Norman Rosten, with whom he kept up an intermittent correspondence until 1954. Rosten had clearly wondered about the meaning and nomenclature employed in the fiction which was enjoying a vogue of popularity amongst left-wing intellectuals in America. He wrote:

61 *Porthkerry Road,*
Barry, Glam.
Oct 30, 50.

Dear Norman Rosten,

Many thanks for your letter. It was a kind and delightful gesture, the sort of pleasant surprise which more than makes up for the almost sombre lack of success, in strictly commercial terms, which the books had when they came out. Fortunately for me, the background and experiences which gave me the material to produce the books gave me also the patient understanding to accept as a sufficient and fine reward the occasional appreciation of isolated and shrewd connoisseurs of the human scene like yourself. 'The Terraces' of course are a fragment of the Rhondda Valley in the mid part of this county where we knew incredibly bitter distress in the 20s and 30s. In a life which has given us few enough things to be glad about, I account myself pleased that a few publishing firms here and one in America have given me the chance, with barely any gains for themselves, to express some part of the spirit of these brave, lyrical and sardonic people.... No, I have never thought of turning the stories into plays. As far as the London theatre is concerned, just the faintest whiff of this type of material would have managers and actors howling for the police. That you, as a playwright, should feel tempted to try an adaptation makes me feel very happy.

*I am sending you, under separate cover, another volume of mine called 'Where Did I Put My Pity?'. This is an early work, not published in America, and, as you will see, very badly produced by a young and unsuccessful firm in the years just after the war when materials were in poor supply. But in this book I think I most vividly express what I felt about the Rhondda. Please accept it from me by way of gratitude for the very nice things you said about the other two books.**

With all best wishes,
I am,

Sincerely yours,
Gwyn Thomas.

---

* *This is not an example of the fulsomeness which is reckoned to be the characteristic vice of the Celt. In the mounting lunacy and desolate hatreds of our time, such intimations of kinship and sympathetic solidarity as I found in your letter are beginning to acquire a lovely and deepening pathos.*

G.T.

In other words Gwyn Thomas' books are a refraction beyond

other people's fiction of his own observed society. There is scarcely any descriptive matter, of landscapes, buildings, rooms, meals or even faces; and politics, strikes and pit explosions, the very stuff of most coalfield literature, either do not figure or have happened, muffled, off-stage. Nothing is brought to a final climax, though some matters are sorted out along the way; the only light that shines is from the minds of those brave enough not to succumb either to mindless temptations (money, the flesh) or to passive acceptance of those who mistake power for value, wealth for wisdom. There is understanding but no forgiveness of those who do. These are the concluding words of his 1946 novella, *The Dark Philosophers*:

> 'You should have known' said Ben 'that if he got worked up he would die.'
> 'Why not?' asked Walter. 'How else would you want it? How else could it be?'
> We shook our heads, saying neither yes nor no, but feeling that wisdom, though sweet, is hard as the hills.

A year later he wrote at the end of his bleakly named work *The Alone to the Alone*: 'And we, for another interlude, went back to our wall, to trace the circular, intricate thoughts that came to us as the down sag of our half baked being found comfort, in the hard, shrewd upthrust of well baked brick.'

This task of imaginative reconstruction of the zany social and economic absurdities of a real world led him to fictional devices as complete, as total in their enclosed way, and as apposite as William Faulkner's invention of Yoknapatawpha County in Mississippi was for *his* defeated, bypassed world. Rhythms and mannerisms of speech, not verisimilitude, in plot or dialogue, re-presented the history that had been articulated positively by political and industrial leaders. He inverted the mirror. Powerless people became 'the voters', harmless observers of life are 'elements' or 'rodneys' or – if their talk becomes 'refulgent with dreams' – 'dark philosophers'. Blighted villages bear grandiloquent names, replete with sylvan charm – 'Ferncleft', 'Moonlea', 'Meadow Prospect', and their undeniable collective presence is softened into 'the Terraces'. His fiction is an adventure into life not a spurious documentation.

As is now well established, Gwyn Thomas' style was modelled on American writers who also had discarded mimetic representation. His direct models in the 1940s were the wits, absurdists and satirists who inverted the urban scene they observed in New York

City – echoes, and more, of S.J. Perelman, Robert Benchley and notably Damon Runyon can be readily detected. But, so too can the harder edge and more laconic prose of Dashiell Hammett and Raymond Chandler, and the early work of Hemingway as it influenced them and so much of modern prose as it fragmented into the glinting shards which alone managed a kaleidoscopic replication of a shattered post-1918 world. Gwyn Thomas as a citizen was a denizen of the wasteland of post-First World War Wales but as an aspiring writer he was the beneficiary of a branch of English-language writing which had no English equivalent. This is what made him a Welsh writer. His society, after all, had been 'American Wales'. His genius was to connect the essence of that meaning to a mode of telling. His work cannot be disassociated from that conjunction of style and social purpose without de-historicising it. Only cloth-eared, ahistorical historians seem unable to hear the evidence before them. Readers at the time knew why American writers of the hard-boiled and the humourist school spoke so eloquently to their own condition. And in the case of one such reader his most creative burst of writing stemmed as directly from that as from his conviction that the history he had to dramatise demanded a new way of being voiced. For a time both writer and society claimed the lead position as their 'world elsewhere' mocked the notion of any centre, geographical or historical, that might delimit their ambition or their reality.

Ann Douglas' summation in *Terrible Honesty: Mongrel Manhattan in the 1920s* (1995) of what happened when 'classic American literature' emerged on the other side of The Great War takes us straight to the apparent enigma of 'American Wales' deepest writer.

With the Great War, America's 'world elsewhere' became the here and now. People always ask from literature the description of their world as they know it; they always want to see their image in the mirror, as Henry James remarked. But the Great War showed much of the West that what the world had seemed to be just prior to the outbreak of the war, the world people still saw out their windows in the postwar decade, the world the English narrative had described with matchless fidelity, inventiveness, and depth, was not, somehow, the 'real world' at all. The indescribable 'world elsewhere' that the American narrative tradition was concerned with was, however unfamiliar or displaced it seemed, the real 'real world'. When the world seems itself to be 'switched' or displaced from its course, the funhouse mirror reflects most accurately the object, or the person, as it really is. Officially to devalue conventional mimesis, as the Great War did, was to create a critical atmosphere in which, though the narrative preferences of Melville and Twain – their refusal or inability to play conventional storyteller, coherent plotter, and consistent delineator of place and character – might still feel like limitations to readers of their work, they could no longer disqualify them from the front ranks of authorship....

If the subject of the English novel had been society, that of the French narrative tradition the mind, that of the German school the metaphysical sensibility, that of Russian literature the soul, the central preoccupation of classic American literature lay in the mood and the psyche where it originates: the abrupt fluctuations and disturbances of people's perceptions of life and themselves, as vague as a malaise and as sharp as a gambler's hunch, the troubling traces of something that leaves many footprints but no trail, that is all clues and no substance, something people know as well and as little as they know themselves.

In his 1946 novella, *Oscar*, we are given a disturbing allegory for the whole of coalfield history. The 'villain' is Oscar, a fat, lecherous drunkard who owns a mountain on which a coal tip has slowly grown. On this tip work the hopeless, passive 'pickers' employed by Oscar. They scrabble for left-over coal from the pits where they once worked. The 'hero' is Lewis, the boy who eventually decides to kill Oscar by pushing him off the mountain.

> I have never felt as fully wise as I felt then. I had never before known when all the old stupidities, all the old doubts, have been laid to rest. And I knew, too, that thousands of people who slept in their cramped, terraced houses on the sides of the mountain would nod their brave, tired, friendly faces in agreement with what I wanted to do.

Lewis does kill Oscar but he has been 'Oscar's boy', taunted, even sexually, because of his willingness to act as a supervisor of pickers and general factotum. No one else has the energy to be offensive, except verbally, as Oscar takes – money, workers, and their women – whenever he wants. But who allows this? The crushed 'picker', called No Doubt because he found this phrase the easiest way to reply to any query, especially official ones, since it 'is quite harmless to governments and kings and bishops and so on'; Danny, who wastes away in working for Oscar; Hannah, his wife, who turns to Oscar for that warmth of well-being which Danny had never been able to provide. But Hannah had intended to beat Oscar's brains in, Danny shoots at him, and even No Doubt, Lewis reflects, 'with all his talk of love for mountains, must hate that tip deeply, but the hates of a voter like No Doubt must be so deep and silent ... they had probably got all tangled and did not mean anything any more, bumping into one another and being battered instead of shooting outwards and battering the things he hated.'

When Lewis has murdered Oscar he feels only the pity of the waste. He is, of course, in his endless waiting in the rain outside the yellow windows of cheery pubs, tied irredeemably to Oscar. They all are, caught in their parody of a relationship to the mode of production, not even cutting coal any more, unemployed, or mere pickers. With their lack of any meaningful work they also lack any chance of control, of individual release. They are trapped. A violent action is only momentarily cathartic because there is no imaginable future.

A response through institutions to the depredations of the 1930s was not the next step the miners were supposed to take, according to the 'syndicalist' tract *The Miners' Next Step* in 1912; indeed it was a clear continuation of the social welfarism so despised by the authors of that pamphlet – the bureaucratic dispensation of pap by those who were set up as leaders. And it is in this sense that the cul-de-sac of *Oscar* is the alter ego of the potential of syndicalism just as, in such a short spell, the image in the mirror of society had been cruelly inverted.

Gwyn Thomas wrote for a people who had voted in the first majority Labour government, intent on social reconstruction and including ex-miners Bevan at the Ministry of Health and James Griffiths, ex-President of the SWMF, concerned with industrial welfare, and with Arthur Horner, leader of the British miners. A time of action, clearly; a time of hope. And also a time to remember, to catalogue, to analyse the social miseries all this urgent reformism was supposedly ending.

Gwyn Thomas looked back in his anger, and the values of religious belief, the rights of property ownership, the worth of love, maternal, paternal and sexual, were, along with a clutch of other faking aids to survival, picked up, mulled over and laid indecently down. The rich comic vein of metaphor and simile scarcely managed, in these early works, to keep the black bile of his ink from staining every page. His terse, accusatory, elliptical language gives us a verbal version of Goya's dark, condemning cartoons. He has no political party to whisk down from the clouds in a burst of light. After all, for most people, that was not what happened. At the same time he is painfully aware of how clearly some people in his South Wales were brought to see, and often how general that vision became. So over 'the Terraces' roams the collective presence of the narrator (Ben, Arthur, Walter, and John) who speaks as 'We'. What they examine are the relationships humanity constructs around sex, money, bureaucracy, the state, fear, greed and poverty. The role of the 'dark philosophers' is to encourage the full revelation of self-deceit and stupidity. They are men of hard minds and, for those who will not or cannot learn, hard hearts.

In *The Dark Philosophers* the Rev Emmanuel Prees is a pre-1914 hell-fire preacher who turns, under threats to his livelihood, to a more quiescent social religion. It is he they eventually drive to his death. The reasons for their final pitilessness are established, in a precise social and historical context, at the beginning of the novella. The battle between them is about 'faking':

> From that point on he developed the gentle, fatherly manner of pulpit talking, which led people to believe he was conversing with them rather than preaching to them. Nor had he any reason to preach, for preaching is passion and with what passion can a man stand up and advance a thousand reasons why the golden rule of life should be devotion to the wealthy and obedience to an order that may be condemning his closest neighbours to a lifetime's diet of worried wondering.
>
> It was he who said, when soldiers were sent into our valley to bring the great strikes to an end, that we should give warm welcome to the soldiers and return forthwith to work, inspired with a dutiful terror. He described as cannibals such people as my friend Ben, who saw no point in these soldiers, and claimed that they could be keeping the peace and passing on the time more profitably elsewhere. Emmanuel argued that the soldier was simply our well-beloved brother, for was he not doing the duty that was imposed upon him by the whole family, which was the State.
>
> Whenever there was upheaval in some foreign land, there would he a procession of refugees from that land filing through Emmanuel's pulpit, with quivers full of piety, singing ballads of a sad and lowering sort like 'Russia, Holy Russia, I will die to set you free', and telling a sackful of stories about their narrow escape from the grip of the half-dozen or so godless persecutors who were at the bottom of all this trouble.
>
> My friend Walter was convinced that these refugees were all people from the next valley, trained in the part by Emmanuel and Mr Dalbie, fitted with shawls, an overborne look and accents that only a police dog could follow, and released in clutches of suitable size as revolt succeeded revolt.
>
> During the first world war, Emmanuel called for the lynching

of so many Germans we wrote to ask him where he thought he was going to get all the time and rope needed for such a heavy programme. Then, during the age of unemployment that came upon us at the war's end, it was Emmanuel, clairvoyant and bland almost to the point of magic, who saw most clearly that golden days were just around the corner, that all we had to do now was trust in the skill and kindliness of our betters, grow stocks of potatoes and have faith in faith.

Another item in this recipe of how to go through ten kinds of social hell and still not feel that anything is amiss, was that we should keep our self-respect fresh and sound during this period of trial, as if self-respect were something you could store away under the bed during such times as you were not using it for ordinary purposes.

In this and other prose fiction Gwyn Thomas wrote down to the early 1950s, all the history of a social formation is taken for granted, as is mass emigration, long-term unemployment and even the return of employment with light industries and war preparation, so that our noses are rubbed up hard both against what he calls 'a lying culture' with its predatory bankers, solicitors, preachers and shopkeepers, and against the dreadful material causation of stupidity, of faking. The opening words of *The Alone to the Alone* parody 'And the greatest of these is charity'.

In the Terraces, we never opposed love. The way we viewed this question was that love must be pretty deeply rooted to have gone on for so long. One would have to be very deep to tinker with so deep a root, deeper than we were. Also, love passes the time. That is a prime feature in any place where there is a scarcity of work for the local men and women to do, a state which prevailed on a high plane indeed during the dark years now being spoken of. Also, love, properly used, keeps people warm. That is a fact of some importance when coal has to be considered as part of the groceries. Also, love, possessing the power of making its subjects see things in a clearer light, creates a desire for beauty. This was interesting to us because if there was one thing the Terraces lacked more than any other it was that very beauty.

Our group which met nightly on the wall at the bottom of our back yard was agreed that never had so little beauty been compressed into so large a space as we saw in the Terraces. It was a clumsy bit of packing altogether. We took this in our solemn way to mean that when men consent to endure for too long the sadness of poverty and decline, beauty sees no point in staying, bows its head and goes. There was much poverty in the Terraces, nearly as much as air, weather or life. It achieved a variety of flavours and shapes that did credit to our originality and patience. Beneath its layers beauty lay in a mess and, no doubt, very dead. Men, like artists who gallop after beauty, should make a new set of divining rods, find out where hell is and put poverty in. Then beauty, rising like a rainbow from man's new dreams, would be pervasive as the mist of pettiness among us now and would come galloping after them for a change.

Among us, in the Terraces, love sometimes broke out. Love, making people see things in a clearer light, had a depressing effect. The Terraces, seen in dim light that softened the curves, could give a man a bellyache that nothing short of a hot water bottle atop the belly could ease. Therefore, to see the Terraces in any hard, revelatory light such as would be given off by a kerosene flare or passion would make the lover wish for the very opposite of the Terraces. That opposite would be beauty. So beneath the dark waters of the stream along whose banks we lived, pinched, scraped and pondered, there would sometimes flash the forms of beauty desired and we got much joy from watching these flashing, brief, uncatchable forms. They were the promise of life in a community that had come as near to a general stoppage of living as any community can come without staging a mass execution.

'The most important thing about love, though', said my friend Walter, 'is that it keeps people warm. That's more important even than love considered as a means to breeding to a man who hasn't got the means to go filling his outhouse with coal. To that man anything that puts him in a position of his outhouse is a very big thing. That's a bigger thing even than man's having been descended from the apes.'

Gwyn Thomas' prose is accumulative, almost incidental, repetitious in its certainty, affirmative in its own sense of itself. It offers the only hope worth having – that of the freedom to probe into the making and faking of human life with an intelligence imaginative enough to create anew.

The alternative, as he argued in the preface to his 1960 play, *The Keep*, is the manipulation of brother by brother:

The last brother, Con, is the archetypal pest of this and all other ages. He is the ungentle shepherd, the manipulator who regards no other life as complete if his nose is not in it. Where most other Welshmen find a fairly cosy tomb in a conjunction of work, sex, singing and ale, Con's nerves cry out for a more sinister sublimation. The people around him he sees, not as people, but as wires which, conjoined with proper cunning, provide just the right light and warmth that will bring Con to his full growth and puissance. Con is a pain in the neck, and if your neck doesn't feel it yet, be sure that Con will be getting in touch with you.

Then of a sudden the stones of the keep begin to crumble. At the same moment, Wallace, Russell, Alvin and Oswald all feel a crazy desire to make an assertion, to give their pallid dreams an airing, to see Con flat on his Machiavellian back. They want to raise their fists and smash a hole in the old, venerable roof and have their first clear view of the sky above. Can their fists reach that high? Is the sky really there? Are their fists really there? So we come to the seminal question in all human affairs. Who is fooling whom?

★ ★ ★

Gwyn Thomas' grandfather had emigrated to the USA where Gwyn's own father, Walter, had been born in 1872. Although trained as a cabinet-maker Walter Thomas, repatriated with his family in booming 'American Wales', worked underground in the Rhondda. It is a teasing irony which was not unique to the Thomas family. Gwyn Thomas, almost at the end of his life, wrote in 1979 – 'My father and mother were Welsh-speaking, yet I did not exchange a word in that language with them. The death of Welsh ran through our family of twelve like a geological fault. Places like the Rhondda were parts of America that never managed to get to the boat.'

If he had been born in America he might have become an American writer. Many people in Wales so disliked his eloquent mind and the windows his prose opened on to cold winds that he might well have been seen by them as alien enough to claim the title by default. He was as he put it himself, no more and no less than a writer who told 'folk tales from the modern Welsh'. That, however, is a complex subject matter. If 'American' Wales is a metaphor far more than it is a reality, then it is still a profoundly suggestive one, acute in its understanding that what had taken place in Wales was not merely industrialisation or urbanisation or anglicisation but rather a process of discovery as profound for Wales as the making of a specifically American identity in the USA was during that country's own dramatic nineteenth century. To be American, then, was to risk much that was already assured elsewhere in time and space. Amongst all the loss there was a quickening of human potential. It may have come in small ways more than in earthquaking gestures but it was unstoppable.

In Place of Wales: A Coda

The student of politics must ... seek neither universality nor
immortality for his ideas and for the institution through which
he hopes to express them. What he must seek is integrity and
vitality. His Holy Grail is the living truth, knowing that being
alive the truth must change.
    Aneurin Bevan, *In Place of Fear* (1952)

In 1944, famously or infamously, Aneurin Bevan the MP for Ebbw
Vale since 1929 rose in the House of Commons during the first
ever 'Welsh Day' debate to declare, in essence, that there was no
'Welsh problem' as such – only those social ills and economic difficulties which beset Wales as they did other, similar parts of the
British Isles. In the summer of 1959 as the Labour Party prepared
itself to fight the last election in which Bevan would play a part he
surprised some of his Welsh parliamentary colleagues by not only
supporting Llanelli MP Jim Griffiths' plea for a Welsh Office but
logically arguing that a Minister meant a seat in the Cabinet with
full cabinet responsibilities for the specific duties to be undertaken
in Wales. And those duties were, largely, those already devolved
administratively. Labour fought and lost that election with the
proposal for a Welsh Secretary of State as one of the planks of its
manifesto. Before the summer of 1960 had ended, Bevan was
dead. In 1964 James Griffiths became that first ever Welsh
Secretary. Since then as commissions deliberated and devolution
became the oval ball of Welsh politics – run with, fumbled, kicked
to touch, kept in the stands, and eventually touched down for a
disputed but given try in the 1997 Referendum – Bevan's frag-
mentary opinions have mattered and have been claimed, justifiably
given their seeming self-contradiction, by both sides in the on-
going debate. All this would be a futile exercise in hero-citation,
and one which Bevan would have scorned, if it were not for one
other factor, one very particular to this politician: he had a philosophy of political action that went beyond the merely contingent.
An apparently contradictory stance may be the result of a change
of mind or of circumstance over a fifteen year period or it may
conceal a stunning indifference to the actual form democratic
politics takes provided it remains accountable and the outcome
liberates more than it controls.

The Welsh Day debate had taken place in October 1944. Bevan's
contribution was typically brisk and unsentimental, sardonic even.
Historians have since cited Jim Griffiths' autobiography *Pages From*

Memory (1969) for its view that Bevan's long-standing doubt about the creation of a Welsh Office stemmed from an antipathy to 'nationalism which divided peoples' and a concomitant fear that Welsh 'political activity' might be divorced 'from the mainstream of British politics'. This is clearly a firm assessment. However, in the context of earlier and later pages in that same autobiography Bevan's actual position is always qualified by the other possibilities he also accepted. In July 1943 Bevan was Vice-Chair (with Megan Lloyd George) of the Welsh Parliamentary Party (representing all MPs in Wales), a body which had Griffiths as its secretary. They wrote to the Prime Minister to indicate that, with the unanimous support of the members, a sub-committee was being established to consider 'the problems of the future government of Wales, and in particular the establishment of a Welsh Office with a Secretary of State'. Undoubtedly Bevan was one of those who would disagree about the desirable extent of 'administrative devolution' but, equally, his signature on the letter indicates he was not far, if at all, from the prevailing view that what should be transferred were 'those departments ... in which there was already some degree of devolution in the form of the Welsh Department of Education and the Welsh Board of Health.' This limited devolvement, after all, is precisely what he also signed up for in 1959. We can interpret his all-Wales Health Service administrative machinery (along with Griffiths' identical Social Insurance system) in the same light: not sentiment but being sensible of the widespread, existing pattern (seventeen government departments with Welsh administrative units by the late 1950s and under, since 1951, a Conservative Minister for Welsh Affairs).

By 1959 there was no conceivable reason why Bevan should have opposed the main planks of a proposal which, in principle, he had accepted as possible in 1943. Admittedly, neither he nor the Labour Governments of 1945-51 had made 'the government of Wales', in a separate sense, any kind of priority. Bevan could not have minted his dictum 'the language of priorities is the religion of socialism' with any better cause in mind than the specific legislative drive of the Labour government during those years and besides, he was clearly on a flood tide of Welsh approbation for his political actions. The Council for Wales, established in 1948 with an old friend of Bevan's at the helm, the trade union leader, Huw T. Edwards, was not especially favoured by Bevan who, rightly, regarded it as a superior talking shop which was neither accountable nor responsible. If you were to have proper responsibility you needs must be accountable. This was the logic Bevan applied in 1959.

The longer term question of his views on further devolution and some kind of elected Welsh political forum is strictly unanswerable. We know that Bevan was a clear, consistent opponent of the Parliament for Wales campaign inaugurated in the 1950s and led, amongst others, by Welsh Labour MPs like Goronwy Roberts and S.O. Davies. But Jim Griffiths was just as committed an opponent of that initiative. Bevan did not live to see the growth in Welsh Office powers under both Conservative and Labour governments. There is no reason to assume he would have been concerned since the same question of cabinet responsibility and parliamentary accountability would have been in place and was answered. Where he would have stood in the referendum debate of 1979 is more of a moot point: his friend and successor as MP for Ebbw Vale, Michael Foot, offered support and loyalty to the Labour government's scheme; his fellow townsman and, by common consent, the nearest thing to an heir apparent we had seen, Neil Kinnock, then MP for Bedwellty, was, along with Leo Abse, MP for Pontypool, a scathing denouncer of the democratic inadequacies of the proposed Assembly; in my view Bevan would have been unlikely to be swayed by the 'patriotic' appeals that Michael Foot could resist less easily and, if at the height of his own powers, more likely to take a scalpel to the flabby arguments used to dress up the proposal. What I think is unarguable is that Bevan would have railed until he dropped at the manner in which an incremental growth in devolved powers, through the 1980s into the 1990s, went hand-in-pocket with a superstructure of un-elected, un-representative bodies and the downgrading of local government power. That might have led him to consider the whole matter of electoral politics with a distinct Welsh dimension in a different manner than the one he certainly professed in his lifetime.

Then, the imperatives of class politics, in and beyond Britain, was what exercised his mind and he consistently depicted Wales, or rather his significant part of it, as at the forefront of those 'advanced movements'. In other words, as with most of the Welsh over the whole period of his life, the question of Wales, *per se*, was not one to which he gave much thought in isolation. It was what had taken place inside Wales through its industrial history which concerned him and, by extension, how the people who had undergone that experience might make dynamic social capital out of their material exploitation. Those factors could not be kept within national boundaries, whether Welsh or any other kind.

However, Bevan was an acute reader of the specificities of lives on the ground and a stern critic of those, whether on the left or the right, who would deprive people of the requirement of self-definition. He would not have failed to notice how for many that had come to include a deeper sense of their Welshness. Provided this was in an inclusive rather than excluding sense Bevan would surely not have applauded the shallow thinking, as evinced by some recent members of his own party, which scorns the only thing we really know about ourselves: the past. He would have been at one with those, on both sides of the argument within his own party, who would wish to restore some measure of control over socio-economic trends, however powerful and trans-national, to the people whose lives are otherwise bent to their impersonal and ahistorical whim. That would not have seemed utopian to him. That was the essence of his political rationale. It is not so abundantly obvious exactly how it is to be done that we should second-guess the way in which Bevan's own stance might have shifted. If, on the other hand, we can tease out what Aneurin Bevan might have preferred in place of the Wales that has actually emerged since 1960 we might come closer to answering a more pressing conundrum: and that is, how do we place the insights Bevan's life and work has left us back into the debate on an emerging Wales.

* * *

There are two ways to examine Aneurin Bevan's actual response to the leading issues of his own time and his projected attitude to those of the immediate future: first, by considering his practice and, secondly, by sifting his views. As so often with Bevan, that reviler of 'romantic biographies', his cool irony had anticipated and deflated the practice. A full year before the war ended, and with Churchill ready for a peacetime dividend that did not come, Bevan reflected: 'This is ... the immortal tragedy of all public life, that the *hero's* need of the people outlasts *their* need of him. *They* obey the pressures of contemporary conditions while *he* strives to perpetuate the situation where he stood supreme. *He* is therefore overwhelmed by a nostalgia for past glory whereas *they* are pushed on by new needs, impelled by other hopes and led by other nascent heroes.'

Since Bevan pointedly dismissed hero-worship as an immature pursuit it is clear where his own instincts lay – with contemporary conditions, change and hope. It is a measure of his continuing importance, now as icon more than influence, to note how, even at the blushing rose-pink dawn of New Labour, his own authority and glory is still claimed across the spectrum and the decades. It was scarcely surprising that Tredegar-born Neil Kinnock, as modernising Leader of a torn Labour Party, should invoke Nye's name, quote his words and assume his mantle at conference after conference in the 1980s: it was a tribute and a comforting necessity so to do as his own name was ironically linked to the legacy of Gaitskell. If, under Tony Blair, that battle was decisively concluded with the refutation of Clause IV and the re-writing of the Party's constitution, there might seem little space left for the man who did, after all, say he owed more to Marxism than any other political creed and never apologised for telling the world in 1948 that so far as he was concerned Tories who had, in the interwar years, 'condemned millions of first class people to semi-starvation' were 'lower than vermin'. Such remarks might have once underpinned the anathema with which Bevan was once regarded by cabinet colleagues like Herbert Morrison but Morrison's highly influential grandson, Peter Mandelson, MP had no hesitation, in 1996, in placing Bevan and Blair on the last page of *The Blair Revolution*. Bevan is quoted for asserting that 'Free men can use free institutions to solve the social and economic problems of the day.' The index tells us to look up the word 'socialism' under the heading for 'New Labour'. What has come uncoupled, as contemporary politicians seek the advantage of a past authority and achievement, is a Bevan floating free from the contemporary conditions which his own life had attuned him to meet.

Aneurin Bevan's own emphasis in *In Place of Fear* (1952) was that his whole life had been shaped and circumscribed by the factors (iron, coal, steel) which had industrialised Tredegar, South Wales, and, of course, comparable places in Britain. His concern was to use the condition as a catalyst to effect change not to see it as a genetic code to excuse stasis or deference. In my *Aneurin Bevan and the World of South Wales* (1993) I argued that imagining his culture – the whole way of life that had formed him, its penumbra of social existence not only the spotlight of biographical facts – was 'an essential pre-condition to comprehending his politics'. I had not quite understood how much of a social closure I had implied by so integrating South Wales' greatest political figure with a declining cultural formation. In a stimulating and challenging essay in *History Workshop Journal* (Vol 41, 1996), Dr Chris Williams reminded me both of that factor and of the further necessity of turning the narrative lacuna into a social and political caesura. He wrote: 'the challenge for the next generation of Welsh historians ... is to come to terms with the South Wales that Bevan, dying in 1960, would never see.'

The full weight of those remarks, however, go way beyond the historical profession even if it is they who will need to clear the social waters we have let grow stagnant with suspended ambition. It is the practice of politics, of defused common purpose as in the miners' strikes of the 1970s and 1980s and of diffused civic intentions as in the palpable turning away from political faith, which has helped atrophy the culture which once gave South Wales its local vibrancy and its wider significance – the culture that moulded the public and representative Bevan as its finest exemplar. Of course, the primary, forcing factors have been deindustrialisation, the decline of heavy, male-dominated single industry communities, the coming of service industries, of white collar work and inmigration, of inward capital investment and the de-skilling of a significant part of the working-class, of spotted but long term unemployment and social-spatial differentials. A sociological, socio-linguistic, socio-economic profile written as bullet points in managerial landscape-style, with the demographic shifts of the politely named Groups A-E clearly outlined, is nowadays an essential snapshot analysis of our new world. Shot from Space, naturally, or wherever minds once were, for all this is to allow Bevan's famous Noun (of description) to subvert his desired Verb (of action). Societies of purpose are what they choose to become not what they settle to be.

Through his own formative period, down to the early 1920s, the dominant regional politics all around Bevan were very different from those that would be espoused in his heyday. This was true of both the Trades Unions and of the County Councils whose committees, in turn, he would join. Nor was he ever a great believer in the inviolability of political institutions. He had a sceptical notion of Parliament and its traditions: not even democratically elected he felt until 1929 and whose televising he ardently promoted in debate decades before it became remotely fashionable to do so. That was in order to maintain a bond between the voters and those they elected. He had no time for tradition if tradition's purpose only served to keep corners of public life away from the democratic gaze. At the same time constitutionalism was a sterile game played by those who had proved incapable of joining in the potentially fertile process of political power-seeking: what he did by accepting a Secretary of State for Wales was cold-eyed, pragmatic, almost indifferent to the nature of the change provided the practice brought results. And that was what his culture, his deep social formation, had taught him.

This, above all, is what continues to make an understanding of Bevan, in all his complexity, relevant to us today – that he fused attachment to a core of principles (his libertarian, democratic and socialist creed) to a politics aligned to the practicalities of what was achievable (for that majority who were not privileged). Where the tension between the two became unbearable he did not retreat from the former but he did resign from the latter. Power had to have meaning beyond itself if it was to be renewable. You could do little without it. You did less if you simply held it. That was what caused him to resign in 1951 and that was also why, after 1955, however reluctantly, he supported Gaitskell. It was the Welsh dimension to his politics which made him want to root that democratic branch in a wider British life.

The Wales of his first decade was recognisably the Wales of his last decade. Momentous changes had occurred but a visitor to Tredegar or Rhondda or even Cardiff in 1956 – the first year of that city's existence as a Capital – would have seen the same basic infrastructure as in 1906. Half a century of coal boom and bust, of a thriving export trade in the huge docks of Barry, Cardiff and Newport, mass unemployment and outmigration of the Welsh people so that population did not rise between 1921 and 1961, and even the welfare security of the 1940s and the shallow affluence of the 1950s, had not altered the basic dependency of the Welsh economy – from Brymbo to Bedwas – on coal extraction and steel production. What had been lost in the thrusting economic terms of a madcap capitalism had been replaced by a really deep sense of societal ownership. Nationalisation was not, as Bevan the old syndicalist, well knew, the panacea – and he had been an early advocate of a mixed economy in which public and private partners took their designated roles – but it was not an advance which would have been rejected at the time. In a sense it was an anchored world, moored for the foreseeable future against the kind of storms which had buffeted it so hard. Only the future was scarcely foreseeable.

A decade after Bevan's death two Labour governments had reduced the coalmining workforce in South Wales from 100,000 to 38,000 and thus, themselves, paved the way for the social defiance which the increasingly militant mining communities, not just the affected workforces, would offer as their sole defence against 'higher' economic wisdom. Now, in 1998, there is, after a perhaps avoidable maelstrom, only one deep-coal mine left as a working pit in South Wales, and that is a worker co-operative. This is still quite unimaginable stuff to those who thought South Wales and those particular communities – whether in coal or any other heavy industry – would always be synonymous. The phrase 'cultural materialism', a concept which encapsulates the profoundly liberating argument (and actual outcome) that men and women could create their own civilisations out of intractable reality, was given vivid life by the history of these people. And, let us be brutal about this, has been submerged in the years since Bevan's death. We have instead been inhabiting an archipelago of historical vanity ringed by coral reefs of nostalgia.

We can, of course, blame Bevan and those he represents for much of this. How can we live up to them? Why weren't they more perfect? How could they be so ambitious? Why did they fall so short? Two men I admired greatly spent large parts of their lives lamenting the fallen deity of Dreams that once was South Wales: the writer Gwyn Thomas (1913-81) who wrote two unperformed plays about Bevan and the historian Gwyn A. Williams (1925-95) who tried to fashion Bevan into the unlikely form of a Welsh Gramsci (a doppelganger role in which Gwyn played the more vocal part). The novelist was in his teens by the time of the General Strike and, essentially, the world had already fired his imagination: after the traumas of 1921 and 1926 survival was the only vitamin deficiency South Wales did not have. Gwyn A. Williams' generation twisted any number of ways in the winds of sectarian fashion, eager to escape the bad news that 1945 And All That was a tidying up job not a blueprint for further advance. Bevan was central to their dreams. Indeed, he not only shared them he lived them. He too felt the despair at what might have been; as he so poignantly told Geoffrey Goodman in 1959 – 'History gave them (the British working class) the chance – and they didn't take it'. Though, to be sure, and as Michael Foot's biographical masterpiece makes clear by context and by quotation, that mood could drift away and even at the very end of his life the challenge to enlarge expectation was to the forefront of his mind. At the Blackpool Conference, an electoral post-mortem, in his last great speech, Bevan informed the delegates, but only reminded himself, that:

> The fact is ... that a very considerable number of young men and women in the course of the last five or ten years have had their material conditions improved and their status has been

raised in consequence and their discontents have been reduced, so that temporarily their personalities are satisfied with the framework in which they live. They are not conscious of constriction; they are not conscious of frustration or of limitation, as formerly they were, in exactly the same way as even before the War large numbers were not sufficiently conscious of frustration and of limitation, even on unemployment benefit, to vote against the Tories.

What is the lesson for us? It is that we must enlarge and expand those personalities, so that they can become again conscious of limitation and constriction. The problem is one of education, not of surrender.

It had been an opportunity for the man who was then the elder statesman of the Labour Party to indicate, however gently, that he (born in 1897) had been this way before. For Bevan had the memory of a real landscape, in political terms, that had not been mapped out, and so reduced in the mind, at all. This was especially true of Tredegar and Monmouthshire where Labour political domination was not secured, at either District or County level, until the late 1920s. The county of Glamorgan, with more intensive and breakneck industrialisation behind it and, except on its southern extremities, devoid of countervailing influence, was embroiled by then in debates about the efficacy of *which* 'socialism' – the communist or the Labour kind. Both the geography and the sociology of Bevan's patch were more diverse. The social and economic constrictions, as he later put it, were nonetheless obvious. They were to be met, by those of Bevan's fiery persuasion, down to the 1920s by a 'direct action' outlook, via the South Wales Miners Federation and its local offshoots. Behind that, at least for the minority who were consciously attempting to channel the workforce's disgruntlement (some 270,000 coal miners in South Wales by 1920), was a programme of working-class education (variously in the Plebs League classes and the Central Labour College) of which Bevan partook voraciously.

There had been no national Labour governments. The Labour administrations in South Wales had been, at best, patchy, and, scarcely at all, of socialist intent. A philosophy of Lib-Labism was deeply ingrained. Autodidactism and union activity were elemental but heavily dependent, for effectiveness, on an almost impossibilist combination of constant mass strife and self-sacrifice. Bevan and various colleagues, maybe by dint of necessity in the company town of Tredegar, began to forge a political culture or rather, as time went on, to let culture shape the political formations they neither possessed nor inherited. Between the rock of the Great Strikes and the hard place of the Welfare State they found a place for the individual life.

Labour lost its temporary control of Monmouthshire County Council in 1923 and in Tredegar Urban District Council did not regain it until 1928. These intervening years were crucial. How would a new Labour party root itself in these drifting and uncertain communities? It was a question the young Bevan directly addressed. Neither the economy nor the social fabric of industrial South Wales was established, as it had been since the 1840s, anymore. Clearly a people, defined by religious persuasion and social custom as much as by aimless aggregation, had not become a proletariat, and in the classically defined sense never would. The brilliance of Bevan's earliest foray into political endeavour lay in his capacity to see the issue as an ethical one that had to be underpinned by a cultural commitment. Defining the latter would not be done in a study – though, notoriously, Bevan read incessantly in these years and, later, was instrumental in building the Tredegar Institute Library into the finest in a coalfield whose every pit village and township would strive to provide access to the Information Technology weapons of the day – books, films, journals, newspapers and radio. Education, to succeed as Bevan wanted it to succeed, could not have the whiff of the schoolroom about it; it should not degenerate into a solo voice and a megaphone of righteousness. He would, therefore, have approved of the Carnegie Trust's plan in 1930 to provide wireless sets in fourteen centres across the coalfield where people could gather and listen – to drama, variety theatre, sport and news.

Now we can grasp why Bevan was not being frivolous when he made one of his earliest interventions as a Monmouthshire County Councillor in 1928 – he wanted local cinemas to be allowed to open on Sundays (thus, his critics alleged, 'ushering in the worst excesses of the Continent'). Popular culture was not an opiate. On the contrary, the pleasure principle was a release trigger that exposed what constriction and frustration really were. Enjoyment of life was a necessity for socialists. Articulation of that necessity became Bevan's mission.

They knew they inhabited an old iron and coal town in a depressed industrial area in the very maw of the world capitalist slump. What should they put in its place? Bevan and the circle of friends in the Query Club – always a question – acted with the intensity of those short of time and behind in the race. Soon they outstripped the rest of South Wales, and thereby Britain. At least they could show the skeleton of ambition. Flesh was for later bones, ones put in the right order of priority. Bevan presided over a range of unprecedented activity, all radiating from the Labour Party. Events proliferated, big and small, from teas and dances to 'the Labour Players' amateur dramatic group, from jazz bands and street carnivals to sports days and choral meetings, from cinema showings of all manner of films, from Europe as well as America, to whist drives and brass band parades. There were regular Sunday evening lectures on socialist culture throughout the winter months of 1924 and an array of visiting speakers. Bevan was justified in boasting that 'in Tredegar they could congratulate themselves upon organising a Labour movement second to none in South Wales and they had every phase of the movement provided for even to an orchestra which was promising to become a very fine one.'

A hallmark of his thinking was heard as early as 1925 when he told fellow councillors, with Independents and ratepayers in the majority, that a 'rabbit warren home led to a rabbit warren life' and that their plans to squash sixteen homes to an acre in blocks of six (instead of the previous Labour council's decision for blocks of two with twelve homes apiece and an extra room downstairs) would create the 'slums of the future'. He was scornful of the cost cutting which had no regard 'to the artistic and aesthetic aspect of the scheme.' Throughout this time he built with words a picture of a town in which amenities were shared and the beauty of a man-made landscape treasured as much as the wilder hills he adored walking.

The flamboyant insolence which this representative Bevan exhibited, as an MP in London, and for which he was much mocked by colleagues and enemies (in his case the distinction was often blurred), was no foolish affectation. It was necessary to have 'enough energy to be rude', he told Durham miners in 1948, in order to 'be rude to the right people'. By then he was at the peak of his confidence in a Labour Britain he saw as only a move in the right direction towards the world he had imagined, and partly created, through his cultural initiatives of the 1920s. If we remove the film over the mind's eye that the powerful images of the Hungry Thirties have induced in Wales we might see that we now have more in common with a Wales that had not been so over-determined. Aneurin Bevan responded to that challenge in his own time.

In our own we could find a ready tick-list of the aspects of life in the 1990s he would rage against – and unnecessary, deep seated family poverty would be high on that list. Nor would he have any patience with that half-baked and quintessentially passive macro-economic theory, of globalisation and money markets, which by-passes uncomfortably persisting notions of exploitation and resistance. He would, after the economic history of his own country in this century, stand amazed at the failure of some political experts to identify self-preening as the parrot's alternative and, at least, self-taught trick. For the rest, my guess is that his own political waters would find their own appropriate levels whether over the idea of Wales as a European region or on the question of a single-European currency. It is not so much that you *could* claim him for both sides as which side will answer his persistent question about community empowerment and individual freedom. Of course they are hard questions. That is why he would have quizzed them long and hard from within his party. Evasion was never his style.

But it is in his life-long quest for a personal voice, a style if you will, with which to express the human dilemmas he first found in Wales that we must settle for proof of his continuing worth to us as thinker and doer. It is that example, more than anything, which we should use as a signifier of how mature citizens should face contemporary uncertainties – not by clutching at identities, antique or freshly drawn, but by embracing our culture, achieved and changing, so that we can celebrate the shape of our humanity in the places where we live.

Bevan's credo was based on such distinctiveness. How he would have despised the shallowness of those who promoted the consumption of the culture of others without supporting the production of our own. It was Bevan who signed on Alun Lewis, the young Welsh poet and short story writer, for *Tribune* in 1942 and Bevan who pulled George Orwell into that orbit. Israel Sieff recorded his friend, the philosopher-politician, shyly reading his unpublished poetry out loud and Jennie Lee emphasised, more than once, how dearly Nye would have enjoyed the equivalent of a university sabbatical. He would scarcely have had difficulty in agreeing that, in the late twentieth century, his fellow citizens will need re-training and re-skilling to find a niche in the global markets so transformed by the new, and coming, technology; nor would Bevan have rejected for an instant the drive to sustain economic well-being; but he would, surely, have asked then as he always did – for what purpose beyond the material do we propose these measures? Confronted by the quantum leap in the technology of communications made since 1960 Bevan, above all others, would have been amazed at the indifference or cynical disregard with which the elected have treated English language broadcasting in Wales for Wales. Here still is the most potent opportunity to articulate the voices of the people he chose to represent decade after decade. Amidst the post-industrial uncertainties of South Wales in the 1990s, held afloat by no indigenous industry and on a geographical margin where once it had been a hub-and-spoke centre, Bevan would not have been content with the necessary support of one dependent, linguistic culture whilst a majority languished as cultural supplicants. One of his favourite novels was Stendhal's *Red and Black*, perhaps because of its exquisite dissection of greed and snobbery, perhaps because in the character of Julien Sorel, conformist rebel and sexual predator, he detected the ambiguous careers of any number of Welsh parliamentarians, but, for certain, because he would see in that prophetic book the need for a rounded society to express its individuality by allowing its individuals social expression in a common pursuit.

Naturally, with Bevan attached to a project this could be no narrow pursuit. Nationalism was never a perspective he would adopt. To an extent his opening salvo in the Commons against David Lloyd George was directed against the facility of the professional patriotism employed by the ex-Prime Minister as much as against his chicanery in the miners' strike of 1919. Emblematic of Bevan's own relationship to a specifically Welsh culture was his pride in welcoming Paul Robeson, whose civil rights cause had been upheld by the South Wales miners, to the National Eisteddfod when that peripatetic body visited Ebbw Vale in 1958. Bevan then said that the Eisteddfod, an all-Welsh language occasion which had caused controversy by going to 'anglicised' Ebbw Vale, was 'a Monument to civilisation'. Civilisation was here rooted in one of Wales' languages; like all creative human acts it was to be cherished. It was an Eisteddfod which did seek to unite the linguistic communities of Wales. Bevan was there on equal terms, symbol of what could be done if Wales 'spoke to the world'.

Despite financial losses, largely the result of bad August weather, it was a triumph. Not least for Bevan himself who was, for once, lauded in both the Conservative and the Welsh-language press. It seemed he could do no wrong and, one year before he shelved all formal doubts about the proposal for a Secretary of State for Wales, he responded to the focus of a Welsh language world with warmth and generosity. Perhaps his geniality had been inspired by the presence of Robeson whom he introduced to a crowd of 8,000

in the Eisteddfod Pavilion, with another 1,000 in an overflow
venue to hear, if not see, the two together. But, completely at ease
and amongst his own in every sense, he went further and in
welcoming the festival to his constituency, as *The Western Mail*
reported on 4th August 1958, he stressed that although 'We in
Monmouthshire ... speak English and no Welsh we are essentially
a part of Wales [for].... [i]ts characteristics are Welsh, its legends
are Welsh.' So how should the duality of 'Wales and Monmouthshire' be ended? Why, by ignoring the foolish distinction and
striking 'it out of official documents'. And that done, he appealed
to local authorities to use the Parliamentary Act 'which gave them
the power to spend money on cultural purposes ... (to lead) ... to
an artistic revival in Wales.' Vintage Bevan on his own patch.

Full circle. Gwyn Thomas caught that echo in the title of the
first play he wrote on Nye – *Return and End* (1963). His second
attempt in 1975 was *A Tongue for a Stammering Time* and, again,
he returns Bevan to his beginnings, to the open moorland of the
Waun above Tredegar where his three memorial stones now stand
in perpetuity. This Aneurin is not looking to make his own end any
kind of terminus for others. His past is what should help us to a
future. The play's time is 1958:

> It began here. I feel I'm hitting a new stride. I give you a pledge
> ... I'm going to live another twenty years. I'm going to catch the
> world's ear. I'm going to switch the light on in rooms that have
> been dark for ages.... Let us improve the slum of our beginning.
> Let us put contempt for others at the top of the list of deadliest
> things. We shall unclench our fists and minds. Let's stop fright-
> ening each other to death in shadows of our own creating. Let's
> make a happy morning and make a new kind of fuel of joy.

Almost uncannily, except that it penetrates to the essence of the
meaning of Bevan, another distinguished socialist playwright,
Trevor Griffiths, was drawn to a connected imagery of renewal. He
closes *Food For Ravens*, his RTS award winning 1997 screenplay
for BBC Wales, by having Jennie Lee reconsider her actual words
about Nye being born old. She is addressing the large crowd gathered to hear her speak at the commemoration of the Stones erected
to his memory:

> ... 'For years and years, I would say that Nye Bevan never had
> a childhood in the conventional sense, that somehow he came
> into this world full grown. But I see now there is something to
> add to that judgement; for if it is true he was born a man, it is

equally true he died a boy...;'
She turns, takes the urn ... spills the ashes onto the wind.

★ ★ ★

In place of the Wales that was Aneurin Bevan imagined the Welsh who might show the world how to live fulfilled lives in a country of their own making. His flaunted style of highly conscious being did not take away a people's sense of their own worth; it suggested what was latent in their wider consciousness. In place of Wales as an abstract entity he offered up a subtle, endlessly modulated language of citizenship to hold the quicksilver nature of a changing society. In place of a Wales which suffocated in provincial garb in either of its languages he stressed the links between 'a rich local life and a wide cosmopolitanism' since the one 'gives meaning and particularity to the other'. In place of Wales as a country which possesses us he taught us to create the Wales we desire.

Bibliographical Update

Since *Wales! Wales?* was published by Allen & Unwin in 1984 there has been a continuing interest in a number of the subjects and events dealt with in that edition. Notably Idris Davies' work has received full critical and scholarly attention in *The Complete Poems of Idris Davies* (University of Wales Press, 1994), edited by Dafydd Johnston; Gwyn Thomas' work has been well served in recent years by Seren who re-published under his biographer Michael Parnell's editorial eye, *Three Plays* (including *The Keep*) in 1990, then *Selected Short Stories* (1988) and *Meadow Prospect Revisited* (1992). BBC Wales produced and broadcast a new version of *The Keep* in 1996 and in an accompanying publication *Opening Up The Keep* (edited by Anna-Marie Taylor and Rob Humphreys) can be found a number of revelatory essays, especially that of Rob Humphreys, '*The Keep*: Text and Contexts' and Victor Golightly's 'Gwyn Thomas & America'; Seren also published Alun Richards' *Selected Stories* in 1995 whilst the evergreen *How Green Was My Valley* attained the status of a Penguin Twentieth Century Classic in 1991.

Welsh Writing in English, a periphrasis that speaks eloquently of the unease of some of its protagonists, began its annual appraisal as 'A Yearbook of Critical Essays' in 1995 and usefully supplements the more regular lit. crit. to be found in *New Welsh Review* and *Planet*. Ian Bell edited *Peripheral Visions: Images of Nationhood in Contemporary British Fiction* (University of Wales, 1995) and 'Aztecs in Troedrhiwgwair: recent fictions in Wales' by Tony Bianchi is the best thing in it. A more general survey of writing can be found in Ned Thomas' chapter 'Wales' in *The Oxford Guide to Contemporary Writing* (edited by John Sturrock, 1996).

The historiography, and some of its implications, is surveyed in the essay 'Wales' by D.W. Howell and Colin Baber in *The Cambridge Social History of Britain* (Vol 1), Edited by F.M.L. Thompson (Cambridge University Press, 1990); by Angela V. John in 'Sitting on the Severn Bridge: Wales & British History' in *History Workshop*, No. 30, Autumn 1990; by Neil Evans in 'Writing the social history of modern Wales: approaches, achievements and problems' in *Social History*, Vol. 17, No. 3, (1992); and by R. Merfyn Jones in 'Beyond Identity? The Reconstruction of the Welsh' in *Journal of British Studies*, Vol. 31, Oct. 1992. All three historians have been stalwarts of *Llafur* where, along with the *Welsh History Review*, the real quarrying continues. Evidence of my own labours at the professionals' work face can be traced, for the chapter 'A Place in the South of Wales' in *Past and Present* (87), 1980, where detailed archival and newspaper references are given in 'Tonypandy, 1910: Definitions of Community'. References to other sources and works are, for this book, embedded in individual chapters or can be found in 'Sources of the World of South Wales' in its companion text, *Aneurin Bevan and the World of South Wales* (University of Wales Press, 1993).

Finally, and perhaps most encouragingly given the weight of importance this present edition of my book claims for the subject, historical analysis can indeed enliven debate in Wales. Numbers 26 and 27 of *New Welsh Review* from Autumn to Winter of 1994/95, indicated how history can still serve to bring fire to the skin. Hopefully, it can bring the best enlightenment possible, too, and since that is a co-operative endeavour, often undertaken over many years by researchers who build on each others' work, I want to end by mentioning the underpinning which my interpretation of Welsh history owes to an exceptionally gifted group of men and women who came under my supervision at the University of Wales. 'Who built the seven gates of Thebes?' – the Brechtian question deserves, as always, a collective answer:

1. Stuart Broomfield 'South Wales During the Second World War: The Coal Industry and its Community', Ph.D., University of Wales (Swansea), 1979.

2. W.D. Jones 'Wales in America: Scranton and the Welsh c. 1860-1920', Ph.D., University of Wales (Cardiff), 1987 and, in 1993, as his book *Wales in America* (University of Wales Press).

3. Andrew Chandler 'The Re-making of a Working Class: Migration from the South Wales Coalfield to the New Industry Areas of the Midlands, c1920-40', Ph.D., University of Wales (Cardiff), 1988.

4. Susan Demont, 'Tredegar and Aneurin Bevan: A Society & its Political Articulation, 1880-1929', Ph.D., University of Wales (Cardiff), 1990.

5. T.I. Williams, 'Language, Identity & Education in a Liberal State: The Anglicisation of Pontypridd, 1818-1920', Ph.D., University of Wales (Cardiff), 1990.

6. D.K. Davies 'The Influence of Syndicalism and Industrial Unionism on the South Wales Coalfield, 1898-1922: A Study in Ideology & Practice', Ph.D., University of Wales (Cardiff), 1994.

7. Chris Williams 'Democratic Rhondda: Politics & Society, 1885-1951', Ph.D, University of Wales (Cardiff), 1991 – and, in 1996, as his book *Democratic Rhondda* (University of Wales Press).

Dai Smith

Publisher's Acknowledgements

The publisher is grateful for permission to quote from the following copyrighted work:

Ron Berry *This Bygone* (Gomer, 1997) by permission of the publisher; **Idris Davies** *Gwalia Deserta*, 'A Carol for the Coalfield', *The Angry Summer*, 'The village of Fochriw' by permission of the estate of Idris Davies; **J. Kitchener Davies** 'Sŵn y Gwynt' by permission of the estate of J. Kitchener Davies; **John Davies** *History of Wales* (Penguin, 1990) by permission of the publisher; **Ann Douglas** *Terrible Honesty: Mongrel Manhattan in the 1920s* (Macmillan, 1997) by permission of the publisher; **Trevor Griffiths** *Food for Ravens* by permission of the Peters, Fraser and Dunlop Group Ltd; **Saunders Lewis** 'The Deluge' by permission of the estate of Saunders Lewis; **Richard Llewelyn** *How Green Was My Valley, Green, Green My Valley Now* by permission of the estate of Richard Llewelyn; **David Mamet** *The Cabin* (Vintage USA, 1993) by permission of the publisher; **Alun Richards** 'The Former Miss Merthyr Tydfil' by permission of Aitken and Stone Ltd; **Edward Said** *Culture and Imperialism* (Vintage, 1984) by permission of the publisher; **Josephine Tey** *The Daughter of Time* (Heinemann 1951) by permission of the publisher; Gwyn Thomas *All Things Betray Thee, Sorrow for Thy Sons, The Dark Philosophers, Oscar, The Alone to the Alone, The Keep, A Tongue for a Stammering Time*, letters by permission of Felix de Wolfe; **Ned Thomas** *The Welsh Extremist* (Y Lolfa, 1972) by permission of the publisher; **Raymond Williams** *The Long Revolution* by permission of the estate of Raymond Williams; **Gwyn Alf Williams** *When Was Wales?* (Penguin, 1985) by permission of the publisher.

Every effort has been made to contact copyright holders. If any have been overlooked, the publisher will be pleased to make the necessary arrangements.

Index

About the Author

Dai Smith is one of Wales' leading historians. He has a rare gift for communicating his stimulating and challenging analyses of modern Welsh politics, culture and society. Born in the Rhondda town of Tonypandy in 1945, Dai Smith was educated at Porth County School and Barry Grammar School. He read History and novels at Balliol College, Oxford, and novels with History at Columbia University, New York, where he wrote an MA thesis on Joseph Conrad. He went on to research for a PhD on the South Wales miners at the University of Wales, Swansea. Between 1969 and 1993 he taught history, first at the University of Lancaster, then at the University of Wales, Swansea and, from 1976, at the University of Wales, Cardiff. He was awarded a personal Chair by the University of Wales in 1986. He joined the BBC as Editor of Radio Wales in 1993 and is now Head of Broadcasting (English Language) at BBC Wales. He combines his career in broadcasting with a continuing commitment to Welsh academic life and he is an Honorary Professor in the Department of Adult Continuing Education at Swansea.

Dai Smith's latest book is *Aneurin Bevan and the World of South Wales* (1993), an appreciation of Bevan's political philosophy and of the vibrant South Walian culture which was its wellspring. In 1980 he edited *A People and A Proletariat: Essays in the History of Wales, 1780-1980* which includes his own seminal essay, 'Wales Through the Looking Glass'. In the same year he published two authoritative works: *The Fed: A History of the South Wales Miners in the Twentieth Century* and *Fields of Praise: The Official History of the Welsh Rugby Union* (co-authored with Hywel Francis and Gareth Williams). His *Lewis Jones*, a study of the novelist and leader of the unemployed in 1930s South Wales followed in 1982 and, in 1984, his book *Wales! Wales?* was associated with six films under that title which he wrote and presented for BBC 2. He is well known as a broadcaster on radio and television: his film *A Class Apart: Aneurin Bevan and the Labour Party* was shown on BBC 2 in 1988 and he has been a presenter of Radio Wales' weekly Arts programme, *Firsthand*. He is currently writing a biography of Raymond Wiliams.